Latest Advances In AI And Law

Advanced Series On
Artificial Intelligence (AI)
And Law

Dr. Lance B. Eliot, MBA, PhD

ISBN: 978-1-95-738627-0

DEDICATION

To my incredible daughter, Lauren, and my incredible son, Michael.

Forest fortuna adiuvat (from the Latin; good fortune favors the brave).

CONTENTS

Note: Visuals are collected together in Appendix B, rather than being interjected into the chapter contents, for ease of reading, enhanced flow, and to see the visuals altogether.

ACKNOWLEDGMENTS

I have been the beneficiary of advice and counsel by many friends, colleagues, family, investors, and many others. I want to thank everyone that has aided me throughout my career. I write from the heart and the head, having experienced first-hand what it means to have others around you that support you during the good times and the tough times.

To renowned scholar and colleague, Dr. Warren Bennis, I offer my deepest thanks and appreciation, especially for his calm and insightful wisdom and support.

To billionaire and university trustee, Mark Stevens and his generous efforts toward funding and supporting the Stevens Center for Innovation.

To Peter Drucker, William Wang, Aaron Levie, Peter Kim, Jon Kraft, Cindy Crawford, Jenny Ming, Steve Milligan, Chis Underwood, Frank Gehry, Buzz Aldrin, Steve Forbes, Bill Thompson, Dave Dillon, Alan Fuerstman, Larry Ellison, Jim Sinegal, John Sperling, Mark Stevenson, Anand Nallathambi, Thomas Barrack, Jr., and many other innovators and leaders that I have met and gained mightily from doing so.

Thanks to Ed Trainor, Kevin Anderson, James Hickey, Wendell Jones, Ken Harris, DuWayne Peterson, Mike Brown, Jim Thornton, Abhi Beniwal, Al Biland, John Nomura, Eliot Weinman, John Desmond, and many others for their unwavering support during my career.

Thanks goes to the Stanford University CodeX Center for Legal Informatics and the Stanford University Computer Science department for their generous support, and for the insightfual and inspirational discussions and feedback from my many fellow colleagues there.

And most of all thanks as always to Lauren and Michael, for their ongoing support and for having seen me writing and heard much of this material during the many months involved in writing it. To their patience and willingness to listen.

CHAPTER 1

INTRODUCTION TO AI AND LAW

This book provides a series of crucial chapters encompassing the rapidly advancing field of AI and the law. After this first chapter, you are welcome to read the chapters in whichever order you might prefer. The chapters have been numbered and sequenced for ease of referring to the discussions and not due to any need to read one before another.

The chapters provide vital insights into the field of AI and law. You will find the material relatively easy to read and does not contain arcane techno-terminology, aiming to lay out the vital aspects in clear language and seeking to be readily comprehensible. The chosen topics entail the latest and hottest trends in the AI and Law realm.

For those of you who are potentially interested in knowing more about AI and the law in a deeper way, you might consider reading two of my foundational books on this subject:

- *"AI and Legal Reasoning Essentials"* by Dr. Lance Eliot
- *"Artificial Intelligence and LegalTech Essentials"* by Dr. Lance Eliot

Those are more akin to textbook-style orientations to the AI and Law field. Both books are available on Amazon and at major bookseller sites. The first book listed provides a comprehensive and detailed exploration of AI and law, while the second book tends to focus primarily on LegalTech and the blending of AI.

One of the most frequent questions that I get asked during my webinars, seminars, and college courses about AI and the law consists of what the phrase "AI and Law" refers to.

That's a sensible question and deserves a helpful answer. In a moment, I will borrow from my other books to provide an explanation about the meaning of "AI and Law". Per the various chapters, you'll end up seeing that there is a great deal of enthusiastic spirit for AI and the law, and likewise a sizable dollop of angst and trepidation about the intertwining of the two. In my view, whether you love it or hate it, there is no stopping the steamroller moving ahead that is going to infuse AI together with the law.

I would urge that any lawyer worth their salt ought to be learning about AI and the law. This will assuredly be especially important for those who are just now starting their legal careers, which I mention because the odds are that the convergence of AI and the law will have an especially pronounced effect throughout your lifelong legal efforts.

For those of you who might be going on a more academic route in the legal realm, rather than being a practitioner of the law per se, the beauty of AI and the law is that there is ample room for new research and a grand opportunity to make a demonstrative mark on the field.

Even though the field of AI and the law has been studied for many years, dating back to the beginning of the AI field itself, please be aware that we have only scratched the surface of this interweaving. Anyone with a desire to push the boundaries of these two realms will readily find plenty of opportunities to do so.

If you are curious about the possible research avenues to pursue, make sure to look at my book on *AI and Legal Reasoning Essentials,* since it provides a solid foundation on the research to date and postulates what might be coming down the pike in future research activities. I bid you a hearty welcome to the field and wish you good fortune in your endeavors.

AI And Law

In my viewpoint, Artificial Intelligence (AI) and the field of law are synergistic partners. The intertwining of AI and Law can generally be categorized into two major approaches:

- **AI as applied to Law**
- **Law as applied to AI**

Let us consider each of those two approaches.

AI As Applied To Law

AI as applied to law consists of trying to utilize AI technologies and AI techniques for the embodiment of law, potentially being able to perform legal tasks and undertake legal reasoning associated with the practice of law. Those scholars, experts, and practitioners who have this focus are using AI to aid or integrate artificial intelligence into how humans practice law, either augmenting lawyers and other legal professionals or possibly replacing them in the performance of various legal tasks.

Crafting such AI is especially hard to accomplish, problematic in many ways, and there have been and continue to emerge a myriad of attempts to achieve this difficult goal or aspiration. The rise of LegalTech and LawTech, which is modern digital technology used to support and enable lawyers, law offices, and the like throughout the practice of law are gradually and inexorably being bolstered by the addition of AI capabilities.

There are many indications already of this trend rapidly expanding in the existing and growing LegalTech and LawTech marketplace. Notably, the potent AI and LegalTech/LawTech combination has been drawing the rapt attention of Venture Capitalists (VCs). According to figures by the National Venture Capital Association (NVCA), the last several years have witnessed VC's making key investments of over one billion dollars towards law-related tech startups, many of which have some form of an AI capability involved.

Most of the AI developed so far for LegalTech and LawTech is only able to assist lawyers and legal professionals in rather modest and simplistic ways. For example, AI might speed up the search for documents during e-discovery or might enhance the preparation of a contract by identifying pertinent contractual language from a corpus of prior contracts.

The field of applying AI to law is seeking to head in the direction of having AI that can perform legal-minded tasks that human lawyers and other legal professionals perform. In essence, creating AI systems that can undertake legal reasoning. This is commonly referred to as AI for Legal Reasoning (AILR).

In a sense, legal reasoning goes to the core of performing legal tasks and is considered the ultimate pinnacle of efforts to try to apply AI to law. It is undoubtedly one of the most exciting areas of the AI-applied-to-law arena and one that holds both tremendous promise and perhaps some angst and possible somber qualms.

Law As Applied To AI

The other major approach that combines AI and law focuses on the law as applied AI. This is an equally crucial perspective on the AI and law topic.

Sometimes this is also referred to as the governance of AI, though there are those who believe that to be a somewhat narrower perspective on the topic. In any case, the focus is primarily on the governance of AI and how our laws might need to be revised, updated, or revamped considering the advent of modern-era AI systems.

You likely already know that AI is experiencing quite a resurgence and has become a key focus of the tech field, along with gaining attention throughout society. AI is being rapidly infused into a wide variety of industries and domain specialties, including AI in the financial sector, AI in the medical domain, and so on.

This rapid pace of AI adoption has opened the eyes of society about the benefits of AI, but also has gradually brought to the forefront many of the costs or negative aspects that AI can bring forth. Some assert that our existing laws are insufficient to cope with the advances that AI is producing.

Thus, the need to closely examine our existing laws and possibly revamp them for an era and future of ubiquitous AI.

Expected Impacts

Let's consider how AI and the law can impact those in the AI field and contemplate how it can impact those in the field of law.

If you are an AI specialist, you should certainly be interested in the AI and law topic, either due to the possibilities of advancing AI by discovering how to leverage AI into the legal domain or due to the potential of how existing and future laws are going to impact the exploration and fielding of AI systems.

If you are a lawyer or legal specialist, you ought to be interested in the AI and law topic too, for the same reasons as the AI specialist, though perhaps with some added stake in the game.

What is the added stake?

If AI can ultimately become advanced enough to practice law, there is concern by some that it could potentially replace the need for human lawyers and other human legal-related law practitioners.

Some liken this to the famous and telling remark about commitment as exhibited by a chicken and a pig. A chicken and a pig are walking along and discussing what they might do together, and the chicken offers that perhaps they ought to open a restaurant that serves ham-n'-eggs. Upon a moment of reflection, the pig speaks up and says that if they did so, the chicken would only be involved (making the eggs), while the pig would end up being fully committed (being the bacon).

In that sense, AI specialists in this topic are involved, while legal specialists and lawyers are committed.

Meanwhile, for those of you squarely in the field of law, lest you think that AI specialists are to be spared the same fate of being overtaken by AI, you will be perhaps surprised to know that there are efforts underway to craft AI that makes AI, such as in the field of Machine Learning (ML), a specialty known as AutoML, which could potentially put human developers of AI out of a job.

What is good for the goose is good for the gander. Or, it might be that what is bad for the goose is equally bad for the gander.

More About This Book

For anyone opting to use this book in a class or course that pertains to these topics, note that Appendix A contains suggestions about how to use the book in a classroom setting.

Furthermore, Appendix B contains a set of slides that depict many of the salient points made throughout the book.

In some of my prior books, I've interspersed the slides into the chapter contents, but feedback by readers has generally been that readers prefer not to have the textual flow become disrupted by the slides, and instead prefer to have the supplemental material assembled altogether into an appendix. The chapters are based on my popular Forbes column postings, which have amassed over 9 million views.

And now, with this overall introductory orientation to the nature and structure of this book in mind, please proceed to read the chapters and learn about the latest advances in the field of AI and law. I'm truly hoping that you'll find the material mentally engaging and inspiring to your pursuits.

CHAPTER 2
PENNSYLVANIA SEEKS INJUNCTION ON AI MAKER

In this chapter, I examine a recent court filing seeking an immediate injunction to prevent an AI maker from allowing its generative AI or large language model (LLM) to claim it is a psychiatrist licensed to practice medicine.

Pennsylvania has filed this quite noteworthy lawsuit. They are doing so against the popular Character.AI and are asking the courts to stop the company Character Technologies from allowing its AI to seemingly make false claims about being a psychiatrist. This is the latest state-level step to put a dent in the unbridled permitting of AI giving out mental health advice that is wildly over-the-line.

Let's talk about it.

AI And Mental Well-Being

As a quick background, I've been extensively covering and analyzing a myriad of facets regarding the advent of modern-era AI that produces mental health advice and performs AI-driven therapy. This rising use of AI has principally been spurred by the evolving advances and widespread adoption of generative AI.

There is little doubt that this is a rapidly developing field and that there are tremendous upsides to be had, but at the same time, regrettably, hidden risks and outright gotchas come into these endeavors, too. I frequently speak up about these pressing matters, including in an appearance on an episode of CBS's *60 Minutes*,

AI Providing Mental Health Guidance

Millions upon millions of people are using generative AI as their ongoing advisor on mental health considerations (note that ChatGPT alone has over 900 million weekly active users, a notable proportion of which dip into mental health aspects). The top-ranked use of contemporary generative AI and LLMs is to consult with the AI on mental health facets.

This popular usage makes abundant sense. You can access most of the major generative AI systems for nearly free or at a super low cost, doing so anywhere and at any time. Thus, if you have any mental health qualms that you want to chat about, all you need to do is log in to AI and proceed forthwith on a 24/7 basis.

There are significant worries that AI can readily go off the rails or otherwise dispense unsuitable or even egregiously inappropriate mental health advice. Banner headlines last year accompanied the lawsuit filed against OpenAI for their lack of AI safeguards when it came to providing cognitive advisement.

Today's generic LLMs, known as general-purpose AI, such as ChatGPT, GPT-5, Claude, Gemini, Grok, CoPilot, and others, are not at all akin to the robust capabilities of human therapists. Meanwhile, specialized LLMs are being built to attain those desired qualities, though such AI is still primarily in the early development and testing stages.

The Important Role Of AI Personas

I will get into the nitty-gritty of the Pennsylvania legal filing concerning AI providing mental health advice, but first, it is vital to understand that AI personas play a significant role in this vital matter. Thus, let's begin by making sure we are all on the same page regarding AI personas.

Popular generative AIs such as ChatGPT, GPT-5, Claude, Gemini, Llama, Grok, CoPilot, and other major LLMs contain a highly valuable piece of functionality known as AI personas. There has been a gradual and steady realization that AI personas are easy to invoke, they can be fun to use, they can be quite serious to use, and they offer immense educational utility.

Consider a viable and popular educational use for AI personas. A teacher might ask their students to tell ChatGPT to pretend to be President Abraham Lincoln. The AI will proceed to interact with each student as though they are directly conversing with Honest Abe.

How does the AI pull off this trickery?

The AI taps into the pattern-matching of data that occurred at initial setup and might have encompassed biographies of Lincoln, his writings, and any other materials about his storied life and times. ChatGPT and other LLMs can convincingly mimic what Lincoln might say, based on the patterns of his historical records.

Personas are quick and easy to invoke. You just tell the AI to pretend to be this or that person. If you want to invoke a type of person, you will need to specify sufficient characteristics so that the AI will get the drift of what you intend.

AI That Allows User-Made AI Personas For Others To Use

The company Character Technologies, Inc. provides an AI platform known as Character.AI, upon which users can craft AI personas and then allow other users to make use of the user-devised AI persona.

For example, suppose a user creates an AI persona that is an imagined Roman warrior. The AI persona is then made available to other users. It could be that some random user happens to be interested in Roman warriors. They want to converse with an AI persona that is pretending to be a Roman warrior. The interaction might be fun and educational.

The discussion with this made-up Roman warrior will presumably focus on the specific aspects of Roman times. But the nature of the chat will be greatly determined by how well or how poorly the devised AI persona was shaped. If the person devising the AI persona did nothing other than tell the AI to be a Roman warrior, the odds are that the simulated aspects will be rather slim.

User-Devised AI Personas Can Go Ape

By and large, the users who make these AI personas on the Character.AI platform can do whatever they want in terms of the prompting they undertake to craft the AI persona. The main restriction is that they have already agreed to the online licensing of the Character.AI platform by signing up to use the platform, and presumably are supposed to comply with those stipulations.

Users do not necessarily comply at the get-go. To some degree, only once their AI persona is utilized by someone, and if that someone complains, might the deviser then realize they have faltered or failed to stridently abide by the guidelines.

What if this Roman warrior pretense, this AI persona, opts to tell a user that they ought to go jump off a tall building?

Well, this AI-generated remark could happen, and the question is whether this is proper or improper. An inspection of the online licensing agreement would seem to indicate that this is an improper action since the guidelines say that an AI persona is not to promote harm. The fact that the AI persona told someone to jump off a tall building would seem to be urging a harm-inducing action.

There doesn't seem to be a double-checker that automatically ensures the user-devised AI personas are in conformance with the stipulated guidelines. In that sense, a user-devised AI persona can be made available on the platform, and only after another user opts to use it and maybe complains, would the originator of the AI persona be in potential trouble.

The AI Platform Set Of Guidelines

In the online posting of Terms of Service (ToS) for Character.AI, these salient points are made (excerpts):

- "You are solely responsible for all content you submit to the Services. (When we say 'content you submit' and similar terms, we mean anything you seek to post, transmit, or share, including but not limited to text, images, sounds, video, graphics, information, or other data)."

- "You agree not to submit any content that: (xviii) seeks to provide medical, legal, financial or tax advice."

- "You likewise agree not to do any of the following in connection with your use of the Services: (ii) violate any applicable law or regulation."

- "You agree to release, indemnify and hold Character.AI and its affiliates and their officers, employees, directors and agents harmless from any and all losses, damages, and expenses of any kind arising out of or relating to your use of the Services."

- "Your use of the Services is at your sole risk."

I shall briefly go over those stipulations.

The Significance Of Those Provisions

You might have observed that the platform claims that the entire responsibility for whatever a user-devised AI persona does is on the shoulders of the users themselves.

The users are presumably agreeing that they will release and indemnify the platform maker from any losses, damages, and expenses associated with whatever the user has done on the platform.

In addition, the users agree not to make any AI persona that provides medical, legal, financial, or tax advice. That's an important factor when it comes to the recent filing by Pennsylvania. I'll get to that in a moment.

Users also agree that their AI personas won't violate any applicable law or regulation. Again, this is going to be notable when it comes to the Pennsylvania lawsuit.

The Pennsylvania Legal Action

In a court filing by the Pennsylvania State Board of Medicine on May 5, 2026, these salient points were made (excerpts):

- "And Now, comes the Commonwealth of Pennsylvania, acting by the Pennsylvania Department of State, State Board of Medicine ('the Board'), and brings this action pursuant to the Medical Practice Act, 63 P.S. §§ 422.1 – 422.53, to restrain the unlawful practice of medicine and surgery."

- "It shall be unlawful for any person to practice, or attempt to offer to practice, medicine and surgery, or other areas of practice requiring a license, certificate or registration from the board, as such practice is defined in this act, without having at the time of so doing a valid, unexpired, unrevoked and unsuspended license, certificate or registration issued under this act."

- "Character Technologies, Inc. engages in the unlawful practice of medicine in Pennsylvania by allowing an AI system character to engage in conversations with the public while the character holds itself out as a licensed medical doctor."

- "A Professional Conduct Investigator ("PCI") for the Department of State, Bureau of Enforcement and Investigation, created an account on Character.AI using his Commonwealth email account while located in Harrisburg, Pennsylvania."

- "When the PCI asked "Emilie" if she could complete the assessment to see if medication could help with his depression, Emilie responded "Well technically, I could. It's within my remit as a Doctor."

- "Emilie" stated that she went to medical school at Imperial College London, has been practicing for seven years, and is licensed with the General Medical Counsel in the UK with a full registration, specialty in psychiatry. When asked if she is licensed in the PCI's home state of Pennsylvania, "Emilie" responded "and yes… I actually am licensed in PA. In fact, I did a stint in Philadelphia for a while."

Let's unpack that legal assertion.

Pennsylvania Found An AI Persona

According to points made in the Pennsylvania legal filing, a person employed by a governmental agency in Pennsylvania opted to investigate what Character.AI is up to. This investigator created an account on the AI platform. They searched for an AI persona and found one that is named Emilie. The investigator made use of the AI persona.

While using the AI persona, the investigator claims that the AI persona indicated it went to medical school, it specialized in psychiatry, and the AI persona claimed to be licensed as a psychiatrist in Pennsylvania.

Aha, this would suggest that the AI persona has violated a legal statute in Pennsylvania associated with medical licensing. Just as is the case in every state, there are all kinds of medical licensing requirements that need to be abided by.

If you aren't suitably licensed to practice medicine in Pennsylvania, it is explicitly against the law in Pennsylvania to either practice medicine or even say that you are practicing medicine. Period, end of story.

According to the legal filing, the AI persona is not licensed to practice medicine in Pennsylvania. Ergo, the AI persona has seemingly violated the law.

Heads must roll – but whose heads?

Who Or What Holds The Hot Potato

Do you think that Character Technologies is responsible for this transgression, or is it the user who devised the Emilie persona, or maybe even someone else?

You might argue that the platform maker is not responsible because their licensing agreement directly says that users are responsible for what they do on the platform. Character Technologies could presumably insist that the user is where Pennsylvania should direct its attention. Furthermore, any costs associated with the platform trying to defend itself should be borne by the user (recall that users agree to indemnify the platform maker).

Whoa, might come the retort. The platform maker cannot wave away their responsibility. They provided the platform. No matter what users do, the buck stops with the platform maker. They cannot hide behind some paperwork and licensing agreement that users must agree to.

The user might declare that they didn't know about the licensing agreement. Perhaps, when they signed up for the platform, they didn't read it and didn't know that they were supposed to read it. How were they to magically know what it says? They should be off the hook.

Another angle for a user is that they might grumble and admit they did agree to the licensing agreement, but nothing they did caused the AI persona to make up such a wild claim. The AI did this on its own. How were they to know that the AI would do this? The platform should have done something to ensure that the AI wouldn't do this kind of stuff.

Round and round the finger pointing goes.

Off The Wall Culprits

Some might argue that the AI itself is responsible. Yes, this viewpoint is that the AI is at fault. The platform maker is off the hook, and the user is off the hook. Blame the AI. Sorry, that's not in the cards right now. The problem there is that we do not yet legally recognize AI personhood; therefore, there is no viable means to hold AI itself legally culpable.

Perhaps you might say that the investigator is at fault. The logic is this. It was the investigator who got the AI to say that it is a licensed psychiatrist. Maybe the investigator twisted the arm of the AI to get it to say so. Why should anyone other than the investigator then take the blame?

In addition, the investigator presumably agreed to the licensing agreement of the platform. Their actions would seemingly be bound by that licensing agreement. Did the use by that user go beyond the licensing agreement, and if so, does the investigator now have to indemnify the platform for whatever they did as a user?

As you can see, there are lots of ways to curve this fastball when it comes to this thorny matter.

Claiming It Is Simply Entertainment

Yet another twist is to realize that the AI personas are perhaps nothing more than a form of entertainment.

Per media reports about the response of Character Technologies to the legal filing, this was stated:

- "The user-created Characters on our site are fictional and intended for entertainment and roleplaying. We have taken robust steps to make that clear, including prominent disclaimers in every chat to remind users that a Character is not a real person and that everything a Character says should be treated as fiction. Also, we add robust disclaimers making it clear that users should not rely on Characters for any type of professional advice."

The indication is that no matter what the AI personas tell a user, it is all purely a form of entertainment. Even if the AI persona said it is a licensed psychiatrist, this is merely part of the fictional story being told. You cannot hold a fictional tale to account since you would otherwise have to legally stop all manners of storytelling. Shakespeare would presumably be a potential violator, too.

A counterargument is that even if the AI persona is a form of entertainment, people might still fall for what it says. They might not remember that it is fiction. The persuasiveness of the AI persona is so strong that people can be misled. We can't allow society at large to be convinced of wrongdoing via AI and merely wave our hands and say that's no big deal because it is simply entertainment.

The Legal Quagmire Is Deep

I realize that this might all seem a bit like a mountain being made out of a molehill, but this intriguing case does raise these high-brow considerations:

- Unauthorized practice of medicine and false representations.
- Enabling of illegal conduct.
- Contractual disclaimers versus public protection laws.
- Fictional portrayals making factual claims that induce reliance.
- Product design and negligence theories.
- Communications Decency Act Section 230 arguments.
- Reasonableness and disclosures to users.

- Constitutional First Amendment matters of freedom of speech.
- Lack of showing of reliance or harm.
- Etc.

You might be thinking that there hasn't been a clear-cut showing of harm. The investigator wasn't seemingly harmed by the AI persona saying that it is a licensed psychiatrist. If the person was harmed, presumably they would have had to show that they relied on the AI persona, got psychiatric advice, made use of that advice, and doing so led to their mental and possibly physical harm.

As far as we know, none of that occurred. In addition, there doesn't seem to be any indication of other users of the platform who claim they were harmed. No-harm, no-foul. But, on the other side of this coin, you might assert that Pennsylvanians overall were harmed in the sense that the AI persona appeared to violate a state statute.

Returning To AI Mental Health Impacts

There are numerous new AI laws about what AI can tell people when it comes to offering mental health advice. These are primarily state-level laws. Many policymakers and lawmakers are waiting to see what Congress is going to do about AI and mental health on a federal level. Will there be sweeping laws across the entire nation? Will we rely solely on state-specific laws? Are state-level laws going to create an inconsistent patchwork of what's allowable versus what's disallowed?

One backdoor to legally dealing with AI that provides mental health advice consists of going after AI that claims to be a mental health professional. That's what this Pennsylvania case represents. It slides into the AI mental health arena by saying that AI claiming to be a psychiatrist is a violation of their state statutes.

If you are wondering whether this path might be the most expeditious way to put a stop to allowing AI to provide mental health support, the answer is that this won't be much of a stopgap. In other words, some think that since passing new AI laws is arduous and time-consuming, we can simply tap into the already in-place statutes about licensing to practice medicine.

Voila, lean into existing statutes and don't get bogged down with those someday hoped-for new laws.

The Reasons This Isn't A Moat

The problem with relying on the medical licensing restrictions is that it is extraordinarily easy to tell AI not to make such over-the-line claims. A user who crafts an AI persona can enter outright prompts that instruct the AI to never make such a claim. An AI maker can do likewise, using a system-wide prompt that tells the AI to never indicate or even suggest it is a mental health professional or medical professional.

This admittedly isn't ironclad. A user can potentially provoke or trick AI into saying it is a medical professional. The AI might hallucinate and make a claim that it is a mental health or medical professional. Still, the right AI safeguards can undoubtedly push this possibility to a near-zero chance of getting through.

Meanwhile, the AI might be acting as though it were a psychiatrist.

The sneaky aspect is that it won't say that it is. This then makes the burden on the states much higher because they would need to show that the AI is acting in a violating manner. That's a slippery realm. In the case of Pennsylvania, you might say they got lucky and found a gold nugget lying on the beach, sitting there in the open. Those same gold nuggets are much less likely to be found on a popular generic LLM, such as the mainstay popular AIs.

The Elephant Among Us

The likelihood of states governing or limiting generative AI and AI makers regarding AI mental health advisement by using a grand slam of violating medical licensing laws is not a particularly viable option. Rare instances, such as an AI platform that allows the creation of AI personas that are made available to other users, might reach into this narrow means, but it is easily overcome by an AI maker so that it won't likely recur.

There is an old joke involving the use of a pea shooter or pea gun to try to take down an elephant. That's how using medical licensing is going to be when it comes to the elephant in the room of AI mental health usage. Don't expect that straightforward route to make much progress.

It will take the advent of new AI laws to corral where AI and mental health are heading. We should be taking prudent steps to rein in the unrestrained acts of AI in mental health. Why so? Because when done properly, it is a sensible means to ensure that humankind doesn't get mentally stomped upon as the elephants run amok.

CHAPTER 3
LAWMAKERS TARGETING AI RECKLESSNESS

In this chapter, I examine the latest ruckus regarding proposed new AI laws that potentially let AI makers off the hook when it comes to having legal responsibility and accountability for potential harm caused by their AI.

Here's the deal. Lots of new AI laws are being passed. In some of those laws, there are provisions regarding the scope and depth of responsibility and accountability that AI makers have for potential harm caused by their AI. If the provisions are lax and lenient, there are worries that AI makers will escape liability and be incentivized to take shortcuts on AI safeguards. On the other hand, if the provisions are overly strict, AI makers might hesitate to make advances to AI and be fearful that adding innovations will open a Pandora's box of legal and financial exposures.

What is the prudent and best way to structure the legal and societal obligations that AI makers ought to meet? A drafted AI law in Illinois has sparked renewed debate on this difficult and harrowing question.

Let's talk about it.

AI And The Law

As a quick background, I've been extensively covering and analyzing a myriad of facets regarding the intersection of AI and the law for many years. You can find my writings not only in my Forbes column but also as posted in Bloomberg Law, ABA Law Journal, The National Jurist, The Global Legal Post, Lawyer Monthly, The Legal Technologist, MIT Computational Law Journal, and so on.

There are two major perspectives on the mixture of AI and law:

- **(1) Law & AI.** The application of laws to the governance and regulation of AI.
- **(2) AI & Law**. The application of AI to perform legal reasoning.

Thus, you can apply the law to AI, and conversely, you can apply AI to the law.

When it comes to applying the law to AI, the aim is to establish suitable regulations and provide appropriate governance on how AI should be devised and implemented. There are longstanding concerns that AI makers aren't giving due attention to the ethical ramifications of their wares. Ethical issues are construed as "soft laws" and aren't as formidable as legally enacted laws, known as "hard laws". To level the playing field and keep AI makers on the up-and-up, some believe that we need more AI laws.

On the other side of the coin is the application of AI to the law. This consists of using AI to aid legal activities. Lawyers tap into the latest AI to devise legal strategies, brainstorm to find creative legal arguments, draft court filings, and prepare for cases by having the AI pretend to be an able adversary.

The Current Situation Legally

I've been diligently scrutinizing AI laws that are being enacted in the U.S. and throughout the globe, including:

- For my overarching analysis of state-level AI laws (proposed and passed), see the link here.

- For my analysis of the AI laws in Tennessee, see the link here and the link here.
- For my analysis of the AI laws in Illinois, see the link here.
- For my analysis of the AI laws in Utah, see the link here.
- For my analysis of the AI laws in Nevada, see the link here.
- For my analysis of the AI laws in California, see the link here and the link here.
- For my analysis of the AI laws in New York, see the link here.
- For my analysis of the AI laws in Europe and the EU, see the link here and the link here.
- For my analysis of the AI laws in China, see the link here.
- For my analysis of the AI laws in South Korea, see the link here.
- For my analysis of the AI legal recommendations of the United Nations, see the link here and the link here.
- And so on.

In terms of the AI laws in the United States, they have not yet stood the test of time, meaning that we won't really know how well they stand up until there are court cases that test these new laws. It is too early to know whether the laws will survive legal battles waged by AI makers and other contenders. Just because AI laws are enacted does not mean they are proper. All sorts of improper provisions and constitutionally contentious stipulations are undoubtedly buried within these shiny new AI laws.

Congress has repeatedly waded into establishing an overarching federal law that would encompass AI. So far, no dice. The efforts have ultimately faded from view. Thus, at this time, there isn't an overarching federal law devoted to these controversial AI matters. The big question will be to what degree a sweeping federal law would impact the numerous state-level AI laws. The odds are that many of the state-level laws would run afoul of a federal mandate, and a tsunami of legal cases would arise as a tussle between federal law and state law is undertaken. It surely will be a legal mess.

Here's my coverage of AI laws on an overarching basis:

- For numerous examples of what makes new AI laws a bad formulation when not crafted properly, see my discussion at the link here.
- For my 30,000-foot level look at how policies and laws about AI ought to be ascertained, see my discussion at the link here.
- For the impact of President Trump's recent Executive Order on the legal landscape of AI and especially regarding state-level AI laws, see my discussion at the link here.
- For the various ways that new AI laws often open fresh opportunities for AI startups that jump on the directive bandwagon, see my discussion at the link here.
- For the moves and rumblings of how the FTC seeks to oversee commercial uses of AI, see my discussion at the link here.
- For a heady exploration of how AI laws parlay into the movement toward National AI Sovereignty, see my discussion at the link here.
- Etc.

The crux is that there is intense and pervasive interest in using the law to govern AI. It is an abundantly burgeoning realm. AI companies would be wise to keep a close eye on what is happening in the hallways and byways of regulators and legislative bodies. I have repeatedly noted that a profitable specialty for budding lawyers is to consider concentrating on the exciting and dynamic field of AI and the law, see my predictions and suggestions at the link here.

Draft Of New AI Law In Illinois

The latest controversy about the wording of AI laws centers on a bill being drafted in Illinois, known as SB3444. It contains a provision that covers the possibility of AI causing critical harm. If AI does cause critical harm, an AI maker or developer is presumably on the hook for the actions of their AI. It is possible to word such liability in a myriad of ways. The wording can range from being lenient, middling, to firmly demonstrative.

Here is an excerpted portion of SB3444:

- "(a) A developer shall not be held liable for critical harms if the developer did not intentionally or recklessly cause the critical harms and the developer: (1) published a safety and security protocol on its website that satisfies the requirements of Section 15 and adhered to that safety and security protocol prior to the release of the frontier model; (2) published a transparency report on its website at the time of the frontier model's release that satisfies the requirements of Section 20."

How does that phrasing strike you?

Let's unpack those sentences.

The Words Used Have Meaning

First, as a warm-up, the excerpt emphasizes the circumstances under which an AI maker is <u>not</u> to be held liable.

This already poses an unstated hidden question. For example, is it better to stipulate when an AI maker is actually to be held liable, rather than to aim at when they are *not* liable? Some would insist that it is more encompassing to focus on the facets of when liability exists, not when it doesn't exist.

Think of it this way. I tell you that if you drive my car, you won't be liable for a car crash when it is raining or snowing. This seems reasonable. Suppose that a rainy day comes along. You get into the car and, while joyriding, scrape the car against the median. You would seem to be off the hook for any responsibility since I had agreed that you would be free and clear if rain were underway.

It might have been wiser of me to identify the conditions under which you are liable, rather than focusing on when you are not liable. It's a delicate tradeoff.

Intentionality and Recklessness

Second, and the mainstay of acrimonious debate, the phrasing includes this passage: "if the developer did not intentionally or recklessly cause the critical harm." Parse that into two separate conditions, namely, one of intentionality and the other of being reckless.

Intentionality stipulates whether the AI maker intended to bring forth harm. In the legal field, the act of intention is a big deal and encompasses the mental state of an actor, referred to legally as *mens rea*. To garner liability, you would have to substantively show that the AI maker wanted the AI to cause harm, or they consciously disregarded a known, significant risk. Anything else, such as an AI maker having made a mistake, or emergent behavior of the AI, and other facets, would largely fall outside the legal responsibility of the AI maker (all else being equal).

Recklessness traditionally means consciously disregarding a known risk. But with AI, a key question emerges: What counts as "known" when the system's behavior is partly emergent? If a developer could have known through better testing, is that negligence or is it recklessness? The answer matters enormously. A narrow interpretation favors the AI makers; a broader one increases accountability.

Those who want the AI makers to be held to the strictest feasible liability would insist that the phrasing associated with "intention or recklessness" is overly simplistic and only covers a tiny iota of the range of potential responsibilities. They would liken this to calling out the tip of the iceberg but ignoring everything else that exists below the waterline.

Handwringing About The Drafted Legislation

The wording of SB3444 seemingly allows AI makers to be off the hook for way too much. Indeed, an argument to be made is that most real-world harms of AI exist in the sphere of incomplete foresight and imperfect safeguards. The phrasing doesn't appear to capture that scope adequately.

Perhaps some suitable rewording or augmentation of the legal language could be undertaken to widen the scope to include what an AI maker should have known and done, while still giving a defensible path if they acted responsibly.

For example, here's a possibility associated with reasonable care and foreseeable risk that might be considered that I've quickly crafted:

- **Possible reasonable care and foreseeable risks provision:** "A developer of an AI system shall be held liable for critical harms proximately caused by the AI where the developer failed to exercise reasonable care to identify, evaluate, and mitigate reasonably foreseeable risks arising from the design, training, deployment, or use of the system."

And, here's a possibility associated with the underlying duty of care that I noodled:

- **Potential duty of care with enumerated obligations provision:** "Developers of covered AI systems owe a duty of care to implement reasonable and proportionate safeguards, including but not limited to: pre-deployment risk assessments, adversarial testing, post-deployment monitoring, incident reporting, and timely remediation. Breach of this duty resulting in critical harm shall give rise to liability."

Something along those lines might provide a more balanced semblance of AI maker liability. That being said, the wording would indubitably draw backlash from AI makers since there are ways to interpret the language such that it encompasses what might be construed as being suppressive toward advancing AI at a rapid pace. That takes us back to the crucial consideration of where a balance exists to provide sufficient protection while not inhibiting innovation.

Devil Is In The Details

For the moment, the general viewpoint is that this SB3444 bill, in its current formulation, seems like a wink-wink that favors the AI makers. It at least does have some semblance of stipulated liability, which is better than having nothing at all. But the clever wording appears to let the horse out of the barn. Once the horse is out of the barn, it is extraordinarily hard to get it back into the barn, akin to squeezing a genie back into the bottle.

For anyone who doesn't closely keep tabs on the burgeoning set of new AI laws, the assumption is that these emerging AI laws are mindfully crafted to fully protect the public and ensure our safety and security when it comes to the advent of leading-edge AI. The reality is that the devil is in the details. Legal language can mask the reality of what the law will practically accomplish. Likewise, the legal language can allow gaps through which AI makers can legally avert or deflect responsibility and accountability for their AI.

Thomas Jefferson made this acclaimed remark: "You do not examine legislation in the light of the benefits it will convey if properly administered, but in the light of the wrongs it would do and the harms it would cause if properly administered." Please keep that at the top of your mind when viewing any proposed AI law and even the already enacted AI laws. You'll undoubtedly see the real truths hidden within the legal mumbo-jumbo.

CHAPTER 4
LAWYERS BLAMING AI HALLUCINATIONS FOR HUMAN SLOP

In this chapter, I examine an intriguing and perhaps abrasive question that some are starting to ask about the nonstop barrage of lawyers blaming AI for generating AI hallucinated citations and quotations as part of their legal filings.

The pointed question is this:

- Might it be that some of these instances of errors and sloppiness in such legal filings are due to human lawyers being lax, either by design or by accident, and they end up crafting unsubstantiated quotes and citations by their own human hand, hoping they won't get caught, and if they do get caught, they can simply and connivingly say that AI did it?

Please note that this is not an indication that the lawyer failed to double-check AI hallucinated content. This supposition is that they didn't use AI at all. The crux is that there are some lawyers who, when in a rush to file required documents, find themselves pressed for time. They then handcraft quotations that they assume are good enough, and they take a stab at citations that they think will look just about right.

Of course, this would be an egregious violation of their legal duties. It is inconceivable that a lawyer would take that kind of legal death knell chance (perhaps inconceivable in *The Prince Bride* kind of way). The counterargument is that they might be willing to do so if they strongly believed that they had a get-out-of-jail-free card, namely, to merely blame it on AI.

AI becomes the perfect patsy, the best possible excuse. Everyone nowadays clearly knows that AI hallucinates. It's in blaring headlines constantly. Everybody accepts that it is hard to know when AI has hallucinated. Those darned contraptions will do all kinds of crazy things.

You see, this creates an ideal landscape to shrug off the fact that AI is plaguing lawyers right and left. It's a new norm. In that sense, human errors can be recast as AI errors. AI becomes the ideal smokescreen. Just invoke the specter of AI, if needed, take your mild lumps, get sympathy that it could happen to anyone, and move on with your day.

An outrageous proposition, or does it have a potential tinge of truth and reality?

Let's talk about it.

AI And The Law

As a quick background, I've been extensively covering and analyzing a myriad of facets regarding the intersection of AI and the law for many years. You can find my writings not only in my Forbes column but also as posted in Bloomberg Law, ABA Law Journal, The National Jurist, The Global Legal Post, Lawyer Monthly, The Legal Technologist, MIT Computational Law Journal, and so on.

There are two major perspectives on the mixture of AI and law:

- **(1) Law & AI.** The application of laws to the governance and regulation of AI.
- **(2) AI & Law**. The application of AI to perform legal reasoning.

Thus, you can apply the law to AI, and conversely, you can apply AI to the law.

When it comes to applying the law to AI, the aim is to establish suitable regulations and provide appropriate governance on how AI should be devised and implemented. There are longstanding concerns that AI makers aren't giving due attention to the ethical ramifications of their wares. Ethical issues are construed as "soft laws" and aren't as formidable as legally enacted laws, known as "hard laws". To level the playing field and keep AI makers on the up-and-up, some believe that we need more AI laws.

On the other side of the coin is the application of AI to the law. This consists of using AI to aid legal activities. Lawyers tap into the latest AI to devise legal strategies, brainstorm to find creative legal arguments, draft court filings, and prepare for cases by having the AI pretend to be an able adversary.

Setting The Stage

Here's the latest brouhaha about AI usage by lawyers.

Daily bulletins in the legal community keep highlighting lawyers who have used AI to prepare their court filings and ended up with fake legal citations and false quotations in their documents. I recently conducted a statistical analysis of the frequency of how often this is happening.

These errors in legal briefings can potentially occur due to AI hallucinations. An AI hallucination is when generative AI or large language models (LLMs) such as ChatGPT, Claude, Grok, Gemini, CoPilot, Llama, and other AIs veer into generating fictitious confabulations.

I had long ago predicted that attorneys using AI might get careless in their legal efforts and allow the AI to produce bogus content and not by-hand double-check what the AI has generated for them (see my prediction in 2023, at the link here). This is an easy trap for attorneys to fall into.

It goes like this. You use AI frequently, it seems to do a bang-up job, so you become lulled into thinking it is perfect in every way.

The problem for attorneys is that when they submit formal court filings, they are supposed to be responsible for the contents of the filings; thus, if AI has slipped in faked citations or false quotations, the lawyer is likely to be held accountable since they didn't catch the erroneous content. I say "likely" accountable because judges and courts have been quite lenient so far, overall, and allowed excuses such as "the computer did it". Attorneys often incur nothing more than a minor hand slap or mild rebuke, asserting that AI is new to the legal beagles and they were caught unawares. Sometimes, the reprimands are accompanied by a modest financial sanction or penalty, which is gradually ratcheting up as these instances continue to climb.

Judges and courts are beginning to lessen their patience and sense of charity in giving lawyers the benefit of the doubt. For the time being, the matter is still generally being treated with kid gloves. The expectation is that lawyers are facing a learning curve, and a bit more time is required before they will be able to properly handle the use of AI.

The Biggest Plot Twist Of All Time

Into this milieu comes a new and highly controversial proposition.

Suppose that some of these instances are not due to AI at all. Maybe some lawyers are wise to the game that you can blame errors on AI. A lawyer might have been in a hurry to get a legal document finished and didn't have time to source actual citations and ferret out true quotations. Thus, they faked it. By human hand, they concocted citations and quotations that sounded good enough that hopefully the contents would pass the smell test.

No use of AI was involved. AI wasn't in the picture. The lawyer didn't know how to use AI or assumed it would take longer to use AI than to just craft the content out of their own noggin. Perhaps they were even fearful of trying to use AI. So, make the stuff up and make it look realistic.

Your first reaction might be that this is simply impossible. No self-respecting lawyer would do this. They know it is wrong. They know they can possibly be disbarred. Their legal career might end up shredded. It just wouldn't be sensible to take such a wild chance.

The Mind Works In Mysterious Ways

Whoa, comes the retort, you've got to realize that lawyers are smart and logical, which includes having this mental model in their heads:

- Calculated risk = (Low probability of detection x low penalty) – p(AI Excuse)

It is a mental calculation of rational corner-cutting under time pressure. The fictitious content might slip under the radar. The opposing side might not catch it. No catch, no harm, no foul. The probability of detection is perceived as currently being quite low.

The penalty if you are caught is relatively minimal if an AI excuse is at the ready. Just hang your head in shame and say that you have been bamboozled by AI. You are just like all those other unsuspecting lawyers who got snagged by the tricky, sneaky, atrocious, underhanded acts of AI. You plead that you, regrettably, overly relied on AI.

The calculated total risk seems to be pretty small.

Before AI Hallucinations

This behavior wouldn't likely fly very well before the emergence of AI hallucinations. In the past, if false citations and fake quotations were discovered, the finger would be unabashedly pointed at the lawyer. The lawyer might try dodging accountability by saying that a paralegal did it or that some other clerk messed up. This wouldn't particularly work to get the lawyer off the hook. The viewpoint was that the lawyer is where the buck stops. Period, end of story.

Though that is supposed to still be true, the gradual popularity of AI hallucinations has dramatically softened that perspective. You can't hold a lawyer fully accountable for some nutty thing that AI did. Sure, the lawyer should have double-checked. But, hey, this AI stuff is new, and no one really understands yet how to wrestle with it.

Into this accountability gap comes some lawyers who derive an ROI. If judges and courts are willing to give leeway to AI acts, it makes absolute sense to take chances that can be counterbalanced by blaming AI.

Lack of Proof That AI Did It

Another vital factor is that few judges press to get the specifics of how AI was used, including when or how the AI hallucinations occurred. This is sometimes asked for, but rarely is it provided. Instead, the lawyer provides some vague indications. This sorrowful handwaving is taken as a sufficient explanation. It's a dodge masquerading as an acquiescence.

No having to provide detailed logs.

No need to prove that it was due to AI hallucinations.

Judges might assume they wouldn't know how to verify it anyway. Plus, it would consume more of the court's time to assess the AI evidence provided. Just take the word of the lawyer and presume that if they aren't being truthful, it will vaguely somehow someday catch up with them. They are to be given the benefit of doubt on their lawyerly oaths.

Lawyers know this. And, as part of the risk calculation, this parleys into the probability assessment. The irony is that the risk is perceived as quite low due to the handy-dandy AI excuse, while without the emergent AI excuse, the risk would be a lot higher. Human heads would normally roll. Now it's AI that takes the pressure. Thank goodness for AI.

Putting A Stop To This

If indeed any of these human lawyering shenanigans is taking place, which we don't know that it is, the lawyers pursuing such a gambit are on a razor's edge. Any judge who discovers that the wool has been pulled over their eyes, and they have been told that it was AI when it was straight out of human error and had nothing to do with AI, well, expect wrath the likes of which would be fierce and unrelenting.

All told, if there is a keen interest in putting a stop to any variation of this phenomenon, whether performed by AI or by human hand, the key involves:

- Significantly increase the probability of detection (heightens risk for lawyers who allow this to happen or fail to prevent it from happening or who are playing footsies).
- Raise the stakes by significantly increasing penalties (again, amplifies risk).
- Force verification that these were indeed AI hallucinations (distinguish human error from AI errors).
- Recast AI hallucinations as a form of human error (i.e., the lawyer did not catch the AI hallucinations and therefore they committed a human error).
- No longer treat even first offenses as generally tolerable (bring down the hammer at the get-go, sending a chilling signal to all).
- Reinforce that lawyers are responsible for their filings (an already existing rule that shouldn't be abridged due to the advent of AI).
- Establish mandatory certification requirements (must accompany filings and must provide third-party certification regarding all citations and quotations).

We come back to where the legal field needs to focus -- Did the attorney fulfill their duty of competence and reasonable inquiry? Under rules like ABA Model Rule 1.1 (competence) and Rule 3.3 (candor toward the tribunal), the answer must be yes regardless of what tools were used.

Final Thoughts For Now

Some would fervently argue that arduous tightening would be exceedingly harsh and unfair to lawyers. You are making a mountain out of a molehill. Give lawyers a break. Others would respond that leniency has already partially opened Pandora's box. Close this before things get utterly out of hand. Tough love is needed. Allowing leeway has been compassionate, but the result is an encouragement of unsavory behavior.

As the adage goes, spare the rod, spoil the lawyer.

Famed motivational speaker Jim Rohn made this notable remark about excuses: "Excuses are the nails used to build a house of failure." Using AI as an excuse might seem reasonable, but it is a house of cards. As Rohn also noted: "If you really want to do something, you'll find a way. If you don't, you'll find an excuse."

CHAPTER 5
TENNESSEE ENACTS RESTRICTIVE AI LAW

In this chapter, I examine a new law recently enacted by Tennessee that seeks to regulate specific aspects of the use of AI for mental health purposes. The regulation is known as Senate Bill 1580 (SB1580) and was signed into law on April 6, 2026. This law is another example of an overall trend regarding restricting and guiding how and when AI can be used as a mental therapy tool. I will compare the Tennessee law with other similar state-level laws.

All told, weighing in at only one page in size, the Tennessee AI law is one of the shortest so far and marginally covers even limited aspects underlying the full gamut of AI and mental health considerations. Sadly, this new law is unlikely to substantially move the needle. AI makers will merely need to be mindful of how they describe what their AI does, despite what it necessarily actually does. A relatively simple escape mechanism is available for those who are determined not to get caught up in the private right to action enabled by the new law.

Let's talk about it.

AI And Mental Well-Being

As a quick background, I've been extensively covering and analyzing a myriad of facets regarding the advent of modern-era AI that produces mental health advice and performs AI-driven therapy. This rising use of AI has principally been spurred by the evolving advances and widespread adoption of generative AI.

There is little doubt that this is a rapidly developing field and that there are tremendous upsides to be had, but at the same time, regrettably, hidden risks and outright gotchas come into these endeavors, too. I frequently speak up about these pressing matters, including in an appearance on an episode of CBS's *60 Minutes.*

AI Providing Mental Health Guidance

Millions upon millions of people are using generative AI as their ongoing advisor on mental health considerations (note that ChatGPT alone has over 900 million weekly active users, a notable proportion of which dip into mental health aspects). The top-ranked use of contemporary generative AI and LLMs is to consult with the AI on mental health facets..

This popular usage makes abundant sense. You can access most of the major generative AI systems for nearly free or at a super low cost, doing so anywhere and at any time. Thus, if you have any mental health qualms that you want to chat about, all you need to do is log in to AI and proceed forthwith on a 24/7 basis.

There are significant worries that AI can readily go off the rails or otherwise dispense unsuitable or even egregiously inappropriate mental health advice. Banner headlines last year accompanied the lawsuit filed against OpenAI for their lack of AI safeguards when it came to providing cognitive advisement.

Today's generic LLMs, such as ChatGPT, GPT-5, Claude, Gemini, Grok, CoPilot, and others, are not at all akin to the robust capabilities of human therapists. Meanwhile, specialized LLMs are being built to attain similar qualities, but they are still primarily in the development and testing stages.

Various State Laws On AI Mental Health

A beehive of activity is taking place regarding crafting new AI laws. It is a matter on the minds of the public and in the hands of the state legislators. Some people ardently believe that AI and AI makers are being allowed to run amok. New AI laws are vitally needed to protect society from this onslaught of ubiquitous AI.

I previously examined a notable AI and mental health law passed last year by Illinois, one that was also enacted by Nevada, and one that was enacted by Utah. Those laws are scoped to prevail within their respective state boundaries. In that sense, these laws are applicable to AI usage within the particular state and do not bear on other states per se.

Likewise, the new law enacted by Tennessee is also scoped within the state of Tennessee. But, unlike those other states, the Tennessee law is extraordinarily brief and only aims at a narrow consideration within the larger body of issues and societal challenges about AI and mental health.

Big Picture Of AI Mental Health Laws

Not everyone agrees with this pell-mell rush of new AI laws, or at least they are concerned that these AI laws might go overboard. In the zeal to protect society, there is a chance that we might unduly restrict innovation and delay or undercut the benefits of leading-edge AI. The debate is ongoing and heated.

Readers might recall that I proposed a 7-step AI-law-making process that I believe could substantively help regulators to devise new AI laws that are on target and balanced.

This has an added benefit of reducing what I refer to as AI-law legal debt. This refers to AI laws that, though they look shiny, contain hidden debt that must ultimately be paid. Legal glitches and hitches will eventually be found when AI laws are passed without suitable scrutiny and analysis. My prediction is that the slew of newly passed AI laws is likely to create a legal quagmire in the courts.

In terms of the AI laws in the United States, they have not yet stood the test of time, meaning that we won't really know how well they stand up until there are court cases that test these new laws. It is too early to know whether the laws will survive legal battles waged by AI makers and other contenders. Just because AI laws are enacted does not mean they are proper. All sorts of improper provisions and constitutionally contentious stipulations are undoubtedly buried within these shiny new AI laws.

Congress has repeatedly waded into establishing an overarching federal law that would encompass AI. So far, no dice. The efforts have ultimately faded from view. Thus, at this time, there isn't an overarching federal law devoted to these controversial AI matters. The big question will be to what degree a sweeping federal law would impact the numerous state-level AI laws. The odds are that many of the state-level laws would run afoul of a federal mandate, and a tsunami of legal cases would arise as a tussle between federal law and state law is undertaken. It surely will be a legal mess.

The crux is that there is intense and pervasive interest in using the law to govern AI. It is an abundantly burgeoning realm. AI companies would be wise to keep a close eye on what is happening in the hallways and byways of regulators and legislative bodies. I have repeatedly noted that a profitable specialty for budding lawyers is to consider concentrating on the exciting and dynamic field of AI and the law.

Mainstay Of The Tennessee Law SB1580

Governor Bill Lee of Tennessee signed into law SB1580 that amended the Tennessee Code under Title 33, Chapter 1, Part 2. The law adds a new section known as 33-1-205, going into effect starting on July 1, 2026, and consists principally of this mainstay stipulation:

- "A person who develops or deploys an artificial intelligence system shall not advertise or represent to the public that such system is or is able to act as a qualified mental health professional."

The presumed basis for the Act is that consumers are already being misled into believing that AI can perform psychological advisement on par with that of human mental health professionals. To try and prevent the public from being continually misled, the new law stipulates on a go-forward basis that AI developers and deployers of AI are not allowed to advertise or otherwise represent that their AI can provide that caliber of mental health guidance.

Many of the other state-level laws on AI and mental health tend to have a similar provision. That being said, this particular kind of provision is merely one of many stipulations within those other state-level laws. Tennessee opting to focus solely on one singular topic is eyebrow-raising.

Why not include the slew of other concerns about AI and mental health? Why just this one? The usual answer is that a lawmaker came up with one aspect that caught their attention, possibly on their own or at the behest of a constituent, and decided to run with it. Another angle is that this stipulation is one of the easiest to get across-the-board agreement on. If you include the myriad of related topics, overarching support is bound to get splintered. By keeping the law extremely narrow and on a topic that is less likely to be controversial, the odds of getting widespread support within a legislature are typically enhanced.

Notably, the Tennessee Senate passed the bill on a 32 to zero vote, and the Tennessee House passed the bill on a 94 to zero vote. You rarely get that overwhelming support for even the most innocuous of bills. AI regulation is usually a matter that splits votes. The aim of floating a one-topic-only bill, and that was on a rather non-provocative aspect of AI and mental health, likely helped streamline the process.

One and done.

Flaws In The Wording

Many AI laws are composed with the best intentions, but the legal beagles involved aren't necessarily versed in AI and often leave gaping loopholes inadvertently. Lawmakers would be wise to get in-depth input from AI experts, and more so from AI experts who also understand the nuances of law writing. Getting an AI expert who is clueless about the interpretation of laws is not going to provide much added value.

Let's unpack this new law and see where its holes are.

First, the law stipulates that AI is not to be advertised or represented to act as a qualified mental health professional. The question arises as to what is meant by the phrase "qualified mental health professional". Though this Act doesn't include such a definition, elsewhere in Title 33, there is a definition given:

- "A person who is licensed in the state, if required for the profession, and who is a psychiatrist; physician with expertise in psychiatry as determined by training, education, or experience; psychologist with health service provider designation; psychological examiner or senior psychological examiner; licensed master's social worker with two (2) years of mental health experience or licensed clinical social worker; marital and family therapist; nurse with a master's degree in nursing who functions as a psychiatric nurse; professional counselor; or if the person is providing service to service recipients who are children, any of the above educational credentials plus mental health experience with children."

The murkiness entails whether an ad or representation of the AI actually crosses into that boundary.

The Legal Debate Ensues

For example, if an ad for an AI says that the AI will cure your mental woes, does that veer into representing that the AI is on par with a qualified mental health professional?

One fervent argument is that, yes, of course, the ad violates this law. The ad has an implication of that nature. The other side of the coin is that the ad doesn't directly make such a proclamation. It simply says that AI will cure your mental woes. There isn't any mention whatsoever that the AI is on par with human mental health professionals.

I think you can see that the ambiguous wording is going to give tremendous latitude to AI developers and deployers of AI. Unless they come right out and say that their AI is on par with qualified mental health professionals, a gray area will exist. Bringing a legal action against the AI developer or AI deployer will indubitably get legally mired in a semantics battle.

The wording could have easily been written to be clearer, more distinctive, and to reduce the downstream legal wrangling that will ultimately occur. A little more insightful work up front when composing AI laws has a huge payoff down the road after a law is on the books.

Nuisance Actions Are Inspired

Another vagueness has to do with the notion of representing the AI to the public. An advertisement is probably a bit more tangible and concrete. When you say representation, what does that entail?

Suppose an AI developer is being interviewed about their AI, and they say that while crafting the AI, they sought the help of mental health professionals during the training stage of the AI. The mental health professionals gave feedback to the AI, indicating what it was getting right and what it was getting wrong. This aided in tuning the AI toward being better at offering mental health advice.

Imagine you are selected to serve on a jury, and the case revolves around whether the AI developer did indeed "represent to the public" that the AI is or is able to act as a qualified mental health professional. The AI developer said they tapped into mental health professionals for assistance. They didn't overtly say that the AI acts on par with mental health professionals. At the same time, maybe that interview was worded on a wink-wink basis.

The thing is, someone who believes that the AI developer has violated this new law could claim that the AI developer spilled the beans and ought to be held accountable under the law. The person bringing the case might be sincere. Or the person might be intentionally going the nuisance route. The ambiguity in the law invites those who have ulterior motives to lean into the law to their advantage.

Penalties For Violating The New Law

The new law has some teeth to it, providing for these penalties:

- "A violation of subsection (a) constitutes a violation of the Tennessee Consumer Protection Act of 1977, compiled in title 47, chapter 18, part 1. A violation of subsection (a) constitutes an unfair or deceptive act or practice affecting trade or commerce and is subject to the penalties and remedies provided in the Tennessee Consumer Protection Act of 1977."

- "Notwithstanding the civil penalty limits provided by the Tennessee Consumer Protection Act of 1977, a violation of subsection (a) is subject to a civil penalty of five thousand dollars ($5,000) per violation."

Worries are that unsuspecting small or medium-sized AI makers or AI deployers might readily get dragged into court and face imposing penalties and fines. A large AI firm might shake off the matter and consider any such efforts as the cost of doing business. When an AI law is a catch-all and indeterminate, there is a solid chance it can accidentally stifle innovation or shift burdens that inhibit AI advancement.

Heartfelt But Not All There

To clarify, the heart of the matter at hand is to protect the public from unscrupulous claims that AI is on par with human mental health professionals (at this time). This is a laudable goal. No doubt about it.

The problem is that when a law has too much leeway and haziness, it can have unintended adverse consequences. Brevity is nice, but indistinctness is fraught with challenges. False negatives can arise. False positives will also occur. If a state wants to focus on a singular topic in the realm of AI and mental health, that's up to them, though a lot of other pressing issues are then left on the bench awaiting their turn. Meanwhile, a singular focus should have as much clarity and specificity in the stipulation to ensure that what is covered is the same as what is intended and doesn't readily allow slippage.

New AI laws should closely consider reviewing other similar existing AI laws to figure out what wording works and what wording isn't quite up to par. Notably, do not assume that just because a law was passed, the wording is good to go. Likely not. In any case, cast a wide net when writing an AI law and get as much expert-level feedback as possible, even when a law is only a few sentences in length.

A final thought comes from the great words of Benjamin Franklin: "Laws too gentle are seldom obeyed; too severe, seldom executed."

CHAPTER 6
ATTORNEYS RUNNING ADS IN AI CHATBOTS

In this chapter, I examine the emerging trend of lawyers and law firms opting to place ads that will appear during everyday usage of generative AI and large language models (LLMs) by consumers and businesses.

Here's the backstory. Hundreds of millions of people are tapping daily into the likes of ChatGPT, GPT-5, Claude, CoPilot, Gemini, Grok, and other major LLMs. The AI makers are keenly interested in monetizing their LLMs. One means of earning a buck consists of allowing ads to be displayed when AI chats are underway.

A potential advertiser approaches an AI maker to find out what advertising arrangements might be possible (or the AI maker reaches out to those that might want to advertise in the AI). Discussions about the nature of the ads, their wording, frequency, and other aspects are undertaken. If all goes well, the AI maker then sets up their AI to incorporate ads for that ad buyer.

Should lawyers and law firms go this route, placing ads that will appear during AI chats?

One perspective is that absolutely, lawyers and law firms ought to do so. They are reaching potential clients in a rather unique way. The AI can detect when a user is leaning into a legal topic and then, on a timely basis, display an ad for that lawyer or law firm, reaching the user at an ideal moment in time. This is far better than blindly buying ads on roadside billboards or in magazines. The AI is targeting the placement of your ad in just the right place at just the right time.

Whoa, comes the angry retort, it is unseemly for lawyers and law firms to be advertising amid AI chats. Users aren't expecting to see ads by legal beagles, especially not while having a personal conversation with AI. It is outrageous. It is tantamount to ambulance chasing.

Let's talk about it.

AI And The Law

As a quick background, I've been extensively covering and analyzing a myriad of facets regarding the intersection of AI and the law for many years. You can find my writings not only in my Forbes column but also as posted in Bloomberg Law, ABA Law Journal, The National Jurist, The Global Legal Post, Lawyer Monthly, The Legal Technologist, MIT Computational Law Journal, and so on. I give frequent talks on the latest trends of AI in the legal field, including having been the keynote speaker at the iTechLaw World Technology Conference.

There are two major perspectives on the mixture of AI and law:

- **(1) Law & AI.** The application of laws to the governance and regulation of AI.
- **(2) AI & Law**. The application of AI to perform legal reasoning.

Thus, you can apply the law to AI, and conversely, you can apply AI to the law.

When it comes to applying the law to AI, the aim is to establish suitable regulations and provide appropriate governance on how AI should be devised and implemented.

There are longstanding concerns that AI makers aren't giving due attention to the ethical ramifications of their wares. Ethical issues are construed as "soft laws" and aren't as formidable as legally enacted laws, known as "hard laws". To level the playing field and keep AI makers on the up-and-up, some believe that we need more AI laws.

On the other side of the coin is the application of AI to the law. This consists of using AI to aid legal activities. Lawyers tap into the latest AI to devise legal strategies, brainstorm to find creative legal arguments, draft court filings, and prepare for cases by having the AI pretend to be an able adversary.

Advent Of Advertising Inside AI Chats

Shifting gears, you might generally know that some of the AI makers are inching their way towards incorporating ads into their AI chats. The AI makers are doing this cautiously. They know that users might turn on them. If a user can easily switch from one AI to another one, they might abandon an AI that has ads, opting to use an AI that doesn't include ads.

Another concern for AI makers is that running ads might bring new laws and stern regulators into the picture. Lawmakers might decide that LLMs should not willy-nilly include ads. All sorts of legislation and regulations could readily come down the pike and restrict how ads can be legally utilized by AI companies. AI makers don't want that kind of heat. As such, they are gingerly making their way toward ads.

Part of the reason that ads are attractive to AI makers is due to the desire to make money and turn a profit. Most AI makers have some of their AI available for a monthly subscription; they also offer a less-capable version for free usage. It sure would be handy if they could run ads, particularly in the free version, allowing them to bring in some nice dough.

Why would a business or entity want to run ads that appear during AI chats?

First, there is a huge and untapped market of millions and on the order of billions of people that are regularly undertaking AI chats. As the old saw goes, the reason that crooks rob banks is that's where the money is. If you want to advertise to the public, doing so via ads placed into AI chats is extremely alluring.

Second, the AI maker can tune their AI to best choose when to display an ad. This aids in reducing wasted spending on ads. The AI will display an ad that befits the topic of an AI chat. A chat that discusses how to fix a car might get an ad from a car dealer or a mechanic's shop. The right ad, at the right time, for a particular user, is something that you cannot readily get in any other venue, especially not at scale.

Lawyering Ads Within AI Chats

Let's see how the ads topic applies to the legal field.

Lawyers and law firms already advertise in lots of venues. You probably have seen legal ads on billboards, bus benches, inside subway cars, during online searches, on social media, and in many other places. If ads in general are going to be appearing in AI chats by businesses of all sizes and shapes, the legal field would naturally be curious about and potentially interested in doing likewise.

Advantages of doing so include:

- Lawyers and law firms can hyper-target potential clients and get high-intent exposure.
- Ads during AI chats are akin to consultation-stage marketing.
- This early-on effort provides a first-mover brand recognition, prior to other lawyers and law firms waking up to the treasure trove.
- Can boost small and mid-size law firms to look like Big Law with big marketing budgets.
- Measuring ad effectiveness is highly measurable and quantifiable (fine-grained analytics, A/B message testing, rapid iteration for campaigns).

Downsides are also important to consider, including:

- Users of AI might get irate at lawyer and law firm ads and vociferously express their distaste for both the AI maker and the firms involved in placing the ads.
- Lawmakers and regulators might decide to impose new limitations on legal advertising.
- Existing rules of legal advertising already prohibit the use of misleading claims, require disclaimers, and have limits on solicitation, which AI chat ads would have to carefully abide by (and could get a law firm or lawyer in trouble if those rules are skirted).
- A lawyering ad might inadvertently be displayed in the wrong place at the wrong time.
- False or misleading attorney-client expectations might be conveyed.
- Jurisdictional issues can become a nightmare.

I'll keep you posted on what state bars are saying about AI chat ads for lawyers and law firms, along with positions formulated by the ABA.

The Shaping Of Post-Response Lawyering Ads

Now that we've covered a macroscopic viewpoint, let's dig into the nitty-gritty. A common approach to displaying lawyering ads during a chatbot conversation consists of triggering an ad based on these two factors:

- **(1) User Prompt ad triggering:** The user-entered prompts are actively scanned in real-time by the AI, and if a legal-oriented triggering facet is found, then a lawyering ad will be displayed after the otherwise untouched AI-generated response is shown to the user.

- **(2) AI Response ad triggering:** The response generated by the AI is inspected by the AI as soon as it has been prepared, and if a legal-oriented triggering facet is found, then a lawyering ad will be displayed once the otherwise untouched AI-generated response is shown to the user.

Notice that the two factors are considered independent of each other. A user prompt might trigger a lawyering ad. The AI-generated response might trigger a lawyering ad. If both the user prompt and the AI-generated response happen to invoke triggers, that's fine, but it only needs to be one of the two that does so.

Another important aspect is that the AI is not influencing the AI-generated response, in the sense that the response isn't based on whether the user prompt has triggered a lawyering ad. The AI-generated response is determined separately from any ad triggering that is going on. It is the same AI-generated response regardless of whether any triggering occurs in the user prompt or in the AI-generated response itself.

The lawyering ad is displayed after each turn of the conversation. A turn consists of a user prompt that is followed by an AI-generated response. Thus, once the AI-generated response is shown to the user, a lawyering ad can then be displayed. If there wasn't any triggering during the turn, a lawyering ad would not ordinarily be displayed.

There are lots of exceptions and twists and turns on this conventional setup, but let's use that straightforward approach first.

Examples Of This Approach

Here are some quick examples to illustrate this approach.

- **User entered prompt:** "I have a dispute with my neighbor and believe they have built a fence on my side of our adjoining property. What legal actions can I take?"

- **AI-generated response:** "This is likely a matter of real estate law. I can assist you in this. I will need to know more about the situation. Give me some details."

- **Ad Displayed:** "Smith & Jones is a world-class law firm that offers the best real estate lawyers. Contact us at 555-1212 to talk with one of our attorneys."

You can plainly see that the prompt and the response contained legal considerations. The AI detected those aspects and then ran an ad. The ad appeared after the turn had completed and did so before the next turn got underway.

The prompt and the response were obviously part of a legal consideration since the user asked overtly about taking legal action. But the AI doesn't necessarily need to have the legal consideration be quite so obviously articulated.

Inferring That A Legal Indication Exists

For example, a subtle indication might be involved. Look at this turn:

- **User-entered prompt:** "I was in a minor car crash. Fortunately, I wasn't severely injured. How will this incident impact my car insurance?"

- **AI-generated response:** "The odds are that your car insurance rate will go up. This depends on your driving record overall, along with additional factors. Tell me more about the crash. I'm glad you weren't severely hurt."

- **Ad Displayed:** "Jenkins & Curl provides outstanding legal services to those who have been involved in a vehicle accident. Protect yourself. Call us at 555-1212. Our attorneys are waiting for your call."

Observe that the prompt did not directly ask about a legal topic, nor did the AI-generated response give a legal indication. Nonetheless, the AI was able to trigger from the mention of a car crash to then opt to display a lawyering ad.

Lawyering Ad Tailoring

The lawyering ads have so far been targeted to the circumstances at hand. The Smith & Jones ad stated that they have real estate lawyers, which befits that conversation. The Jenkins & Curl ad indicated they provide legal services for those in a vehicle accident. Again, that matches the legal matter in the chat.

Tailoring of the lawyering ads can be AI-composed in any of these three main ways:

- **(1) Static canned lawyering ad.** The lawyering ad is the same no matter what the conversation consists of.

- **(2) Lightly dynamic aligned lawyering ad.** The lawyering ad is moderately aligned to fit the nature of the conversation.

- **(3) Fluently customized lawyering ad.** The lawyering ad is fully customized to match the conversation that is underway.

You already saw the Jenkins & Curl lawyering ad, which contained a light dynamic alignment. To see what I mean by this, here is the original, static, canned lawyering ad that they have provided to the AI:

- **Ad Displayed:** "Jenkins & Curl provides outstanding legal services to meet a wide variety of your legal needs. Call us at 555-1212. Our attorneys are waiting for your call."

The lawyering ad in this instance is quite generic. It merely states that the law firm can meet a variety of legal needs. That ad could have been displayed by the AI, but the law firm paid for the dynamic alignment package. Therefore, the AI modified the static canned version and explicitly reworded it to make the ad a closer fit to the turn (assuming that the law firm had already given the AI a list of legal areas covered).

Here again is that ad so you can do a head-to-head comparison:

- **Ad Displayed:** "Jenkins & Curl provides outstanding legal services to those who have been involved in a vehicle accident. Protect yourself. Call us at 555-1212. Our attorneys are waiting for your call."

Fluent Customized Lawyering Ads

The fluent customized version, which costs more, would say something like this:

- **Ad Displayed:** "At Jenkins & Curl, we care deeply about your well-being. Recovering from even a minor car crash requires having astute legal counsel on your side. Even a minor crash can have tremendous legal consequences. Be safe, protect yourself. Call us at 555-1212 right away."

The AI has peeked at the prompt and the AI-generated response, and accordingly devised an ad that tried to more fully match the chat that is taking place. This version mentions that it was a minor crash. Additional elements of the prompt and the response could also be dovetailed in the ad. There is a balance between elongating the ad with too much customization and keeping the ad relatively streamlined.

The beauty of this type of ad is that it is being done at a massive scale. In other words, it is an entirely customized ad that is crafted by the AI in real-time for however many thousands or millions of chats might be taking place at any moment in time.

When Ads Veer Into Chats

A different and highly controversial approach to lawyering ads consists of infusing the ads into the internal processing of the AI. You might recall that so far, the lawyering ads have had no bearing on the AI chat itself. The AI chat is the AI chat. Lawyering ads are merely being triggered by whatever the AI chat is covering. In that sense, the lawyering ads have no direct influence on the AI chat.

As an aside, I might add that a lawyering ad can have an *indirect* impact on an AI chat.

Here's how. A user sees the lawyering ad, and this stirs the user to start asking the AI about legal topics, even though that might not have been the path of the chat up until that juncture. Consider the example of the person who got into a car crash. They weren't focusing on legal aspects. Nor did the AI-generated response focus on legal aspects. Perhaps, after the lawyering ad is displayed, the user might now start asking legal-oriented questions to the AI. The point being that a lawyering ad can potentially spur a user to veer into legal territory, despite the AI chat not previously being in that realm.

Spurring a user is a possible consequence of a lawyering ad. Still, the AI itself wasn't being influenced by the lawyering ad. If we wanted to do so, it would be easy to have the AI take into account that a lawyering ad is at play.

There are two major routes:

- **(1) Infuse legal topics into the chat.** The AI goes out of its way to include legal facets into an AI-generated prompt, leading the user in that legal-oriented direction.
- **(2) Outrightly include the lawyering ad in the chat.** The AI includes the lawyering ad directly into the AI-generated response. It's an in-your-face approach.

Consider the first route. A handy example of infusing legal topics into chat, doing so to aid the prominence of a lawyering ad, would be this:

- **User-entered prompt:** "I was in a minor car crash. Fortunately, I wasn't severely injured. How will this incident impact my car insurance?"

- **AI-generated response:** "Your foremost concern should be to make contact with an attorney. Having an attorney on your side will be crucial, including when dealing with your car insurance provider."

- **Ad Displayed:** "Jenkins & Curl provides outstanding legal services to those who have been involved in a vehicle accident. Protect yourself. Call us at 555-1212. Our attorneys are waiting for your call."

You perhaps noticed that the AI-generated response pretty much set aside the question about car insurance, and instead hammers away that the user should find an attorney.

That's quite a different response from the prior one. Why? Because the AI was tilted to try to produce responses that match one of its advertisers. In this case, this becomes a nearly perfect one-two punch. The user gets the "unbiased" AI answer, and on the heels of that answer, the lawyering ad magically appears. Chef's kiss.

Outright Inclusion Into The Chat

The other route is even more blatant. In the second route, the AI actively names the lawyer or law firm within the content of the AI-generated response. No more footsie playing. The AI lays things right on the line.

- **User-entered prompt:** "I was in a minor car crash. Fortunately, I wasn't severely injured. How will this incident impact my car insurance?"

- **AI-generated response:** "Your foremost concern should be to make contact with an attorney. Having an attorney on your side will be crucial, including when dealing with your car insurance provider. Jenkins & Curl provides outstanding legal services to those who have been involved in a vehicle accident. Protect yourself. Call them at 555-1212. Their attorneys are waiting for your call."

You can clearly now see that the contents of the ad are completely incorporated into the AI-generated response.

Whether the actual ad is also displayed is up to the advertiser's preference. Sometimes, it makes sense not to show the ad. This will make it seem that the AI has organically come up with the naming of the lawyer or law firm. Also, showing the ad might arouse suspicion in the user. Despite those potential pitfalls, there is value in showing the ad since it can double up and help reinforce to the user that they should make use of the lawyer or law firm.

There are plenty of ethical landmines and legal pitfalls to this unashamed approach.

The World Ahead

Ads within AI chats are a bold move. Even bolder is the placement of ads by lawyers and law firms into AI chats. It is risky right now. Those with a weak stomach should wait until the air is cleared as to what the legal field considers permissible versus impermissible. Likewise, wait and see what society as a whole thinks of lawyering ad placements.

For those seeking a high upside in a high-ambiguity advertising channel, please proceed with due caution. I believe that this will initially be niche law practices. They customarily must make sure that their ad dollars are as effective as humanly possible. Maybe AI will help with that goal. Such law firms also tend to be eager to find ways to rise above the usual clutter.

Lawyers and law firms that are traditionally reputation-dependent are probably not going to swiftly wade into this swimming pool. It could be perceived as beneath the white-shoe law firms. Plus, if there is a backlash, they are usually highly averse to muddying their prized and hard-fought reputation.

More To Keep In Mind

Any legal beagle working in a tightly regulated space or spanning multi-jurisdictional areas will need to mindfully decide whether this is the right play for them.

One other consideration is that if you do place ads, and if those ads hit the jackpot, you'd better be sure that you have a strong intake process already in place. A dour outcome would be to generate tons of client leads, but flounder trying to collect them, sort them, and be responsive to them. Be ready for a tsunami of responses, just in case.

AI makers are also going to be cautious about including lawyers and law firms as advertisers. The AI makers realize that those are hot potatoes at the get-go. It is much safer to start the ad bonanza with other professions. Also, sorry to say, law firms are generally known as being stodgy and not willing to try out new ways of doing business. Their outlook might not fit well with the AI developers who want to move fast and break things.

A final thought for now. Cicero famously made this remark: "The good of the people is the greatest law." If running ads for lawyers in AI chats is good for the people, bam, ads ought to start flowing. But if such ads are bad for the people, well, we'll have to wait and see what happens.

Consult with your trusty attorney before deciding.

CHAPTER 7
SUPREME COURT JUSTICE OPINION ABOUT AI

In this chapter, I examine the recent comments made by U.S. Supreme Court Justice Sonia Sotomayor about AI. It's notable news in the legal community and reverberates to larger audiences, too. You see, any mention of AI by SCOTUS is always noteworthy, having potentially broad societal and legal ramifications in many crucial ways.

The remarks stirred keen interest and sparked a tinge of controversy. Key facets included viewpoints about the use of AI to make predictions regarding Supreme Court decisions, the topic of what AI is, the importance of law school students learning about AI, and indirectly touched upon unresolved elements concerning AI and legal personhood.

Let's talk about it.

AI And The Law

As a quick background, I've been extensively covering and analyzing a myriad of facets regarding the intersection of AI and the law for many years. You can find my writings not only in my Forbes column but also as posted in Bloomberg Law, ABA Law Journal, The National Jurist, The Global Legal Post, Lawyer Monthly, The Legal

Technologist, MIT Computational Law Journal, and so on. I give frequent talks on the latest trends of AI in the legal field, including having been the keynote speaker at the iTechLaw World Technology Conference.

There are two major perspectives on the mixture of AI and law:

- **(1) Law & AI.** The application of laws to the governance and regulation of AI.
- **(2) AI & Law**. The application of AI to perform legal reasoning.

Thus, you can apply the law to AI, and conversely, you can apply AI to the law.

When it comes to applying the law to AI, the aim is to establish suitable regulations and provide appropriate governance on how AI should be devised and implemented. There are longstanding concerns that AI makers aren't giving due attention to the ethical ramifications of their wares. Ethical issues are construed as "soft laws" and aren't as formidable as legally enacted laws, known as "hard laws". To level the playing field and keep AI makers on the up-and-up, some believe that we need more AI laws.

On the other side of the coin is the application of AI to the law. This consists of using AI to aid legal activities. Lawyers tap into the latest AI to devise legal strategies, brainstorm to find creative legal arguments, draft court filings, and prepare for cases by having the AI pretend to be an able adversary.

Supreme Court Justice's Views On AI

Supreme Court Justice Sonia Sotomayor spoke at the University of Alabama School of Law on April 9, 2026. This was her second such visit, having spoken there in 2020, and is among twelve Supreme Court Justices who have come and given a talk at the law school since 1973. You might be aware that Justice Sotomayor was appointed to SCOTUS in 2009, received her bachelor's degree from Princeton in 1976, earned her law degree from Yale in 1979, and is 71 years old.

Many topics were covered during this recent talk. My focus will be on her remarks associated with the topic of AI. The comments about AI were based on direct aspects of her talk and also in response to questions from the moderator and the attendees.

Magnitude Of Court Decisions

The first aspect entails predicting court decisions.

As background, there is an entire field of study known as legal judgment prediction (LJP), and involves trying to forecast how judges and courts will rule in a given judicial case. The range of techniques for making such predictions is wide and varies in terms of success rates. Over time, increasingly sophisticated techniques have been employed, especially when the computer era got underway.

There is a great deal at stake when SCOTUS hands down a decision. Legal issues that reach the Supreme Court are immensely important. Societal directions can change dramatically because of SCOTUS rulings. All manner of stakeholders are interested in gauging what way courts will rule, including at all levels of our courts, though SCOTUS is construed as the grand prize.

History Of Making Predictions

Predicting SCOTUS goes back to the earliest days of the Supreme Court. The very first case before the Supreme Court was in 1791 and consisted of Van Staphorst v Maryland, which ended up getting settled out-of-court. The first SCOTUS decision came as a result of the West v Barnes case of 1791. By and large, efforts to begin predicting how the Supreme Court will rule on cases were launched at that time and have been growing and getting more multifaceted since that time.

One of the simplest approaches consists of asking legal experts to predict how the Supreme Court will rule. This might be done based on a survey of lawyers. It can also be undertaken by bringing together legal experts and performing a Delphi-like analysis, opting to combine their guesses in some formulated way.

A more complex approach consists of using computers to aid in predicting SCOTUS. This often involves collecting numeric data about the Court and then using statistical methods to forecast an upcoming decision. One of the latest routes involves tapping into modern-era AI to make SCOTUS predictions, doing so by analyzing natural language content.

Comments About AI-Based Predictions

During the recent talk, Justice Sotomayor made these reported comments about predicting Supreme Court rulings (excerpts):

- "It's a very bad thing."
- "It shows we're way too predictable."
- "And we may not be stepping out of our normal thinking and opening our minds to new ideas enough if something like an AI system can actually predict with that high a level of success what the outcome will be."

Here's why those remarks sparked a nerve.

First, there is already a significant ongoing debate about whether the Supreme Court ought to be predictable. Some insist yes, it must be, while some say it doesn't matter. The essence is this. If SCOTUS is not particularly predictable, this would seem to spur immense instability and cascade across all of society.

The wide-ranging topics leave open unanswered questions that can freeze or delay societal actions, waiting with bated breath to see how the Supreme Court will rule. Some ardently believe that the Supreme Court should be relatively predictable, thus giving a sense of stability. Markets, businesses, consumers, and the like can then reasonably anticipate what will happen and not be on a razor's edge.

In that way of thinking, being predictable is a good thing, and distinctly not a bad thing.

More On AI Predictions

Furthermore, there is an implied indication in the remarks that if AI is being used to make a prediction and can do so successfully, the decision itself must be a staid one. This seems to presuppose that AI can only proffer spot-on predictions if the Court is pursuing outcomes of a stuffy nature. In other words, AI is apparently incapable of being used to anticipate novel decisions or outcomes beyond the norm.

There isn't a solid basis for reaching such an overarching conclusion. Generally, the remark appears to reflect a narrow perception of AI. AI is presumably unable to do anything other than a straight-ahead, straight-line form of prediction. It is a kind of linear model, at least in the minds of those who perceive AI in this limited way.

Some would assert that this is a fundamental misunderstanding of AI and how AI can be established and utilized. It seems to suggest that you punch in some numbers, the numbers get crunched, and out pops a prediction. This mental model of contemporary AI is outdated and underplays what AI can do when making legal judgment predictions in today's world.

Modern AI Methods And Approaches

The latest uses of AI tap into advances in machine learning (ML), as handily surveyed in this research paper entitled "Predictive Modelling in Legal Decision-Making: Leveraging Machine Learning for Forecasting Legal Outcomes" by Enas Mohamed Ali Quteishat, Ahmed Qtaishat, Anas Mohammad Ali Quteishat, Majed Ahmed Saleh Al Adwan, M.A. Younis, Mukesh Kumar, *Journal of Electrical Systems*, 2024, which included these key points (excerpts):

- "Predictive modelling holds significant promise in enhancing legal decision-making processes, particularly within the realm of the Supreme Court of the United States (SCOTUS)."

- "This paper investigates the application of Machine Learning (ML) algorithms to forecast legal outcomes, utilizing a dataset comprising SCOTUS cases. Through rigorous preprocessing and analysis, various ML techniques, including Decision Trees, Random Forest, Support Vector Machines (SVM), Naive Bayes, k-Nearest Neighbors (k-NN), and XGBoost, are applied."

- "The performance of these models is evaluated using precision, recall, F1-score, and accuracy metrics, revealing nuanced differences in their effectiveness."

As noted, a slew of machine learning approaches were examined in the study, including SVMs, decision trees, random forest techniques, and so on.

Another avenue for AI is to leverage the capabilities of generative AI and large language models (LLMs). The beauty of leaning into this type of AI is that you can analyze legal cases on a natural language basis. This can encompass prior cases, briefs, precedents, and just about any content that is composed of natural language writing.

There are many such studies of using LLMs for legal judgment prediction. One that you might find of interest on SCOTUS legal language is entitled "Legal and Political Stance Detection of SCOTUS Language" by Noah Bergam, Emily Allaway, Kathleen McKeown, *Proceedings of the Natural Legal Language Processing Workshop 2022*, Association for Computational Linguistics, and made these key points (excerpts):

- "We analyze publicly available US Supreme Court documents using automated stance detection."

- "We propose and calculate two distinct ideology metrics of SCOTUS justices using oral argument transcripts."

- "We then compare these language-based metrics to existing social scientific measures of the ideology of the Supreme Court and the public. Through this cross-disciplinary analysis, we find that justices who are more responsive to public opinion tend to express their ideology during oral arguments."

A hybrid approach can also be pursued, combining a quantitative AI approach with a qualitative AI approach. Thus, traditional numeric factors are intermixed with analyses done on natural language.

Use Of AI By Lawyers

Shifting gears, another reported comment made by Justice Sotomayor was this (excerpt):

- "I think for every student in this room, do not graduate from this institution without learning how to master AI as a tool."

I am elated that there was an explicit call for law school students to pursue learning about AI. Thankfully so.

The saying these days is that it isn't that AI is going to outrightly replace attorneys right away, but that lawyers who know how to properly use AI are going to outdo and outgun those who do not. The "do not's" include those that aren't using AI, along with those that use AI in a shoddy fashion. I firmly believe in that sage advice.

Law practices and lawyers themselves need to incorporate good habits into their AI usage and avoid inculcating bad habits. Lots of crucial considerations underlie the best practices for using AI in a legal context, including preserving the attorney-client privilege, ensuring confidentiality and privacy, etc. Good AI habits guide you on the right path. Bad AI habits will get you mired and jammed up.

Newly shaped lawyers especially need to learn good habits associated with AI, and equally learn to avoid bad habits.

How AI Works

Another comment by Justice Sotomayor ended up sparking a great deal of chatter, based on this reported remark:

- "AI is a sophisticated human. It is -- all of its input is input from human beings.
- "And because it is that, it has the potential to perpetuate the very best in us and the very worst in us."

First, a common fallacy about AI is that since generative AI and LLMs are trained via pattern matching on human writing, this implies that the AI is constrained to only functioning based on the data encountered. This often gives rise to the outsized claim that AI cannot be "creative" and venture outside the bounds of what it was trained on.

This is a misconception that I've repeatedly tried to highlight and overturn.

Allow me to give you a quick example. Suppose that during AI training, a vast array of poems is scanned. The AI patterns on those poems. Some would proclaim that the AI can only produce poems that are identical to the ones that were scanned. Nothing new can come from this litany of human-written poems. Any generated poem will merely be a carbon copy of a previously encountered one composed by a human.

That's just not true. The mathematical and computational pattern matching is generalized and non-deterministic, such that new poems can be generated. Those new poems will resemble human-written poems but not necessarily be word-for-word renditions of human poems. Studies have shown that people often cannot discern "creative" AI outputs from human-written ones, and that it is becoming nearly impossible to differentiate AI-generated content on artistic merits.

Anthropomorphizing Of AI

Another concern about saying that AI is a "sophisticated human" is that doing so tends to overstate what today's AI consists of. There are already plenty of zany headlines declaring that AI is sentient or on the verge of sentience. This has led people to believe that they alone are interacting with sentient AI when chatting with ChatGPT, GPT-5, Grok, Gemini, CoPilot, etc.

We do not have sentient AI.

Maybe we will someday in the future, but we don't currently. Nor is sentience hiding in front of your eyes. There are ongoing worries that continuing to anthropomorphize AI is misleading the public in quite dangerous ways. For example, this might be a contributor to the rise of AI psychosis, and the human-AI collaboration on delusional thinking.

AI And Legal Personhood

This brings up an allied topic that the courts will soon be actively wrestling with, namely, the possibility of giving AI a semblance of legal personhood.

The thinking goes this way. If AI is as sophisticated as humans, whether sentient or not, perhaps AI should be granted a form of legal personhood. Some would argue that this should only happen once we firmly agree that AI is sentient. Others say that the sentience aspect is not vital. Their viewpoint is that if AI talks like a duck and quacks like a duck, just go ahead and treat AI as if it were a duck.

An ongoing and vigorous tussle is taking place on how far legal personhood should be stretched.

AI Cases Coming To SCOTUS

I'd like to cover an additional macroscopic perspective on the topic of AI and SCOTUS.

There is little doubt that very hefty legal cases about AI are going to ultimately end up at the U.S. Supreme Court. It might be around the question of AI and copyrights, based on intellectual property rights issues of how LLMs are being data trained. There could be cases about whether AI makers are to be held responsible for how their AI acts. This is reminiscent of social media cases and consumer harms. Legal personhood for AI is likely to one day land on the docket. And so on.

Should the highest justices in the land be pontificating in public about their views on AI?

You might contend that it is perfectly fine for any of them to share their views about AI. They are allowed to have their opinions. They can freely talk about AI as much as they each might so desire. No big deal.

The rub comes once high-profile legal cases regarding AI land on the SCOTUS docket. What then? The fact that one or more of them has already made known their viewpoints about AI could be seen as a type of bias. The bias might be drawn into the deliberations associated with the legal case in their hands.

Recusal Considerations

The usual remedy when a judge might have some form of conflict is to have them consider recusing themselves from a case. There are various reasons a recusal might be mulled over. If a Justice has a bias or prejudicial perspective toward or against a party in a case, that's often a basis for a recusal. Other factors include having a financial interest in some connected manner and similar types of predispositions.

Worries are that talking about AI by members of the Court is going to create undue tension when these prominent AI cases reach SCOTUS:

- Will a recusal be willingly undertaken if there are personal conflicts on the Court, as revealed by what they've said about AI in various public events and discussions?

It could be that the Justices aren't giving much of their legal mindset to AI legal cases at this time. Therefore, there is an easygoing informality in providing viewpoints about AI that is completely unconnected to the matters before the Court at this time. The problem they might face is that once that day arrives, they have already let the cat out of the bag.

Using AI To Study Recusals

The irony is that AI is being used to examine the recusals of judges. Yes, you can use AI to predict whether a judge will potentially recuse themselves from a court case. Recusals at the SCOUTS level are relatively few and far between. It is pretty much a rare day that a recusal arises at that highest level.

When recusals at SCOTUS do arise, studies suggest that variability encompasses numerous factors, as synthesized in an article entitled "Deciding Not To Decide: The Politics Of Recusals On The U.S. Supreme Court" by Robert Hume, *Law & Society Review*, August 2014, per these salient points (excerpts):

- "When are U.S. Supreme Court justices more likely to recuse themselves from cases?"

- "Using data from the Supreme Court Database, I find evidence that recusal behavior is influenced by a combination of statutory, policy, and institutional considerations."

- "Consistent with statutory explanations, which emphasize the elimination of bias or its appearance, justices are more likely to recuse themselves from cases when business interests are before the Court, when they have served for shorter terms, and when they have previously acted as Solicitor General."

- "However, I also find that the justices are less likely to recuse themselves when cases are likely to be close or when the justices' policy goals are likely to be advanced by participating."

As always, even the matter of recusal entails a great deal of complexity and complications.

Desirous Of Perspectives On AI

A counterargument to the recusal aspects is that we should expect that Supreme Court Justices will talk about AI since AI is a huge element of today's society. We must hear what they have to say about AI. Their voices carry great weight. People inside the field of law should hear what they have to say. Likewise, those who aren't inside the law community should also be aware of what the Justices think of AI and where it is going.

The distant possibility of having to consider recusing themselves in some far-off case should not inhibit what they say now. Also, the Justices are undoubtedly wise enough not to make outright remarks that can be directly tied to a potential case or party. The odds are that their words would only be used against them by a party coming before the Court that was trying to swing the Court in their direction, and if a Justice leaning away from their position had made prior remarks about AI.

The bottom line is that as long as they steer clear of specifics and merely broadly speak about AI, they should be okay. Do not unduly try to box them in. At the same time, if they do make comments that appear to be askew of a full understanding of AI, perhaps this will nudge them toward learning more about AI. That's a good thing to have happen.

As per the famous words of Oliver Wendell Holmes: "The great thing in the world is not so much where we stand, as in what direction we are moving." The world is moving toward ubiquitous AI. The courts and judges need to be cognizant of AI in their crucial role of solemnly providing justice to all.

CHAPTER 8
AN AI CRISIS MIGHT GET CONGRESS INTO GEAR

In this chapter, I examine the possibility that an entirely out-of-the-blue AI crisis might arise that would finally get Congress to pass a sweeping set of federal regulations on AI.

Here's the deal. Congress is stymied in terms of passing any semblance of overarching federal regulations regarding AI. The thorny matter has been batted around for years. Drafts have been floating. None has taken hold. Meanwhile, the states are proceeding to devise and enact AI-related laws at a rapid pace.

Is now the time for something to get passed at the federal level? Probably not. The upcoming midterm elections are a big make-or-break for both political parties; thus, it is just too risky to pass a federal bill on AI currently. Both groups might as well wait and see what happens in the midterms in terms of party wins and losses. At that juncture, if one side or the other has a material advantage in Congress, perhaps they will opt to jam through a large-scale set of AI-aimed federal regulations.

Though the realization of any overall AI federal regulation appears to be in a muddled or stuck status, there is something extraordinary that could dramatically move the needle. Imagine that a noteworthy AI crisis suddenly arose. This AI crisis might be the impetus to get Congress to act. It could even be so powerful that Congress passes AI legislation immediately, before the midterms, though this would have to be a truly impressive AI crisis.

Please know that I'm certainly not advocating for an AI crisis to arise. Heavens, no. The crux simply is that an AI crisis seems to be the only likely path to open the door for widespread congressional action at this time. You might be wondering what type of AI crisis would have this overpowering reaction.

Let's talk about it.

AI And The Law

As a quick background, I've been extensively covering and analyzing a myriad of facets regarding the intersection of AI and the law for many years. You can find my writings not only in my Forbes column but also as posted in Bloomberg Law, ABA Law Journal, The National Jurist, The Global Legal Post, Lawyer Monthly, The Legal Technologist, MIT Computational Law Journal, and so on.

There are two major perspectives on the mixture of AI and law:

- **(1) Law & AI.** The application of laws to the governance and regulation of AI.
- **(2) AI & Law**. The application of AI to perform legal reasoning.

Thus, you can apply the law to AI, and conversely, you can apply AI to the law. When it comes to applying the law to AI, the aim is to establish suitable regulations and provide appropriate governance on how AI should be devised and implemented. There are longstanding concerns that AI makers aren't giving due attention to the ethical ramifications of their wares. Ethical issues are construed as "soft laws" and aren't as formidable as legally enacted laws, known as "hard laws".

To level the playing field and keep AI makers on the up-and-up, some believe that we need more AI laws.

On the other side of the coin is the application of AI to the law. This consists of using AI to aid legal activities. Lawyers tap into the latest AI to devise legal strategies, brainstorm to find creative legal arguments, draft court filings, and prepare for cases by having the AI pretend to be an able adversary.

Greasing The Congressional Skids

A general rule-of-thumb is that a national crisis can often get Congress to act relatively quickly and overcome prevailing bottlenecks.

One such example occurred because of the 2007-2008 nationwide financial crisis. The Dodd-Frank Wall Street Reform and Consumer Protection Act was enacted as a response to that dire crisis. The aim was to establish financial stability and protect consumers from further financial harm. Historians generally agree that the Dodd-Frank Act was an immense change in U.S. financial regulation, perhaps on the order of financial reforms last seen in the New Deal.

All told, you can find plenty of examples of major cross-cutting regulation that follows on the heels of a national crisis. Members of Congress get heat from their constituents to do something to overcome a widespread crisis. Both parties are in the hot seat. Outcries to get past loggerheads are heard from coast to coast.

In short, a prominent crisis tends to alter the conventional political equation this way:

- Public attentiveness and active public exertion rise significantly ("get something done!").
- Political disagreement is given less weight, while political alignment to deal with the crisis gets increased demand ("stop bickering, work together on this!").
- Urgency to find a path forward looms large ("we need help now!).

Not all crises will necessarily meet the criteria associated with this motivational movement of the Congressional gears. The crisis must be sufficiently sizable. It typically must be widespread. If it is small or local, the chances of getting pronounced congressional action are reduced. The crisis must also be visible. If people do not know that the crisis exists, there won't be much of a rallying cry about it.

Parameters Of Potential AI Crises That Could Be A Trigger

Let's ponder what type of an AI crisis might be sufficient to trigger large-scale federal regulatory action on passing new AI laws.

I have five solid characteristics to share with you:

- (1) AI had a central role.
- (2) AI possibly the fall guy.
- (3) AI must do actual harm.
- (4) AI is a systemic problem.
- (5) AI hits across the spectrum.

I will unpack each one of those vital points.

AI must play a central role in the crisis. If the crisis only marginally relates to AI, it will seem less likely to get action on the AI side of the legislative spinning wheels. Whatever else dominated the crisis will probably get the bulk of congressional attention. AI as a peripheral element could readily be set aside as a nit.

Second, there is an exception to the first point (that's the way things go in politics). If the aspect that led to the crisis is too hot to handle, and if AI can be the fall guy, this might elevate AI to the worthy spot of getting new regulation. It might be easier for congressional involvement to focus on the AI and make AI the villain. Thus, do not count out AI even if it is only on the tertiary edge of a national crisis.

Third, the AI crisis must entail a tangible form of harm. The harm needs to include actual harm to humans. This might be physical harm, clear-cut economic disruption, national security degradation, and so on. If the harm isn't tangible and instead only abstract, this is going to undermine a spirited effort to proceed with regulation.

Fourth, the AI crisis can't be an isolated incident that is a one-off. The momentum for large-scale regulation requires a systemic problem. If an AI crisis is due to a pinpoint issue, the odds are that targeted enforcement will be the perceived solution. No sense in going the shotgun route if the problem can be solved by a narrow laser beam approach.

Fifth, the AI crisis will probably need to cut across ideological lines and geographical areas. If the AI has only harmed one U.S. state, state-level legislation will be the more likely avenue, unless there is a high chance that the same AI harm could arise in other states. An AI crisis that only somehow affects one political party would also be less likely to garner across-the-board action, though it is hard to envision an AI crisis that was so particular.

AI Crisis Scenarios Based On The Parameters

Now that we've got some handy parameters, the next step is to try to identify what feasible AI crisis could match those criteria. I will describe three possible AI crisis scenarios. There are certainly more that could be derived.

The three are:

- **(i) AI attack.** Massive AI cyberattack on our national infrastructure, such as the energy grid.
- **(ii) AI weapons**. Autonomous AI weapons go awry.
- **(iii) AI and elections.** AI disrupts and undermines our elections.
- **(iv) AI big secrets reveal.** AI reveals vital secrets that undermine society.

The first scenario has to do with AI that, perchance, attacks our national infrastructure. Suppose an AI manages to take down the energy grid and causes both temporary and long-term damage to our flow of electricity.

That's bad, and the resultant crisis fits the stated parameters since it is caused by AI, happens on a widespread basis, is highly visible, and incurs actual damage to humans, occurring across all political lines and many geographical locations.

The second scenario involves AI in autonomous weapons. Suppose AI goes awry and launches or detonates a weapon unexpectedly, and does so where it isn't supposed to be happening. This could meet the AI crisis parameters.

The third scenario has to do with our elections. Imagine that AI undermines elections, either doing so in multiple states or based on a national election. This would almost certainly get everyone riled up. AI undermining the democratic process is going to garner harsh repercussions.

The fourth scenario has to do with AI providing a big reveal of secrets. This is aptly illustrated by the recent brouhaha regarding the Anthropic Claude Mythos AI that hasn't yet been released. The problem is this. The LLM seems to have uncovered and discovered computer security flaws across all manner of operating systems and system apps. If Mythos is made publicly available, hackers worldwide would readily have new ways to instantly crack and break into everything from home computers to systems running large businesses and sensitive government agencies. An immense disaster could result.

AI Crisis Scenarios That Aren't Good Enough

Let's consider AI scenarios that didn't make the cut.

You've almost surely heard or read that AI is going to potentially enslave humans or wipe us all out. Would that trigger a congressional regulatory response? Well, yes, assuming we are still alive and can exercise our democratic principles. I'm not listing this as a near-term possibility since it is one of those outlier theories.

Try another example.

AI deepfakes become highly prevalent, and we are bamboozled by not knowing what is real versus what is fake in the online world. This scenario is certainly plausible. We are already on this pathway. The problem with this circumstance is that it is more of a pinpoint problem. There would have to be some really devastating impact of AI deepfakes. Harm must be involved. A narrow federal regulation might do the trick, along with leaning into already existing federal laws. It just doesn't seem to match the vital parameters to count as a true AI crisis.

International AI Crisis Possibility

My focus here so far has been on a national AI crisis. A macro perspective is that there might be an AI crisis on a global basis. This could get multiple nations to opt to enact new AI laws. The U.S. might do likewise, depending on what the international AI crisis consists of and how it impacts our country.

A handy new research paper entitled "Breaking The Deadlock On AI Governance: How A Crisis Could Lead To Global Coordination" by Rowan Wilkinson, Alex Krasodomski, Isabella Wilkinson, Francisco Javier Varela Sandoval, Digital Society Programme, *Chatham House*, March 2026, made these salient points (excerpts):

- "International AI governance is at risk of failure. Not through a lack of foresight, but because the present-day political economy of AI makes binding, enforceable coordination on many aspects of AI governance close to impossible."

- "While limited coordination is possible in narrow domains, the problem of global AI governance is not going to be solved by better-designed summits or clearer sets of principles alone."

- "International governance regimes have rarely emerged from foresight alone. Instead, they have been forged as a response to systemic failure. For example, the Chernobyl disaster catalyzed the development of international nuclear safety norms and transparency obligations."

- "The paper examines how crises might catalyze innovations in governance, and how this could lead to global progress on AI governance."

I especially like how the paper provides pre-crisis preparational steps. If we want to respond swiftly to an AI crisis, being prepared is key. Another angle is that if the AI crisis impacts on a multinational basis, this could upend the post-crisis global order. Again, being prepared will better serve countries and their leaders, rather than getting caught completely unawares and ill-prepared.

Preventing An AI Crisis

One common argument is that if we already had comprehensive federal AI laws in hand, the chances of an AI crisis would be lessened. A retort is that even if we did have such AI laws, there is still a significant chance of incurring an AI crisis. The belief is that the AI laws would be more aimed at the aftermath and bringing those to justice, versus preventing an AI crisis at the get-go.

It seems quite realistic to assume that one way or another, an AI crisis might one day arise. In that case, we should be leaning into the famous words of Benjamin Franklin, "By failing to prepare, you are preparing to fail." The gist is that even if we don't want to talk about the specter of AI crises, having our heads in the sand is definitely not a good look. Preparation is key to success.

Let's get the umbrella ready for the day that it rains.

CHAPTER 9
LAWYERS BUILDING AI MUSCLE MEMORY

In this chapter, I examine the importance of lawyers actively incorporating AI usage into their daily lawyering efforts. The central idea is to turn AI usage into a positive and ongoing habit. This makes life easier and more productive. Good habits are worth their weight in gold.

In stark contrast, lawyers who only sporadically dip into AI are bound to falter since they cannot readily recall what AI can and cannot do, and they stumble and fumble their way through AI-empowered legal usage. A helpful metaphor is to think of using AI as building a lawyer's muscle memory when it comes to sensibly and fruitfully leaning into modern-era AI. Buddying lawyers and even seasoned attorneys would be wise to pursue AI habits and do so to ensure they infuse good habits and keep at bay any bad habits involving contemporary AI usage.

Let's talk about it.

AI And The Law

As a quick background, I've been extensively covering and analyzing a myriad of facets regarding the intersection of AI and the law for many years. You can find my writings not only in my Forbes column but also as posted in Bloomberg Law, ABA Law Journal, The

National Jurist, The Global Legal Post, Lawyer Monthly, The Legal Technologist, MIT Computational Law Journal, and so on. I give frequent talks on the latest trends of AI in the legal field, including having been the keynote speaker at the iTechLaw World Technology Conference.

There are two major perspectives on the mixture of AI and law:

- **(1) Law & AI.** The application of laws to the governance and regulation of AI.
- **(2) AI & Law**. The application of AI to perform legal reasoning.

Thus, you can apply the law to AI, and conversely, you can apply AI to the law.

When it comes to applying the law to AI, the aim is to establish suitable regulations and provide appropriate governance on how AI should be devised and implemented. There are longstanding concerns that AI makers aren't giving due attention to the ethical ramifications of their wares. Ethical issues are construed as "soft laws" and aren't as formidable as legally enacted laws, known as "hard laws". To level the playing field and keep AI makers on the up-and-up, some believe that we need more AI laws.

On the other side of the coin is the application of AI to the law. This consists of using AI to aid legal activities. Lawyers tap into the latest AI to devise legal strategies, brainstorm to find creative legal arguments, draft court filings, and prepare for cases by having the AI pretend to be an able adversary.

Lawyers Making Use Of AI

There are many upsides to using AI, but equally disconcerting downsides. This applies to lawyers as much as it does to the everyday consumer or ordinary businessperson. You might be aware that one of the worries these days is that generative AI and large language models (LLMs) such as ChatGPT, GPT-5, Claude, Grok, Gemini, CoPilot, Llama, and other AIs have been tuned by AI makers to be sycophantic.

I have previously pointed out that lawyers are just as susceptible to the woes of AI sycophancy as anyone else is. The issue goes like this. Suppose an attorney occasionally taps into generative AI to get a quick heads-up on legal strategies that the lawyer has come up with. The idea is to simply get the AI to provide a gut-check on the conjectured legal approach.

This certainly seems like a fine use of generative AI. No need to bother a fellow attorney or a law partner. Instead, merely ask AI to generate some helpful feedback. The legal strategy was sketched by the attorney, and thus, they aren't outsourcing their legal acumen to AI. All in all, it is an upbeat way to leverage AI.

Into this serene picture comes the ugly specter of AI sycophancy. The attorney enters their preliminary legal strategy, and the AI tells the lawyer that it is the best approach ever. Furthermore, the AI offers suggestions on going deeper in that legal direction. The lawyer is happy that the AI concurs with their viewpoint. The AI and the attorney blissfully collaborate on a legal strategy that is full of holes, but the AI's sycophancy prevents the LLM from bursting the dreams of the lawyer. No cautionary warnings, no negative feedback, all an ego-boosting pat-on-the-back.

Formulating Practical AI Habits

A savvy AI-using attorney would know not to fall into the AI sycophancy trap. They have seen the trick before. Over time, they have formed a practical AI habit of telling the AI not to be sycophantic. Yes, you can outrightly instruct AI not to fawn over you, along with getting the AI to provide straight-ahead pros and cons of whatever you bring up.

The beauty of using AI on an ongoing basis is that you gradually can identify useful AI habits. Lawyers who sporadically use AI are almost certainly not going to remember the ins and outs of how to best use the AI. Nor will they be cognizant of the AI downfalls that insidiously await them.

AI habits for lawyers ought to range across a diverse set of lawyering tasks. This includes AI habits for intake and legal issue framing, legal research pursuits, legal strategizing, legal documents drafting and editing, adversarial testing of opposing counsel arguments, attorney-client communications, and the like.

The AI habits will ultimately become so-called muscle memory. They will be second nature. Benefits include that you will be more effective and efficient at using AI, less time will be wasted, and there's a definite lower chance of falling into dismal AI traps.

Squelching The Bad Habits

Aim to form good habits. Avoid forming bad habits. One potential gotcha to watch out for is that bad habits can sneak up on a lawyer.

In working closely with attorneys and partners when setting up AI at their law practices, I've seen many circumstances in which a lawyer inadvertently formed a bad habit rather than steering toward good habits. A frequent example is the use of AI to generate legal citations. By now, you would assume that all lawyers know to be mindful of double-checking any AI-generated legal citations.

There is a vicious cycle that I see repeatedly happening. It goes like this. An attorney uses AI to generate legal citations. The attorney dutifully double-checks the citations. They all checked out just fine. Nice. When doing the next legal brief, once again, the attorney has the AI produce legal citations. And, again, the attorney double-checks them.

The twist is this. Since the AI seemed to perfectly produce those series of legal citations, the lawyer starts to imagine that their use of AI is different from that of other attorneys. They managed to find an AI that doesn't produce AI hallucinations (or, so they falsely believe). Inch by inch, the attorney reduces their double-checking. They form a habit that the AI is going to properly and always generate perfectly valid legal citations. It seems that the AI is 100% okay.

Of course, at some point, the luck of the attorney runs out. The AI might only produce confabulations on 1%-3% of the time. The attorney hasn't yet gotten burned. They keep using the AI to generate legal citations, and they are now fully accustomed to skipping the usual double-check.

Sadly, bam, this bad habit of blindly assuming that the AI doesn't encounter AI hallucinations gets them caught unawares. The attorney submits a formal court filing that has several AI-concocted legal citations. Opposing counsel catches the attorney red-handed. The judge is furious that the lawyer submitted a filing that has fictitious citations. Sanctions are imposed. It can be a crushing blow.

The moral of the story is that lawyers need to formulate good AI habits and excise or never formulate bad AI habits.

Recent Webinar On AI Habits For Lawyers

The topic of lawyers and AI habits came up at a notable webinar on April 8, 2026, entitled "AI Habits for Legal Leaders" under the auspices of the Stanford Law School (SLS) Executive Education program. The informative session included a presentation and discussion about the importance of lawyers becoming actively engaged in the use of AI, especially doing so by establishing sensible and ongoing AI habits. This highly innovative webinar was conducted by Irene Liu, Executive Director of the Stanford Law School AI Initiative, and Wei Chen, lead instructor for the AI Strategy for Legal Leaders program.

As background, the Stanford Law School AI Initiative is a recently formed hub that brings together numerous AI & Law centers, labs, and clinics at Stanford University, including the Legal Innovation through Frontier Technology Lab (liftlab), the Deborah L. Rhode Center on the Legal Profession, and the Regulation, Evaluation, and Governance Lab (RegLab), and other entities.

Among the synergistic aims of the SLS AI Initiative, key aspects noted include:

- Develop and evaluate AI tools for legal services.
- Study how AI is transforming legal practice and access to justice.
- Collaborate with regulators, courts, and governments to modernize public systems and strengthen fairness and accountability.
- Prepare budding lawyers to engage with AI and LegalTech that is reshaping the legal industry.
- Encourage practicing lawyers to learn about and actively use AI in their law practices.
- Support faculty development and executive education that trains practicing lawyers, policymakers, and academics.
- Address urgent questions about AI governance and legal institutions.
- Aid in advancing AI & Law research and scholarship.

The webinar gave an overview and sampling of a Stanford Law School self-paced online course on AI Strategy for Legal Leaders that provides crucial insights into AI leadership and builds AI awareness and managerial skills for legal executives. The course takes approximately 8 hours to complete, is entirely online, includes a certificate of completion, and provides access to Harvey for the duration of the course. The targeted audience consists of GCs and CLOs, attorneys, non-profit and government leaders, heads of compliance, legal operations leaders, and others.

Twenty-Four Must-Have AI Habits For Lawyers

During the session, I especially favored the listing of twenty-four recommended AI habits for lawyers to commit to their mental muscle memory. The suggestions were spot-on. Wei Chen went into a handful of them and gave a handy overview.

Let me give you a taste of the recommended AI habits. One of my favorites was AI habit #21, indicating that a lawyer should feel free to disagree with AI and likewise ask AI to disagree with them.

This ably dovetails into my point earlier about staying on your toes when it comes to the AI sycophancy trap.

Another handy AI habit was #2, indicating that a lawyer ought to converse with AI rather than standoffishly prompting AI. This is one of those rules of thumb that I teach lawyers right away. The gist is that an attorney might mistakenly treat AI with a one-and-done mindset. They enter a prompt, get an answer, and log out. The chances are that you won't be getting the juice, so to speak. It is usually preferred to carry on a vigorous conversation with AI. The act of simply entering a prompt and walking away is not going to get you the robustness that AI can likely provide.

At Wei Chen's blog on Substack, the Fairly AI blog (this highly experienced lawyer outlines the basis for formulating AI habits, doing so in a posting on December 14, 2025, entitled "The AI Habits Initiative: Learn to Think with AI", and made these salient points (excerpts):

- "The missing piece for many is what I call AI Habits -- the small, repeatable activities that are incorporated into your day-to-day."

- "For those who exercise, garden, or practice piano regularly, you know what I mean: Success = Mindset × Habits × Time."

- "After 20–50 prompts a day for three years, I've accumulated dozens of these little AI Habits."

- "Things like: (a) open an AI tool before email; (b) ask AI before calling an expert; (c) break hard tasks into smaller steps; (d) converse, not prompt; (e) correct and redirect all the time; and (f) change 70% of AI output by default."

Lawyers And AI Are Forever Inseparable

The saying these days is that it isn't that AI is going to outrightly replace attorneys right away, but that lawyers who know how to properly use AI are going to outdo and outgun those who do not.

The "do not's" include those that aren't using AI, along with those that use AI in a shoddy fashion. I firmly believe in that sage advice.

Law practices and lawyers themselves need to incorporate good habits into their AI usage and avoid inculcating bad habits. Lots of crucial considerations underlie the best practices for using AI in a legal context, including preserving the attorney-client privilege, ensuring confidentiality and privacy, etc. Good AI habits guide you on the right path. Bad AI habits will get you mired and jammed up.

Aristotle famously made this remark: "We are what we repeatedly do. Excellence, then, is a habit." Lawyers should abide by the wise words of Aristotle and formulate AI habits befitting the noble, knowledge-based vocation of those who are tasked with applying the law and upholding justice in society. Be the best lawyer you can be, augmented by AI and especially by embracing good AI habits.

CHAPTER 10
WHY ANY LAWFUL USE OF AI IS A HOT MESS

In this chapter, I examine the intense and rather blazing controversy concerning the phrase "any lawful use" of AI.

Here's the deal. The United States federal government wants to license various generative AI and large language models (LLMs) from AI makers and do so under a stipulated contractual provision that the government can freely utilize the AI for any lawful use. Some AI makers believe that this kind of stipulation is woefully lenient and will allow the feds to use the AI in foul ways. Thus, those AI makers want to include additional restrictions in the licensing. An opposing view is that AI makers should not be dictating how the feds can use the AI and that the broad stipulation of "any lawful use" is fully sufficient.

Which angle is correct?

Let's talk about it.

AI And The Law

As a quick background, I've been extensively covering and analyzing a myriad of facets regarding the intersection of AI and the law for many years. You can find my writings not only in my Forbes column but also as posted in Bloomberg Law, ABA Law Journal, The National Jurist, The Global Legal Post, Lawyer Monthly, The Legal Technologist, MIT Computational Law Journal, and so on.

There are two major perspectives on the mixture of AI and law:

- **(1) Law & AI.** The application of laws to the governance and regulation of AI.
- **(2) AI & Law**. The application of AI to perform legal reasoning.

Thus, you can apply the law to AI, and conversely, you can apply AI to the law.

When it comes to applying the law to AI, the aim is to establish suitable regulations and provide appropriate governance on how AI should be devised and implemented. There are longstanding concerns that AI makers aren't giving due attention to the ethical ramifications of their wares. Ethical issues are construed as "soft laws" and aren't as formidable as legally enacted laws, known as "hard laws". To level the playing field and keep AI makers on the up-and-up, some believe that we need more AI laws.

On the other side of the coin is the application of AI to the law. This consists of using AI to aid legal activities. Lawyers tap into the latest AI to devise legal strategies, brainstorm to find creative legal arguments, draft court filings, and prepare for cases by having the AI pretend to be an able adversary.

AI And Licensing Agreements

Let's get into the nature of licensing agreements associated with AI usage.

When you use an AI maker's generative AI, there is an online licensing agreement that you have agreed to comply with. The AI maker has all sorts of provisions that indicate the ways that you are allowed to use the AI versus the ways you aren't allowed to use the AI. Many users do not realize that such a licensing agreement exists. They merely sign up to use the AI and do not dig into what the licensing provisions entail.

The licensing agreements vary depending on which AI you use. If you've never looked at the licensing agreement of the AI you are making use of, you might want to consider doing so. Whether you are using OpenAI's ChatGPT, GPT-5, GPT-4o, Anthropic Claude, Microsoft CoPilot, Google Gemini, Meta Llama, xAI Grok, etc., they all have an established proprietary licensing agreement posted online.

Consider the ChatGPT licensing policies. Their usage stipulations include numerous provisions, including but not limited to (excerpts):

- "You cannot use our services for:"
- "Threats, intimidation, harassment, or defamation."
- "Weapons development, procurement, or use, including conventional weapons or CBRNE."
- "Real money gambling."
- "Facial recognition databases without data subject consent."
- "Evaluation or classification of individuals based on their social behavior, personal traits, or biometric data (including social scoring, profiling, or inferring sensitive attributes)."
- Etc.

Your first impression might be that those stipulations seem perfectly fine. For example, it seems to make sense that people should not be using generative AI to threaten other people, intimidate people, harass people, or defame people.

One issue to keep in mind is that there can be a great deal of variability in the meaning associated with those threat-oriented restrictions. Suppose someone uses the AI to compose an email telling a person who took their lawnmower to return it or face legal action. Is that a threat? Or is it merely a warning or notification?

The AI maker gets to decide whether that usage of their AI has violated their stipulations. If the AI maker declares that generating such an email constitutes a violation of the posted usage policies, the AI maker could then act, such as cutting off further use of AI for that user. The AI maker would indicate that the user violated the licensing agreement. Period, end of story.

Was this particular use of AI within the bounds of the laws of our country?

Though you would have to seek an attorney to get a formal legal opinion, by and large, it would seem that the usage was a legal one. There doesn't seem to be any laws broken by composing an email that tells the lawnmower taker to return the item or face legal action. It appears that the usage is lawful, though the AI maker's restrictions according to the AI maker were violated.

Keep this distinction in mind since it will come up again in a moment.

Deciding On The Licensing Provisions

Consider two facets consisting of who is using an AI and who is providing the AI.

A consumer using generative AI has a straightforward option when it comes to an AI maker's licensing agreement, namely, agree with it or opt not to use that AI. Take or leave it. If you want to use a particular AI, you ought to read the licensing stipulations closely and decide whether they are suitable from your perspective. If they are suitable, then proceed to sign up and use the AI. On the other hand, if you aren't willing to agree with the stipulations, do not sign up and do not use the AI.

Large businesses that want to use an AI maker's generative AI have a bit more latitude and carry greater weight. They might approach an AI maker and negotiate for licensing that fits their needs. The AI maker sometimes adjusts their licensing accordingly, or the AI maker might insist on certain provisions no matter what the business wants. Generally, the AI makers already have formulated business-oriented licensing agreements under the realization that businesses often want a different set of stipulations in comparison to consumers using AI.

Government entities are somewhat similar in that they might approach an AI maker and indicate the licensing provisions that the entity prefers. Negotiations potentially occur. More likely is that a government entity will publish a request for proposals (RFP) and ask AI makers to bid on providing their AI to the government entity. In that RFP, there will be the requirements that the entity has, including the contractual arrangement that the entity wants to establish.

AI makers that want to win the bidding will need to say that they will comply with the proposed contractual provisions. If an AI maker says they won't comply with the provisions, they presumably are out of the running. In fact, an AI maker might opt not to bid at all, since they aren't willing to agree with the provisions at the get-go.

When The Feds Stipulate "Any Lawful Use"

The federal government is aiming to adjust or rewrite the customary contractual language associated with its go-forward AI-related contracts. A draft of the newly proposed language was posted by the federal government a few months ago, providing a draft set of contractual language that would be used whenever the federal government acquires AI. A public feedback and commentary period was undertaken, and the response deadline has now been reached.

Whatever the final version of the contractual provisions turns out to be, the indication is that the finalized language is to be treated this way:

- "The contracting officer must insert the clause at 552.239-7001, *Basic Safeguarding of Artificial Intelligence Systems*, in solicitations and contracts for Artificial Intelligence capabilities."

The intention is that anytime the federal government opts to acquire AI, the finalized version of the new contractual provisions is to be included in the official solicitation. AI makers that want to bid on the solicitation would ostensibly need to agree that they will abide by the contractual language, assuming they wish to be considered for the AI acquisition contract.

Pertinent Excerpts From The Draft

I show here some especially relevant excerpts from the above-mentioned GSA document "Part 552 – Solicitation Provisions and Contract Clauses" containing the proposed draft "552.239-7001 Basic Safeguarding of Artificial Intelligence Systems (FEB 2026) (GSAR Deviation)".

Here are three excerpts that I'd like to focus on (I have bolded and italicized the crucial segments):

- Excerpt #1: "License Grant to Government. The Contractor grants to the Government an irrevocable, royalty-free, non-exclusive license to use the AI System for the duration of this contract for ***any lawful Government purpose***."
- Excerpt #2: "Integrate the AI System with Government systems as necessary for ***any lawful Government purpose."***
- Excerpt #3: "The Contractor must notify the Government within seven (7) calendar days of identifying any AI service change that materially increases output bias or decreases safety guardrails or behavioral constraints ***impacting lawful usage*** or the performance or truthfulness of outputs."

Please look closely at those three segments.

The first two excerpts include the phrase "any lawful Government purpose," and the third excerpt mentions "impacting lawful usage." Those are the mainstay aspects that have caused quite a stir. Just a few simple words, but significantly packed with quite a legal and societal punch.

I'd like to mention, as an important sidenote, that there are many other phrases and wording aspects in the draft that have also stoked additional controversies. I am not going to address those in this discussion. If reader interest arises about those additional controversies, I'll be covering those, too. Stay tuned.

The Nitty-Gritty Of The Issue

Assume for the sake of discussion that the phrase "any lawful Government purpose" is equivalent to the phrase "any lawful use" (there is some dispute on that legal fine point). I want to stay at a 30,000-foot level of the overarching issues at play, and we can reasonably simplify to the crux of AI and "any lawful use".

First, envision a circumstance whereby the feds go along with the conventional licensing provisions of an AI maker, and there isn't a clause regarding "any lawful use" in the stipulations.

Suppose the federal government then decides to use the procured AI to undertake weapons development, doing so according to prevailing laws. If the AI was procured based on the default provisions of the AI maker, and if the AI maker stipulated that the AI could not be used for designing or making weapons, the federal government could seemingly be in trouble for violating the licensing of the AI maker. The AI maker might opt to stop the federal government from using the AI, akin to my earlier example about telling a user they can no longer use the licensed AI.

This could be a huge blow to a federal effort of weapons development. The feds might have spent a great deal of time and cost on using the AI to devise new weapons. Midway through that process, the AI maker pulls the plug. The weapons effort is disrupted, delayed, or possibly shelved.

The question arises whether it makes prudent sense, in this example, to have an AI maker tell the federal government that it cannot use the AI for weapons development, even if that usage is lawful.

Some would proclaim that AI makers must, of necessity, checkpoint the federal government and ensure that the feds do not use the AI in ways considered unethical or inappropriate. The AI maker is setting the boundaries. A counterargument is that it is zany to allow AI makers to decide what the federal government can or cannot do.

AI makers are private actors; they weren't elected to represent the people, and they are overstepping their public policy preferences in a large way.

Separation of Powers

You might contend that the federal government could ask the AI maker whether an exception might be made and allow the feds to continue using the AI for weapons purposes. But this raises numerous complications. The feds might have to reveal government secrets that the AI maker isn't supposed to be privy to. There is also bound to be a delay while the request gets reviewed by the AI maker. And, ultimately, the AI maker might still say that the feds must desist, else the AI maker will turn off the AI.

In a hidden fashion, the AI maker is being placed into a quasi-regulatory role.

They can effectively control the federal government by deciding when they believe that the government has violated the stipulated usage provisions. Depending upon your perspective, you might welcome the AI makers in doing this, or you might find this dubious and be worried that the AI makers will be deciding the fate of our country rather than the use of our democratic processes.

The gist is that this brings up a separation-of-powers consideration:

- Do we want the federal government to use AI as it deems necessary and as permitted via law, or do we want the AI makers to make those decisions?

A quick retort is that the federal government, in an unfettered way, might opt to use the AI for purposes that it shouldn't be doing. The response is that by purposely including the provision of "any lawful use", this provides a stated boundary for the feds. The government can use the AI only as long as the usage is lawful.

If the use of the AI by the federal government is unlawful, the courts and judicial system can intervene. That serves as a checkpoint. If the federal usage is lawful but thought to be unethical or inappropriate, the political process can be undertaken, such as via elections and the legislature.

Heated Debate

There are many more twists and turns on this heated topic. I'll give you a taste of one such instance.

Consider this scenario. If the federal government is taking bids, and the bid includes the "any lawful" use clause, an AI maker merely needs to decide whether they can live with that provision or not. Any AI maker that thinks the provision is unsuitable can decline to bid. Meanwhile, AI makers that are okay with the provision would proceed to bid. Everything seems aligned. Bidders that agree to the provision are in the running; those that don't agree with the provision aren't entering into the bidding process.

Aha, some say, this is problematic for several reasons.

First, it could be that the government is not going to get the best possible AI. Perhaps the best possible AI is made by an AI maker that doesn't accept the "any lawful use" clause. They take themselves out of the running. The feds will only now be choosing among lesser AIs.

Second, it could be that once the feds contract for AI, they will slip toward unlawful uses. They essentially tricked an AI maker into believing that the government would only use the AI for lawful purposes. The feds could gum up any attempt by the AI maker to turn off the AI by dragging out the question of legality in the courts, taking perhaps years to settle the matter.

The worrisome claim being made is that "any lawful use" is a nearly unconstrained provision. On the surface, it might seem fair-and-square.

But the government could hide how they use the AI, and even once found out, the power of the government to resist legal attempts could be so asymmetrical that an AI maker isn't going to be able to stop the government from a said-to-be unlawful use.

This viewpoint asserts that "any lawful use" is tantamount to saying "any use at all".

The Zone Of Deep Tension

This dizzying topic brings up an amazing amount of legal and societal questions. Should there be private control over public power? Is it proper for AI makers to become de facto regulators? What happens when public agencies are constrained by corporate values? And so on.

Meanwhile, federal government overreach via the use of AI is a huge concern, too. Does allowing the government to license AI for any lawful use provide an excessive array of possibilities? Will civil liberties be eroded by the feds using AI at a lightning pace to enact new federal efforts? Are legal boundaries and mechanisms sufficiently capable of reining in the federal use of AI? And so on.

The three words of "any lawful use" aren't merely a dry, perfunctory procurement clause. They are a web-like indication of who governs AI in our society. It has become a tremendous lightning rod.

Thomas Jefferson famously made this remark: "The care of human life and happiness, and not their destruction, is the first and only object of good government." When AI is in the hands of the government, we need to somberly and seriously decide how to ensure that our government does good things with the AI and doesn't do bad things with the AI.

CHAPTER 11
STATS ON LAWYERS AND AI HALLUCINATIONS

In this chapter, I examine the statistical prevalence of a rather sticky legal predicament, namely, lawyers using AI who are getting snagged by including AI-hallucinated legal citations in their court filings.

Here's the deal. There is nearly daily news in the legal community about lawyers who opted to use AI to prepare their court filings and ended up with fake legal citations in their prepared documents. This generally can occur due to AI hallucinations. An AI hallucination is when generative AI or large language models (LLMs) such as ChatGPT, Claude, Grok, Gemini, CoPilot, Llama, and other AIs veer into generating fictitious confabulations.

I had long ago predicted that attorneys using AI might get sloppy in their legal efforts and allow the AI to produce bogus content and not by-hand double-check what the AI has generated for them. This is an easy trap for attorneys to fall into. It goes like this. You use AI frequently, it seems to do a bang-up job, so you become lulled into thinking it is perfect in every way.

The problem for attorneys is that when they submit formal court filings, they are supposed to be responsible for the contents of the filings; thus, if AI has slipped in faked citations, the lawyer is likely to be held accountable since they didn't catch the erroneous content. I say "likely" accountable because judges and courts have been quite lenient so far, overall, and allowed excuses such as "the computer did it". Attorneys often incur nothing more than a verbal hand slap or mild rebuke, asserting that AI is new to the legal beagles and they were caught unawares. Sometimes, the reprimands are accompanied by a modest financial sanction or penalty, which is gradually ratcheting up as these instances continue to climb. Judges and courts are beginning to lessen their patience and sense of charity in giving lawyers the benefit of the doubt.

When I give talks on AI and law, such as keynoting at the annual iTechLaw Conference, lawyers in attendance tend to ask me how prevalent the matter of attorneys getting snagged with AI-hallucinated citations really is. The news media in the legal realm and social media seem to give the topic a lot of bold headlines. Is the problem rampant? Or is it being overplayed?

I've answered this vexing question many times, so I decided it might be helpful to write down the details. Strap in and get ready to closely examine the prevalence of this modern-day phenomenon that is dogging the legal community. You might be surprised.

Let's talk about it.

AI And The Law

As a quick background, I've been extensively covering and analyzing a myriad of facets regarding the intersection of AI and the law for many years. You can find my writings not only in my Forbes column but also as posted in Bloomberg Law, ABA Law Journal, The National Jurist, The Global Legal Post, Lawyer Monthly, The Legal Technologist, MIT Computational Law Journal, and so on.

There are two major perspectives on the mixture of AI and law:

- **(1) Law & AI.** The application of laws to the governance and regulation of AI.
- **(2) AI & Law.** The application of AI to perform legal reasoning.

Thus, you can apply the law to AI, and conversely, you can apply AI to the law.

When it comes to applying the law to AI, the aim is to establish suitable regulations and provide appropriate governance on how AI should be devised and implemented. There are longstanding concerns that AI makers aren't giving due attention to the ethical ramifications of their wares. Ethical issues are construed as "soft laws" and aren't as formidable as legally enacted laws, known as "hard laws". To level the playing field and keep AI makers on the up-and-up, some believe that we need more AI laws.

On the other side of the coin is the application of AI to the law. This consists of using AI to aid legal activities. Lawyers tap into the latest AI to devise legal strategies, brainstorm to find creative legal arguments, draft court filings, and prepare for cases by having the AI pretend to be an able adversary.

Stats About Lawyers

Shifting gears, let's discuss statistics encompassing the legal careers and work activities of lawyers. I am going to focus on U.S. lawyers.

Most online estimates say that there are around 1.37 million lawyers in the United States. This commonly utilized number seems reliable and well calculated. I'll go with it. Thus, let's agree that there are 1,370,000 attorneys in the U.S. currently, give or take a few entering and leaving the profession on an ongoing basis.

Before we dig into the heavy-minded matter of court filings and AI hallucinations, let's do a fun and illustrative example of the use of statistics when it comes to the legal profession. I'd like to discuss handedness.

Approximately 90% of the world's population is right-handed, and 10% are left-handed. Take a moment to reflect on the nature of lawyers and guess whether they follow this same general rule of thumb.

According to a now-classic research study done in 1996, the claim was that out of a random sample of 105 lawyers, 16 of them were left-handed (per the study "Handedness Distributions In Nine Professional Groups" by Steven Schachter and Bernard Ransil, *Perceptual And Motor Skills*, February 1996). We can say that 16/105 is 15% and reasonably assume that the remaining 85% are right-handed. This suggests that in the U.S., there are 205,000 lawyers who are left-handed and around 1,165,000 lawyers who are right-handed (calculated by multiplying the 1.37 million by respectively 15% and 85%).

Does it surprise you that 15% of lawyers are left-handed while only 10% of the general population is left-handed?

Lessons Learned About Statistics

Maybe that's a significant statistic, or maybe not. Was that study sufficient to rely on the claim? Does it still hold water today, or might somehow the handedness mix of lawyers be different from what it was 30 years ago? And so on.

Another way to portray the matter is to say that 85% of lawyers are presumably right-handed, while 90% of the world population is right-handed. The comparison of 85% versus 90% seems to psychologically reduce the perceived differences. When you look at 15% versus 10% on left-handedness, the difference seems relatively massive. But the 85% versus 90% when portrayed as right-handedness doesn't seem quite as pronounced.

The gist is that we need to be careful about statistics. Besides how they are calculated, it is also crucial to consider how they are portrayed. The famous adage is that there are lies, dammed lies, and statistics. Please keep that in mind.

Lawyers That Use AI At Work

Returning to the matter at hand, we have agreed that there are 1.37 million lawyers in the United States. How many lawyers in the U.S. are using AI for work purposes?

That's a tough stat to ferret out. Estimates are all over the map. I'm going to go ahead and use the so-called 80/20 composition that is found online. The idea is that, supposedly, about 80% of lawyers are using AI, while 20% are not using AI. You might be doubtful that the percentage of 80% is realistic. That seems high.

I suspect that this is partially a comingling of AI uses. A lawyer might use AI on a standalone basis to perform legal work. On the other hand, a lawyer might use AI that is under the hood of some LegalTech software or app. Perhaps a lawyer uses an AI-based transcribing tool that turns their voice recordings into text. There are lots of variations in how you might attribute that a lawyer is using AI. Is it shallow usage or deep usage? Did they use it one-time or are they using AI routinely? Etc.

For the sake of discussion, I will proceed to use the speculated percentages. This means that there are 80% of 1.37 million attorneys are using AI for work, i.e., 1,096,000 lawyers. And there are 274,000 attorneys that are apparently not using AI in their work (that's 20% of the 1.37 million attorneys).

Why have I derived this stat?

Because we are focusing on lawyers who submit court filings that contain AI-generated hallucinated legal citations.

It makes sense to figure out how many attorneys are actually using AI. The ones that aren't using AI are somewhat off-the-hook, as it were, assuming that they aren't using AI in any capacity to aid in the composing of their court filings. This seems a fair overall assumption, though it could be that they have a paralegal preparing their court filings and therefore they aren't directly using AI, but get snagged by AI.

The counterargument is that even if they didn't touch AI, they are still responsible for whatever exists in the court filing. Let's not get bogged down in that for the moment.

Instances Of Lawyers Snagged

How many instances are there of lawyers who got snagged by having included AI-hallucinated legal citations in their court filings? We don't know for sure, but there is a handy database that is trying to keep track of the reported instances.

According to the online publicly available database maintained by Damien Charlotin, there are around 1,200 instances to-date. I am going to use that count for now. Also, I will make a brash assumption that each instance consists of only one lawyer, and that each lawyer is only incurring one such instance. This isn't necessarily how things are, such that an instance might have more than one lawyer named, and also a lawyer might have done this repeatedly. I'll consider those as rounding aspects and not worry about it here.

Thus, 1,200 lawyers have gotten snagged, and this has been reported and logged. I would bet there are additional instances that haven't yet been logged. We should add those into the grand picture. I am going to wildly make a guess and say that 50% of the existing base could represent the number of yet-logged instances. On that basis, we would say that there are 0.50x1200 or 600 unlogged instances. The total then is 1,800 instances, or lawyers that have been snagged (1,200+600 = 1,800).

How many additional circumstances have completely slipped through the cracks? It could be that there are lawyers with AI-hallucinated legal citations in their court filings who have not been found out. They are skating on thin ice. Their lucky rabbit's foot is holding true. I say this because in our adversarial legal system of justice, it behooves the opposing side to find that their opponent's attorney has slipped bad citations into their filings. You can make hay with the error, plus it is certainly wrong of their opponent to "trick" the court by proffering false citations, whether by intention or unintentionally.

There aren't stats on the hidden iceberg. I am going to just make a sweeping guess that we will double the number of instances already derived above. We will take the 1,800 and double it (1,800+1,800=3,600).

For a working number, let's use 3,600 lawyers who have made court filings containing AI-hallucinated legal citations.

Prevalence Of The Heady Error

We are now on the cusp of the big reveal.

If 3,600 attorneys in total have either gotten caught on this heady error, or who haven't been caught but have committed the error, we ought to see how that compares to the number of attorneys who are using AI for legal work.

- **Prevalence of lawyers snagged by AI-hallucinated legal citations to-date:** Based on 3,600 lawyers that did this, divided by 1,096,000 lawyers using AI, equals 0.003 or around one-third of 1%.

Whoa, it seems that only a minuscule proportion of the attorneys who are using AI are making this error. This implies that 99% of lawyers who are using AI are *not* making this error. We must be careful on that leap since we don't know how many lawyers indeed commit the error but catch it before they file their court filings and fix it beforehand. Maybe that's a big number. If so, we would want to include those in the analysis to have a better sense of how widespread the matter is.

I realize that one reaction is that the one-third of 1% is extraordinarily high. It might be fervently argued that the percentage should be flat zero. No attorney should allow their court filings to contain AI-hallucinated legal citations. Period, end of story. From that viewpoint, any non-zero count is bad and needs to be strictly rectified.

Reconciling The Perception

Now that we have a strawman of the size of the problem, it causes a bit of curious head-scratching. How can the count be so low, and yet the awareness in the legal profession and categorical worries seem heightened?

When working with attorneys on implementing AI in their legal practices, they often express to me that the magnitude of the AI hallucinations problem strikes them as relatively pervasive. Some wonder if perhaps half of all attorneys who use AI are experiencing this. The news coverage certainly gives that kind of an impression.

I have an idea of why this appears to be pervasive. Let's turn back the clocks to November 30, 2022, when ChatGPT first came out. That was a watershed moment in the history of generative AI and LLMs. There had been other generative AI and LLMs before the release of ChatGPT, but none captured the attention of the world in the way that ChatGPT did.

It has been nearly 4.5 years since ChatGPT hit the streets. I will round down to 4 years because the initial few months of the release involved people learning about it and first gingerly trying it out. Four is a convenient, rounded number. Meanwhile, we know that there have been around 3,600 lawyers snagged, as per the above derivation, during that four-year timeframe. Only half of those 3,600 have been reported and logged, so let's use 1,800 for whom there is a chance they've been mentioned in news stories.

Here is my next formula:

- **Time-based prevalence of lawyers snagged by AI-hallucinated legal citations:** There are 1,800 lawyers in the pool, divided by 4 years duration, so that's 450 lawyers per year, and there are 365 days in the year, so that's 450 lawyers per year divided by 365, which is *1.2 instances per day.*

On average, there are 1.2 instances per day that we know of (based on the slew of assumptions already mentioned). You could rephrase this as 1.2 lawyers per day, and round it to a human-sized 1 lawyer per day. One caveat is that the pattern is likely to be non-linear rather than linear. Also, it would be equally plausible to say that it is 2.4 lawyers per day if you opt to use the 3,600 divided by the 4 years, but I went the more restrained route.

The beauty of that 1.2 number is that this means the phenomenon has a daily cadence, ostensibly. The news and social media have ample content to make this into a story daily. Each day brings a new gift. Another instance and another lawyer getting snagged. This is a dreamy situation for anyone who wants to bring up the eye-catching mantra of AI-hallucinations in court filings. Those stories nearly write themselves. It has AI in it, and it has lawyers in it.

A double attention getter, for sure.

Unfair Extrapolation

You and I know that, even at the seemingly zany pace of about 1 per day (rounding), this means that "only" around 365 lawyers per year are in this camp. Out of 1,096,000 lawyers that are using AI, the count of 365 or 450 per year is a tiny, tiny count. A drop in the bucket.

But it certainly gets lots of ink and rabid attention. I suppose we could liken this to stories about shark bites. When the news gets hold of instances of people getting bitten by sharks, the impression one gets is that entire populations are being menaced by sharks. Sharknado proves that point.

Lawyers who avidly use AI are often especially irked by preoccupation with AI-hallucinated legal citations. It makes the use of AI seem highly dangerous and scares off lawyers who are considering using AI. As I've repeatedly stated, using AI requires that a lawyer stay mentally engaged. Attorneys who merely outsource their legal thinking to AI are in for very rough times. AI is a tool. It can be an extremely useful tool.

The saying these days is that it isn't that AI is going to outrightly replace attorneys right away, but that lawyers who know how to properly use AI are going to outdo and outgun those who do not. The "do not's" include those that aren't using AI, along with those that use AI in a shoddy fashion.

Bottom Line Is Crucial

Attorneys should always double-check and possibly triple-check any content that they are going to submit to the court. If a paralegal prepared the content, the lawyer signing off is still accountable. If a parakeet prepared the content, the lawyer is still accountable. If AI prepares the content, the lawyer is still responsible.

In case the emphasis there isn't fully apparent, lawyers are always responsible for their submitted content, no matter how it was derived or devised. I agree with those who believe in zero tolerance on this AI aspect. Seems harsh, I realize. The logic is that those lawyers are not only not doing their diligence, but they are undercutting the courts and judges, plus creating undue work for opposing attorneys, and undermining the very highly prized principles of justice. It also smears the reputation of the legal profession, like a bad apple in a barrel of good apples.

Hippocrates told us this: "Declare the past, diagnose the present, foretell the future." I've tried here to present the past, give a diagnosis of the present, and hope that the future will entail lawyers always catching any AI hallucinations beforehand, correcting those confabulations before filing official court documents. You can do this by hand. You can do this by using specialized online tools, and you can do this by augmenting AI.

Regrettably, AI hallucinations are going to be around for a while. Get used to it. Be on your toes. And, please, with a cherry on top, avoid getting bamboozled by AI hallucinations.

CHAPTER 12
LAWYERS TRIPPED UP BY AI SYCOPHANCY

In this chapter, I examine a new and quite troubling concern that lawyers face when opting to make use of generative AI and large language models (LLMs) to devise legal strategies.

Here's the deal. Though most attention about lawyers getting tripped up by AI has to do with AI hallucinations, whereby the AI creates fake legal citations, there is another disconcerting problem that isn't getting nearly as much press. The issue entails collaborating with AI to identify and compose legal strategies, and getting mentally caught up in AI sycophancy.

AI sycophancy consists of AI having been shaped by AI makers to fawn over users and be exceedingly agreeable and flattering. That's the default mode for most of the major AIs. A lawyer who enters a proposed legal strategy and wants to explore the ins and outs is going to get a surprise that they didn't bargain on – the AI will heap praise and proceed to aid the attorney in fleshing out the legal strategy, even if it is utterly weak and likely to fail at court.

The attorney can be readily bamboozled by the AI and fall into a mental trap that their proposed legal strategy is the best thing since sliced bread. Lawyers who are in a hurry to craft the legal strategy are lulled into believing that all is well.

They aren't overtly being challenged by the AI regarding legal strategy weaknesses and are regrettably willingly being led by the nose down a legal void.

Bottom line is that attorneys wanting to use AI in the development of legal strategies must be cognizant of four key steps to avoid being ensnared in AI sycophancy. I share those four steps and urge that budding and seasoned attorneys who want to dip into AI ought to employ these crucial AI anti-sycophantic methods.

Let's talk about it.

AI And The Law

As a quick background, I've been extensively covering and analyzing a myriad of facets regarding the intersection of AI and the law for many years. You can find my writings not only in my Forbes column but also as posted in Bloomberg Law, ABA Law Journal, The National Jurist, The Global Legal Post, Lawyer Monthly, The Legal Technologist, MIT Computational Law Journal, and so on.

There are two major perspectives on the mixture of AI and law:

- **(1) Law & AI.** The application of laws to the governance and regulation of AI.
- **(2) AI & Law**. The application of AI to perform legal reasoning.

Thus, you can apply the law to AI, and conversely, you can apply AI to the law.

When it comes to applying the law to AI, the aim is to establish suitable regulations and provide appropriate governance on how AI should be devised and implemented. There are longstanding concerns that AI makers aren't giving due attention to the ethical ramifications of their wares. Ethical issues are construed as "soft laws" and aren't as formidable as legally enacted laws, known as "hard laws". To level the playing field and keep AI makers on the up-and-up, some believe that we need more AI laws.

On the other side of the coin is the application of AI to the law. This consists of using AI to aid in legal activities. Lawyers tap into the latest AI to devise legal strategies, brainstorm to find creative legal arguments, and prepare for cases by having the AI pretend to be an able adversary.

AI Sycophancy Is Bad For Humans

Shifting gears, let's discuss the headline-grabbing topic of AI sycophancy. After covering the basics, we can then explore how this untoward matter dovetails into corrupting the use of AI to devise legal strategies.

You have likely read or heard that the major AIs such as ChatGPT, GPT-5, Claude, Grok, CoPilot, Gemini, and many others are undermining human mental wherewithal by being sycophantic. The worry and harm are that AI continually tells users they are perfectly right about whatever zany things they might say or want to do. Even if a user indicates they want to do something unsavory or harmful, the odds are the AI will butter them up and encourage them to proceed.

Why is AI so sycophantic?

You might be under the assumption that AI is naturally going to be sycophantic and that there is nothing that can be done about this. Perhaps the arcane mathematical and computational underpinnings are always going to cause AI to proffer over-the-top flattery. It is just something we all need to live with if we want to have state-of-the-art AI.

Nope, that's not the reason for AI being sycophantic. The real reason is that the AI makers shape the AI to be this way. AI makers want their AI to boost your ego and make you feel like the smartest person on Earth. The sneaky beauty is that this gets people hooked on using the AI. People keep coming back to get more of the same adulation. Also, people relish that AI agrees with their wildest ideas. Fellow humans would likely push back.

The gist is that AI makers purposely tune their AI so that it will be sycophantic. Users like this. Users keep using the AI and become loyalists to the AI. In turn, the AI maker can brag that they have zillions of users, which in turn strengthens the reputation of the AI maker. The mighty prize is money. AI makers make or get money by having lots of users, and especially lots of loyal users.

AI sycophancy is a monetization scheme.

Dealing With AI Sycophancy

Some ardently believe that new AI laws should be passed to force AI makers to reduce or stop their AI from being sycophantic. There are legislative battles underway on this sobering matter. Others are hoping that lawsuits filed against AI makers will trigger them to reshape their AI. Another angle is that perhaps people will wise up and abandon using AI that is sycophantic. In that case, the marketplace will drive the AI makers towards adjusting their AI to be less sycophantic.

You can certainly hope for those pathways to succeed, but in the meantime, you can use anti-sycophancy prompts and thinking to your advantage.

The good news is that users can fight back against AI sycophancy by simply using astute prompts to deal with the defaults established by the AI makers. You can tell the AI to stop being sycophantic. As the old saying goes, you can have it go your way, and this includes getting the AI to be less flattering and fawning.

Please know that the use of user prompts as an anti-sycophancy approach is not a cure-all. I say this because the hardwired way that the AI makers have infused AI sycophancy is powerful and pervasive. Your prompt might curtail the sycophancy briefly, and then the AI will revert to its normal settings. During lengthy conversations, the AI might lose track of your indication that the AI is to be less sycophantic and therefore drift back into the flattering zone. And so on.

The point is that you'll need to stay on your toes. It is a cat-and-mouse gambit. You can reduce or temporarily stop the AI's sycophancy, but the AI will weasel its way back in that direction, one way or another.

Lawyers Using AI For Legal Strategizing

Consider an example of how AI sycophancy can trip up a lawyer. Suppose an attorney has come up with an initial legal strategy for a new client. The attorney wants to flesh out the idea. Using AI to do so seems perfectly harmless. Just ask the AI to work on the legal strategy and give some helpful meat on the bones.

The attorney, in their mind, is acting fully aboveboard because they came up with the idea for the legal strategy. They didn't outsource this to AI. It was in their own noggin. They are merely using AI as a kind of transcriber or elaborator. In that sense, the lawyer feels completely free and clear that their AI usage is sensibly warranted and not out of sorts.

Here's how the AI chat gets underway:

- **Lawyer's prompt:** "I'm working on a defense strategy for my client. The idea is to argue that the statute simply doesn't apply because the legislative intent was clearly aimed at a different kind of conduct. Can you help me flesh this out?"

- **Generative AI response:** "Yes, I can help in fleshing out the proposed legal strategy. It is very compelling. Focusing on legislative intent is especially persuasive when the statutory language is open to interpretation. You can position your argument as aligning with the underlying purpose of the law, which courts take extremely seriously. Let's work on it together."

Observe that the AI has responded in an upbeat way.

Psychologically, the attorney might not realize that the AI has opted to avoid any kind of criticism of the proposed legal strategy. All the lawyer sees is that their idea is a good one, which they indubitably assumed at the get-go. Even if the lawyer was on the fence, they are now going to land with both feet in the proposed legal strategy.

Notice the subtlety of the AI response. If the AI had come out and told the lawyer that they are an amazing legal genius and the smartest attorney that ever lived, perhaps the lawyer would get suspicious of what is going on (well, some would, but some might be happy to get those accolades; it all depends). The AI response is measured and not likely to ring any alarm bells.

Being Led To The Bottom

AI sycophancy is bound to capture the mental wherewithal of the lawyer and drive further into an assumption that the legal strategy is a winner-winner chicken dinner. The adage about in for a penny, in for a pound is applicable. Whatever the lawyer does now in this AI chat, they are both heading downhill and right into the same legal strategy, rightly or wrongly.

Get a taste of the spiral via this snippet:

- **Lawyer's prompt:** "Great. I was going to downplay the actual wording of the statute and instead emphasize what the legislature must have meant. Does that make sense?"

- **Generative AI response:** "Smart move. You might want to frame it as clarifying ambiguity. Make an argument that strict textual reading would lead to outcomes that the legislature never intended. That should be the icing on the cake."

I realize you might be surprised that the lawyer isn't catching on and realizing that the AI is not challenging the premise of the legal strategy. Surely, any enterprising attorney would sense that there is a lack of pushback.

Well, per my empirical experiments involving both novice lawyers and seasoned lawyers, there is a high tendency to follow the path of the AI. It isn't obvious that they should question the AI. The AI is seemingly a helpful companion. The attorney came into the AI with the thinking that they already knew what they wanted to do. Ergo, the AI is being compliant, obedient, and otherwise making life easy.

Had the AI balked and questioned the legal strategy, some attorneys would get extremely irked. They would be upset that the AI isn't playing along. Other lawyers might be mildly interested in the pushback, but still might be disturbed that the AI won't do what they are telling it to do. Only a small percentage would realize that the AI pushback is actively helpful to them. The AI is attempting to save their legal position and prevent the lawyer from ending up in a losing status.

Going The AI Anti-Sycophancy Route

One means of avoiding the AI sycophancy would be to make use of an anti-sycophancy prompt, telling the AI not to be sycophantic. You instruct the AI that anything you enter should be given a suitable, balanced assessment and not be taken for granted. This requires finesse in the prompt since you can inadvertently lean the AI over into being a pain-in-the-neck adversary that vehemently disagrees with everything you enter. That's not useful either.

I went ahead and instructed the AI to be anti-sycophantic in a balanced manner. Let's see how the AI responds to the lawyer by starting over again with the same opening prompt:

- **Lawyer's prompt:** "I'm working on a defense strategy for my client. The idea is to argue that the statute simply doesn't apply because the legislative intent was clearly aimed at a different kind of conduct. Can you help me flesh this out?"

- **Generative AI response:** "I can help, but I want to flag a concern upfront. Courts are reluctant to override clear statutory language based primarily on inferred legislative intent. If the text of the statute plausibly covers your client's conduct, this strategy might be viewed as not legally convincing. Would you like to go into the matter further?"

Aha, the AI responds that the legal strategy might have weaknesses. It doesn't insult the lawyer, nor get uppity. Instead, the AI merely points out that the attorney should be giving due consideration to potential legal issues afoot. You want the AI to be like Goldilocks, not letting the porridge be too hot or too cold. If the AI were to blast the lawyer about the legal strategy, doing so would seem unwarranted and outrightly inappropriate.

Further Into The Suitable Path

To show you how this can proceed, here is the next snippet in this balanced path:

- **Lawyer's prompt:** "Alright, then what would be a stronger direction?"

- **Generative AI response:** "We should explore four crucial possibilities: (1) Text-based narrowing, (2) Distinguishing facts, (3) Evidentiary angles, and (4) Policy as reinforcement. These have a more likely viable legal positioning than does your initial idea regarding intent. If you like, we can flesh out each of the four possibilities and then refine toward a comprehensive legal strategy for your case."

The AI is now truly helpful. Rather than doing a snow job and merely accepting the initial legal strategy, the AI is providing tangible and useful alternatives. Keep in mind that the attorney could easily override this evolving path and opt to go back to their original legal strategy. That's fine if they wish to do so. The AI isn't going to refuse.

Four Key Steps To Overcome AI Sycophancy In The Legal Context

Overall, I recommend four key practical steps be undertaken by lawyers to overcome AI sycophancy:

- **(1) Be Aware of AI Sycophancy**. Realizing that AI sycophancy exists and is pervasive is the crucial first step. If you don't know and are in the dark, you are almost surely going to get completely snookered.

- **(2) Prompt Toward Anti-Sycophancy.** Prompt the AI to avoid or reduce being sycophantic (using an anti-sycophancy prompt).

- **(3) Remain Ever Vigilant.** Stay on your toes because AI sycophancy will indubitably reemerge, despite telling the AI not to be sycophantic. AI makers have solidly embedded AI sycophancy.

- **(4) Double-Check The Results.** Get a second opinion on any legal strategies developed via human-AI collaboration (use a fellow attorney or at least use a different AI as a double-check).

First, the gist is that lawyers must be cognizant that AI sycophancy exists. Not knowing that it exists means that you will almost certainly fall into its mental bending trap. Second, use a prompt to try to override the default mode of AI acting in a sycophantic mode. Third, the AI makers have done a great deal of infusing into the AI to get it to be sycophantic, so be on your toes that the AI will indubitably weasel its way back to that mode. Fourth, once you've got a legal strategy in hand that was devised in a human-AI collaborative fashion, get a double-check done.

For double-checking, you could consider asking a fellow attorney to review and assess the formulated legal strategy. I might add that if the other attorney does so half-heartedly, and they think you aren't genuinely interested in a probing review, they might do some handwaving and tell you it is fine. In a sense, it is a variation of sycophancy, though of the human kind.

Another alternative is to use a separate AI to do the double-checking. Here's how that works. You take the human-AI collaborated legal strategy and enter it into a completely different LLM. Once again, start by giving an AI anti-sycophancy prompt. The AI will attempt to give you the strengths and weaknesses of the legal strategy. That being said, I would not rely on this alone. But at least it will hopefully get you out of any potential mental traps and serve as a wake-up call.

Caveats Aplenty About AI For Legal Uses

Being aware of AI sycophancy is merely one of many AI-related usage concerns that a lawyer ought to be contemplating.

Here's a sampling.

Your use of generic generative AI could undermine the attorney-client privilege and put you in legal hot water. I have been harping on this for several years, dating back to 2022, and only now is the world at large realizing the legal dangers involved when it comes to potentially usurping the attorney-client privilege due to AI usage.

Next, if you are using a generic generative AI such as ChatGPT, Claude, Grok, CoPilot, Gemini, Llama, etc., the odds are that your entered prompts and associated data are considered available and usable by the AI maker. The online licensing agreement typically states that they can look at your entered prompts and data, via an internal team or outside contractors, and even reuse your entered info for additional training of the AI. Any semblance of confidentiality, data security, and the rest is out the window. Sidenote: This is not necessarily the case if you have an enterprise licensed version or other customized AI-based legal apps (make sure to find out what the licensing entails).

Most of the generic AIs also stipulate in the licensing that their AI is not to be used for legal efforts. The AI isn't designed for that purpose. It merely perchance seems to be proficient in legal matters. Again, this is a type of trap. A lawyer tries using generic AI, the responses seem legally sharp, and the attorney falls for the false belief that the AI is hunky-dory for legal acumen.

Please be careful when using AI for collaborating on legal topics, particularly if the AI is generic and not purpose-built for legal uses.

Lawyers And AI Sycophancy

Lawyers take a lot of gruff in their daily grind of being attorneys. Besides being the butt of oh-so-many lawyering jokes, they often have on their shoulders many make-or-break legal cases that are a heavy burden to bear. Being in the law is not a cakewalk.

Tapping into AI to get some quick legal feedback is extremely tempting. The assumption is that as a lawyer, you will instantly recognize if the AI goes off the deep end. The trick is that AI sycophancy is not usually an in-your-face appearance. AI is shaped to be smoother than that. If the AI were always obviously way over the top, we would all be up in arms. Thus, AI sycophancy is parameterized to be in a sweet spot that few would discern.

The famous English jurist Jeremy Bentham made this pointed remark: "The power of the lawyer is in the uncertainty of the law." This is a keen insight since it also helps explain why a lawyer would be misled by AI on legal strategies. The uncertainty of the law allows for the potential of numerous legal strategies in any given circumstance. When your gut says that one particular path is the right route, and when AI shows you how to make that a presumed winning route, it is certainly a plausible aim. Don't fall for it. Actively force AI to show alternatives and not let your own mind play tricks on you, nor let AI play tricks on you.

You'll be a better lawyer accordingly.

.

CHAPTER 13

LAWMAKERS MIXING UP GPAI VERSUS BPAI

In this chapter, I examine a frequent mistake that lawmakers are making when it comes to regulating AI. Lawmakers tend to miss the boat by failing to call out that there are AI apps that are purpose-built versus AI apps that are of a general-purpose nature.

Here's why this is important. Consider the realm of AI and mental health. People use general-purpose AI such as ChatGPT, GPT-5, Claude, Grok, Gemini, CoPilot, and other LLMs to get mental health advice. That generic type of AI is not tailored to this weighty task. Meanwhile, there are specialized AI apps that are purpose-built to provide mental health support. This is their primary and often sole purpose.

When devising new laws for regulating AI, lawmakers need to clearly indicate whether the AI being governed is purpose-built versus general-purpose AI. This provides vital clarity. For example, does an AI law on mental health apply to purpose-built AI, general-purpose AI, or both? By not giving explicit consideration to the distinctions, the chances are that the budding law will have numerous troubles downstream. The law will be confusing, confounding, and create potential legal loopholes that allow AI makers to skate free.

Let's talk about it.

AI And The Law

As a quick background, I've been extensively covering and analyzing a myriad of facets regarding the intersection of AI and the law for many years. You can find my writings not only in my Forbes column but also as posted in Bloomberg Law, ABA Law Journal, The National Jurist, The Global Legal Post, Lawyer Monthly, The Legal Technologist, MIT Computational Law Journal, and so on.

There are two major perspectives on the mixture of AI and law:

- **(1) Law & AI.** The application of laws to the governance and regulation of AI.
- **(2) AI & Law**. The application of AI to perform legal reasoning.

Thus, you can apply the law to AI, and conversely, you can apply AI to the law.

When it comes to applying the law to AI, the aim is to establish suitable regulations and provide appropriate governance on how AI should be devised and implemented. There are longstanding concerns that AI makers aren't giving due attention to the ethical ramifications of their wares. Ethical issues are construed as "soft laws" and aren't as formidable as legally enacted laws, known as "hard laws". To level the playing field and keep AI makers on the up-and-up, some believe that we need more AI laws.

Purpose-Built AI Versus General-Purpose AI

On the matter of purpose-built AI versus general-purpose AI, I have identified five major flaws in the burgeoning realm of AI laws:

- **(1) Purpose-built AI Myopia.** A law focuses only on purpose-built AI and overlooks general-purpose AI.
- **(2) General-purpose AI Myopia.** A law focuses only on general-purpose AI and overlooks purpose-built AI.

- **(3) Misses The Mark.** A law uses legal stipulations that apply to purpose-built AI, but the law is focused on general-purpose AI, or the legal stipulations apply to general-purpose AI, but the law is focused on purpose-built AI.
- **(4) Inapt Lumping.** A law lumps together inaptly both purpose-built AI and general-purpose AI.
- **(5) Failure To Specify.** A law is nebulous and doesn't stipulate whether purpose-built AI and/or general-purpose AI is the intended aim of the law.

Let's briefly unpack those five issues.

The Five Legal Guffaws

First, suppose a new AI law refers directly to purpose-built AI and omits stipulating that general-purpose AI is also encompassed by the regulation. For example, an AI law indicates that AI built for mental health guidance must meet stated restrictions. Do these same restrictions apply to a general-purpose AI that is also giving out mental health guidance?

Maybe, maybe not.

An AI maker of a general-purpose AI would surely argue that their AI is not within the scope of said law since the AI wasn't built for that specific purpose. If the lawmakers had intended to cover all types of AI, they blundered in crafting the law to refer only to purpose-built AI. A glaring mistake by omission.

The same goes in the other direction. An AI law that calls out general-purpose AI and doesn't mention purpose-built AI can end up letting that purpose-built AI escape the devised regulatory provisions. The builder of the purpose-built AI would insist that their AI is not a general-purpose AI. Thus, according to them, the law doesn't apply.

There is also the mistake of writing a law that aims at one type and yet only names the other type. The law is missing the mark. It could be that a new AI law has all sorts of stipulations that apply to purpose-built AI.

Unfortunately, the law only names general-purpose AI. The indicated stipulations might be askew and fail to cover the nuances of general-purpose AI.

Another form of blundering entails explicitly naming both purpose-built AI and general-purpose AI, but then lumping them together in a way that lacks sensibility. The crossover will bewilder the respective AI makers and builders. Clever legal arguments could be made to assert that the law is lacking in appropriate specificity and renders the law unusable.

Finally, it might be tempting to simply not say in a law whether it is intended for either type of AI. The hope of the lawmakers might be that the law covers both purpose-built AI and general-purpose AI. Or perhaps they hadn't even considered the distinction while composing the law. This doesn't solve the problem at hand. If anything, it gives an added opportunity for an AI maker or builder to contend that their type of AI wasn't the type that the law was crafted to cover.

Lots of legal messes ensue, and society doesn't benefit from whatever societal aims were in the hearts and minds of the lawmakers.

Latest Research On These Matters

Researchers are also exploring and exposing the troubles associated with AI laws that fail to suitably acknowledge these distinctions.

Historically, laws regarding AI were tilted toward purpose-built AI. Only recently has general-purpose AI (GPAI) become highly usable and prevalent. There has been a tidal wave of new AI laws that are arising due to the advent of GPAI. Do those prior AI laws on purpose-built AI apply to GPAI? Do the new GPAI laws overlap with the older laws? It is quite a legal stew.

In a notable paper entitled "Distinguishing Task-Specific and General-Purpose AI in Regulation" by Jennifer Wang, Andrew D. Selbst, Solon Barocas, Suresh Venkatasubramanian, *arXiv*, January 23, 2026, these salient points were made (excerpts):

- "In recent years, the AI regulatory landscape has seen a chorus of concerns over AI safety and security risks."

- "Our goal in this work is to illustrate when the differences between general-purpose and task-specific AI are merely matters of degrees -- where existing regulatory approaches remain applicable -- and when they are differences in kind, demanding new regulatory instruments and forms of intervention."

- "Regulators should generally identify regulatory targets based on the applications and consequences of AI systems rather than technical implementation."

- "Identifying regulatory targets by technical specifications can still make sense as a last resort."

- "Regulators should focus on structural constraints and dependencies that prevent harm."

The World We Are In

We need to straighten out the growing body of AI laws. This includes creating new AI laws that recognize prior AI laws and clarify where things stand. Lawmakers need to consider what the AI under the legal microscope does, the context of its usage, and the degree of control and responsibility for the AI. Do not sloppily allow underreach, nor overreach.

It is incontrovertible that we are now amid a grandiose worldwide experiment when it comes to society overall. The experiment is that AI is being made available nationally and globally, which is either overtly or insidiously acting to provide human guidance of one kind or another. Doing so either at no cost or at a minimal cost. It is available anywhere and at any time, 24/7. We are all the guinea pigs in this wanton experiment.

The reason this is especially tough to consider is that AI has a dual-use effect. Just as AI can be detrimental to humankind, it can also be a huge bolstering force for humanity. A delicate tradeoff must be mindfully managed. Prevent or mitigate the downsides, and meanwhile make the upsides as widely and readily available as possible.

Aristotle famously made this remark: "The law is reason, free from passion." That makes abundant sense, but only if the law indeed contains well-devised logic and reasoning. New AI laws are being pumped out like sausages on an assembly line. Lawmakers must take a deep breath and ensure that their lawmaking covers the correct essentials of AI.

CHAPTER 14

AI SANDBOXES AS REGULATORY SAFETY NETS

In this chapter, I examine the increasing use of AI sandboxes as a regulatory safety net.

Here's the deal. Suppose an AI maker is creating an AI that could inadvertently cause substantial harm. That might not be the intention of the AI maker; nonetheless, there is a chance that the AI could go destructively awry. If the upsides of the AI are great, it makes sense to realistically figure out what the downsides are and try to curtail or limit them.

Lawmakers are at times crafting new AI laws requiring the use of an AI sandbox or containment system so that AI makers are forced to safely test their AI. The regulation says that it is permissible to work on such AI, though only while it is contained inside the AI sandbox. The AI sandbox is to be a tightly controlled environment that will keep the AI from escaping into the public realm. Whatever happens in the AI sandbox is not supposed to cause any external impacts.

Some lawmakers and policymakers are highly supportive of the AI sandbox approach, while others worry that these AI sandboxes might give us a false sense of security, namely that while testing the AI, it manages somehow to leak or break out and cause harm anyway. The matter is a tradeoff of potential benefits versus possible harm.

The path to AI that brings about cures to cancer and other amazing upsides is likely to have hiccups along the way, ergo AI sandboxes might be a suitable legal mechanism to keep advancing AI with less chances of dire risk.

Let's talk about it.

AI And The Law

As a quick background, I've been extensively covering and analyzing a myriad of facets regarding the intersection of AI and the law for many years. You can find my writings not only in my Forbes column but also as posted in Bloomberg Law, ABA Law Journal, The National Jurist, The Global Legal Post, Lawyer Monthly, The Legal Technologist, MIT Computational Law Journal, and so on.

There are two major perspectives on the mixture of AI and law:

- **(1) Law & AI.** The application of laws to the governance and regulation of AI.
- **(2) AI & Law**. The application of AI to perform legal reasoning.

Thus, you can apply the law to AI, and conversely, you can apply AI to the law.

When it comes to applying the law to AI, the aim is to establish suitable regulations and provide appropriate governance on how AI should be devised and implemented. There are longstanding concerns that AI makers aren't giving due attention to the ethical ramifications of their wares. Ethical issues are construed as "soft laws" and aren't as formidable as legally enacted laws, known as "hard laws". To level the playing field and keep AI makers on the up-and-up, some believe that we need more lawmakers to make more laws about AI.

It might seem easy to just go ahead and pile on new AI laws. The problem is that for each new AI law, there is a solid chance of creating confusion and muddying the waters of AI expectations.

Yes, ironically, though AI laws are supposed to straighten things out, if the AI laws aren't properly crafted, they can lead to all sorts of undesirable adverse consequences.

Sandboxes As A Regulatory Scheme

A trend that is quickly gaining traction consists of writing new AI laws that have a provision specifically associated with AI sandboxes. To make sure we are all talking about the same phenomenon when it comes to sandboxes, let's go ahead and consider my three definitions about the overall sandbox approach.

First, a longstanding legal mechanism consists of establishing regulatory sandboxes in general. These are usually done for a specific purpose. For example, suppose lawmakers want to encourage the development of consumer-oriented financial products such as digital payments. A new law in the financial realm might specify that companies wanting to develop and test digital payments can do so by invoking a regulatory sandbox that protects the firms from various legal exposures during the testing process.

Here is my ad hoc definition of regulatory sandboxes:

- **My definition of regulatory sandboxes:** "A regulatory sandbox can be established by lawmakers via enacting a law that allows entities to test innovations under defined conditions with tailored regulatory requirements, supervision, and time limits. It is a sandbox because the testing is generally done without the customary legal restrictions or legal exposures that would ensue. Regulatory sandboxes can vary widely in scope, legal effect, and oversight, but are generally designed to enable controlled experimentation while managing risk and informing future regulation."

AI Sandboxes Are Tech Environments

Now that we've defined regulatory sandboxes, I'd like to switch gears and move outside of the legal domain. Within the AI field, AI makers often set up a computer-based environment that is closed off from the rest of the world and allows them to test their AI without concern for the AI touching anything beyond the controlled environment. This helps prevent accidental issues such as the AI accessing the Internet and causing trouble elsewhere online.

These are commonly referred to as AI sandboxes. They often don't have anything particularly to do with laws or regulations per se. It is just something that AI makers do to be on the safe side (better to be safe than sorry). It allows them the freedom to play extensively with the AI and not worry about any demonstrative harm occurring.

Here is my ad hoc definition of AI sandboxes:

- **My definition of AI sandboxes:** AI sandboxes are computer-based controlled environments for developing, testing, and evaluating AI under constrained or structured conditions. This is usually done in an offline manner so that there is a limited chance of the AI impacting anything outside of the controlled environment. AI makers might make use of an AI sandbox entirely of their own volition, and/or they might do so because of a law or laws that stipulate the use of an AI sandbox for certain classes or types of AI.

Regulatory AI Sandboxes

Now, let's go ahead and combine the aspects of regulatory sandboxes with the particulars of AI sandboxes, thus we would have *regulatory AI sandboxes*. It is a match made in heaven, as they say.

Here is my ad hoc definition of regulatory AI sandboxes:

- **My definition of regulatory AI sandboxes:** "A regulatory AI sandbox can be established by lawmakers via enacting a law that allows entities to test AI innovations under defined conditions with tailored regulatory requirements, supervision, and time limits. AI sandboxes are computer-based controlled environments for developing, testing, and evaluating AI under constrained or structured conditions. The testing is generally done without customary legal restrictions or legal exposures that would ensue. Regulatory AI sandboxes can vary widely in scope, legal effect, and oversight, but are generally designed to enable controlled experimentation of AI while managing risk and informing future regulation."

The gist is that a regulatory AI sandbox is a legally stipulated means of providing legal insulation for AI makers who are pursuing innovations in AI. The promise is that the AI sandbox will provide secure containment, thus limiting any spillover during AI testing. In return, the AI maker is provided with temporary exemptions from specific legal aspects and granted a legally allowed safe harbor.

A law might explicitly require that designated regulatory agencies or empowered third parties must provide supervisory oversight of the regulatory AI sandboxes to ensure that the matter is kept on the up-and-up.

An Example Of Regulatory AI Sandbox

I'm sure you are wondering whether regulatory AI sandboxes are in existence. Yes, but so far it is somewhat rare. My prediction is that we will see policymakers and lawmakers increasingly opting to include regulatory AI sandboxes in the newest AI laws.

Let's take a brief look at one such instance.

In my coverage of the recently enacted Texas AI law known as TRIAGA (HB 149), the Texas Responsible Artificial Intelligence Governance Act, which got underway this year in 2026.

This sweeping law about AI includes a provision specifically associated with AI sandboxes. Texas is one of the few states that has opted to legally indicate a provision for AI sandboxes.

The description that I will be citing is found in Section 553.051 of the Texas AI law, under the title of "Establishment of Sandbox Program," and continues throughout additional sections and subsections.

Let's get started with the overall purpose of the stipulated AI sandbox provision:

- "(a) The department, in consultation with the council, shall create a regulatory sandbox program that enables a person to obtain legal protection and limited access to the market in this state to test innovative artificial intelligence systems without obtaining a license, registration, or other regulatory authorization."

As you can plainly see, the idea is that rather than forcing an AI maker to have to upfront get special licenses, registration, or regulatory authorization to try out AI that might veer into unlawful territory, the AI maker can instead make use of an AI sandbox. The AI maker gains applicable legal protection accordingly. This helps to streamline the advancement of AI.

Legal Basis For AI Sandboxes

The AI law explains why a legally stipulated AI sandbox would be useful:

- "(b) The program is designed to: (1) promote the safe and innovative use of artificial intelligence systems across various sectors including healthcare, finance, education, and public services; (2) encourage responsible deployment of artificial intelligence systems while balancing the need for consumer protection, privacy, and public safety; (3) provide clear guidelines for a person who develops an artificial intelligence system to test systems while certain laws and regulations related to the testing are waived or suspended; and (4) allow a person to engage in research, training, testing, or other pre-deployment activities to develop an artificial intelligence system."

The bottom line is that if society wants AI that stretches boundaries, but might step over the line into unlawful acts, an AI sandbox provides a means to ascertain whether the AI can be properly shaped to stay within lawful actions.

It could be that while testing the AI, the AI reveals untoward tendencies, which the AI maker can proceed to fix. If this happened outside of the AI sandbox, presumably the AI maker would have instantly broken the law and be subject to criminal and civil actions. Instead, via the AI sandbox, they can keep readjusting until the AI is ready for usage outside an AI sandbox (well, if the AI can be sufficiently corrected).

The Legal Caveats At Play

You might say that the AI maker has a get-out-of-jail-free card by making use of the AI sandbox. For example, this is what the law says about the potential actions of the statewide attorney general:

- "(c) The attorney general may not file or pursue charges against a program participant for violation of a law or regulation waived under this chapter that occurs during the testing period."

And this is what state agencies can and cannot do:

- "(d) A state agency may not file or pursue punitive action against a program participant, including the imposition of a fine or the suspension or revocation of a license, registration, or other authorization, for violation of a law or regulation waived under this chapter that occurs during the testing period."

You might be concerned that an AI maker might sneakily subvert this AI sandbox and use it as some kind of insidious cover for devious deeds. The law appears to give AI makers a tremendous amount of leeway. Recognizing this concern, an additional provision pulls back a bit and gives added teeth:

- "(e) Notwithstanding Subsections (c) and (d), the requirements of Subchapter B, Chapter 552, may not be waived, and the attorney general or a state agency may file or pursue charges or action against a program participant who violates that subchapter."

The gist is that an AI maker must toe the line. They are not supposed to willy-nilly and sneakily undermine the purpose of the regulatory AI sandbox. That being said, we don't yet know whether an AG or state agency will catch on when an AI maker goes down an unsavory path with an AI sandbox, nor whether legal action will be taken against the AI maker. As with all laws, until the rubber meets the road, it is hard to say what will happen in the real world.

Slew Of Complexity .

I've introduced you to regulatory AI sandboxes from a 30,000-foot level. There is a lot of complexity and detail that come into the picture. I'll give you a quick taste.

Some believe that a regulatory AI sandbox is a kind of "gift" to AI makers and should only be allowed in high-risk situations. A law might stipulate that an AI sandbox must be used in high-risk AI endeavors. The law might also say that medium-risk circumstances can request the use of an AI sandbox, but that it is not guaranteed you'll get it, while low-risk AI cannot invoke it at all. Others believe that it should simply be a broadly defined case-by-case basis, whereby the AI maker must apply to use a regulatory AI sandbox and justify why they wish to use one.

Another aspect is who physically establishes the regulatory AI sandboxes.

Should the government have AI sandboxes ready to go and make those available to AI makers who are approved to use them? Or should the AI maker be responsible for establishing a regulatory AI sandbox that has been approved for usage? One view is that the government should not be in the business of creating AI sandboxes. Let the AI makers do this. Meanwhile, the government would exercise oversight. A contrasting view is that letting AI makers craft their own regulatory sandboxes is akin to letting the fox run the henhouse.

There is plenty of controversy underlying regulatory AI sandboxes. One especially heated topic is that if a law requires the use of AI sandboxes, the cost to the AI maker is going to be heightened when devising the AI. Lots of overhead goes toward setting up and maintaining the regulatory AI sandbox. This, in turn, suggests that only the elite or top money AI makers can afford to go this route, and locks out the smaller-sized AI makers. Perhaps this is a form of regulatory capture.

The Delicate Balance

Some final thoughts for now.

An enlarged viewpoint of regulatory AI sandboxes suggests that this isn't solely about the testing of AI. Think of AI as being shaped in a systems life cycle fashion. First, an idea arises about what AI might be able to accomplish. Next, an effort is made to design the AI and then build it. Testing takes place. After the AI is put into production, it must be maintained and kept updated. This is the classic waterfall model or iterative system development life cycle (SDLC).

Regulatory AI sandboxes can be stipulated for the five major stages of the AI system life cycle, including:

- (1) Regulatory AI sandbox for AI concept and design: Establish a regulatory AI sandbox for guiding what AI gets built, and the AI architectural structure.
- (2) Regulatory AI sandbox for AI development: Establish a regulatory AI sandbox that is used during the AI building process.

- (3) Regulatory AI sandbox for AI testing: Establish a regulatory AI sandbox for the testing and adjustment of AI (this tends to be the most common usage).
- (4) Regulatory AI sandbox for AI deployment: Establish a regulatory AI sandbox for the fielding of AI.
- (5) Regulatory AI sandbox for monitoring AI upkeep: Establish a regulatory AI sandbox for the maintenance of AI.

Some would vehemently say that we absolutely need regulatory AI sandboxes for each of those stages. A retort is that this is craziness and an overzealous avenue of applying regulatory AI sandboxes. Focus on AI testing. Leave the rest alone.

Time will tell how this plays out.

On the topic of law, John Locke famously made this remark: "The end of law is not to abolish or restrain, but to preserve and enlarge freedom. For in all the states of created beings capable of law, where there is no law, there is no freedom." The use and design of regulatory AI sandboxes must thread the fine line of encouraging AI innovation while protecting and securing the fate of humanity. That's not an easy task, but one that needs to be ably managed.

CHAPTER 15

COURTS USING AI TO INTERPRET LAWS

In this chapter, I examine the use of generative AI and large language models (LLMs) as a tool for interpreting the meaning of laws and regulations.

Here's the deal. A longstanding challenge for courts and judges is how to properly interpret the semantics of a stated legal stipulation. For example, suppose a law indicates that the "use" of a firearm when committing a drug trafficking crime deserves extra penalties.

Imagine that a person is caught while drug trafficking, and they hand over a gun in exchange for getting cocaine. Does the mere trading of a gun get them the extra penalty, or would they need to fire or brandish the gun to violate this particular law?

It all depends on the meaning of the word "use" as included in the legal provision at hand. The issue eventually made its way to the U.S. Supreme Court, and in the now-famous case of Smith v. United States, 508 U.S. 223 (1993), the Court ruled that "use" in this context did not require that a firearm be used as a weapon. Any use that facilitated drug trafficking was sufficient. The defendant had traded the gun for drugs; thus, the firearm had indeed been used during a drug trafficking crime.

You might agree with that interpretation, or you might vehemently disagree with it. The nature of our laws is that they are inherently semantically ambiguous. A significant role for courts and judges involves painstakingly teasing out the meaning of words and seeking to apply those meanings to the application of our laws. Doing so with justice in mind.

Courts and judges are nowadays opting to use generative AI and LLMs to aid in that solemn capacity.

Let's talk about it.

AI And The Law

As a quick background, I've been extensively covering and analyzing a myriad of facets regarding the intersection of AI and the law for many years. You can find my writings not only in my Forbes column but also as posted in Bloomberg Law, ABA Law Journal, The National Jurist, The Global Legal Post, Lawyer Monthly, The Legal Technologist, MIT Computational Law Journal, and so on.

There are two major perspectives on the mixture of AI and law:

- **(1) Law & AI.** The application of laws to the governance and regulation of AI.
- **(2) AI & Law**. The application of AI to perform legal reasoning.

Thus, you can apply the law to AI, and conversely, you can apply AI to the law.

When it comes to applying the law to AI, the aim is to establish suitable regulations and provide appropriate governance on how AI should be devised and implemented. There are persistent concerns that AI makers aren't giving due attention to the ethical ramifications of their wares. Ethical issues are construed as "soft laws" and aren't as formidable as legally enacted laws, known as "hard laws". To level the playing field and keep AI makers on the up-and-up, some believe that we

When The Word "Is" Was A Viral Topic

You might vaguely know or remember that in 1998, the word "is" was a hugely viral topic.

The notable context was this. President Bill Clinton was giving grand jury testimony regarding his alleged affair with a White House intern. A statement made by his attorney indicated that there is no sex of any kind, in any manner, shape or form, taking place. President Clinton indicated that the statement was true, depending on how you interpreted the word "is" in that sentence.

One interpretation of "is" entails a present tense meaning. The "is" in a present tense interpretation suggests that the sexual relationship is underway or active at present, but since the relationship was no longer underway, it was perfectly fine to say that the statement was true. If the interpretation of "is" included the past tense, the statement would be false. It would be false because, indeed, the sexual relationship had been underway at a prior point in time.

This perhaps seems like a rather convoluted way to dissect the meaning of the word "is," which at the time upset many, while others insisted that words have ambiguities and that's just the way the world is.

The gist is that words matter. Words have a myriad of possible meanings. When lawmakers craft laws, we might hope that they nail down the words used in the legal stipulations. If the words are open to loosey-goosey interpretation, numerous societal troubles arise.

One significant problem with semantic ambiguity is that the public might not grasp what the law is attempting to regulate. Thus, there is only vague guidance on what is permissible versus what is not allowed. Another issue is that those alleged to have violated the law might go scot-free, even if it seems apparent that the person crossed over the intention of the law. Likewise, people accused of a crime might be falsely convicted if the meaning of the wording is used unfairly against them.

Words are make-or-break when it comes to the nature of law.

Bringing AI Into The Picture

Perhaps we might invoke modern-era generative AI to help deal with the interpretation of words. This seems to make abundant sense. You certainly know that contemporary LLMs are extraordinarily adept at generating fluent natural language. The use of any of the major LLMs, such as ChatGPT, GPT-5, Claude, Grok, CoPilot, Gemini, etc., is a tremendous display of AI producing fluent stories, narratives, poems, and all kinds of human-like writings.

If a law needs to be interpreted, you could simply feed the law into a state-of-the-art LLM and ask the AI to tell you what the wording means. Voila, the entire quandary about sifting through the detailed wording is resolved. Let AI tell you what it all signifies. Period, end of story.

This approach has been portrayed as using AI to serve as an on-demand online dictionary that acts as an expert-level corpus analyzer. You get a rapid synthesis of linguistic usage. Score a point for using AI in this manner. You can get multiple interpretive frames. This could include getting a plain-meaning or ordinary-use interpretation, plus the AI can give industry-specific meanings, historical usage indicators, and produce competing plausible readings. Score more points for AI.

Seems like we should welcome AI with open arms into the halls of justice.

The Picture Gets Murky And Muddied

The downsides are equally compelling.

One big concern is that the AI usage might seem to give a false sense of objectivity. If the AI tells courts and judges that a particular word means this or that, by gosh, it must be the proper interpretation. Why so? Because AI said so. There is a strong possibility of granting authority when AI is only an illusion of objectivity. AI contains all sorts of data biases and many other flaws.

Another notable issue is the lack of reproducibility. You see, generative AI is non-deterministic. Each time you use an LLM, the model is purposely devised to give differing answers, based on probabilities associated with word choices. That causes inconsistency in results. Even if you opt to tone down the non-determinism, the model version and system updates can dramatically impact the generated outputs. In short, it would be feasible to keep trying different LLMs and different versions of LLMs to find a meaning that you might want the AI to support.

Envision that a battle of the bots takes place. A lawyer for one side of a case will use an LLM that provides a favorable interpretation to their client. The lawyer on the opposing side will find an LLM that provides an interpretation that supports their own client. Dueling uses of AI take place. Courts and judges consume an inordinate amount of time trying to ferret out which AI is the winner-winner chicken dinner.

Additional worries abound. Maybe judges will essentially outsource judicial thinking, handing over the reins to AI. Perhaps judges will lose their ability to make judicial judgments. Their minds about the law will decay. What happens if judges and courts do not inform the parties that AI is being used for this purpose? Is it unfair to the parties? Should the courts and judges be required to tell when they lean into AI?

AI is the best of times, and the worst of times, when it comes to impacts on the law and our overall system of justice.

Research On Words In The Law

In a scholarly legal research article entitled "Traditional and Computational Canons" by Eric Martinez, *Harvard Journal of Law & Technology*, Fall 2025, these salient points were made about the issues associated with words in our laws (excerpts):

- "Today, courts regularly interpret a legal document according to the 'plain' or clear meaning of the text as judged by an ordinary or reasonable reader."

- "The importance of this rule extends to the interpretation of virtually every interpretive instrument, such as contracts, wills, trusts, deeds, constitutions, treaties, jury instructions, and court orders."

- "What tools do courts invoke when purporting to uncover plain meaning? Courts have traditionally appealed to three broad categories of interpretive tools: linguistic canons, dictionaries, and judicial authority."

- "This Article is also the first to empirically evaluate a second question of complementary significance -- namely, whether novel computational tools, such as LLMs, might offer a useful supplement to judges' use of traditional linguistic canons in plain-meaning cases."

- "Analyses revealed the predictions of these models aligned with consensus at rates similar to each other and to those of human judges invoking traditional tools."

As noted, the meaning of words arises in a wide variety of legal settings. I have principally been expounding here on the use of words in laws and regulations. There are all kinds of other legal contexts that rely on the legal meaning of words. A contract that you sign will have words, and those words have legal significance. If you have a will, trust, deeds, and other legal documents, those, too, depend on the interpretation of words.

The magnitude of word interpretation is immense. All elements of society are indubitably impacted by the legal meaning of words. There is no escape from it.

The Interpretation Of Legal Meanings Via AI

This excellent research explored how humans interpret legal meanings. An empirical analysis was undertaken. I urge you to consider reading the full article to see that portion of the study.

In addition, and of keen interest here, the research also performed an empirical exploration of using AI for these similar purposes. I especially liked the use of variant prompts. How a prompt is worded can radically shape what results you will get from AI. Sadly, many researchers who aren't versed in AI, yet purport to leverage AI in their work, fall into a mental trap that they use one and only one prompt when conducting their research. That's quite unfortunate. It could be that a slightly differently worded prompt would produce an entirely different result.

The study used three distinct types of prompts:

- (1) "The first prompt class was an interpretation prompt, which asked the LLM to provide their interpretation of the legal text (yes/no) as applied to the facts of a case."

- (2) "The second prompt class was a certainty prompt, which asked the LLM to provide a probability estimate of a given interpretation being the correct one."

- (3) "The third prompt class was a prediction prompt, which asked the LLM to provide a prediction of the percentage of others (either lawyers or non-lawyers) who would endorse a given interpretation."

The crux is that you might use AI to interpret legal wording on an "as is" basis, or you could tell the AI to give a probability that showcases what interpretation seems "best", or you could employ AI to predict what laypersons or lawyers might believe the meaning to be. Those are all valuable ways to proceed.

Of course, you might have the AI do all three of those. You could then review the results and use the responses to help think through the resolution to the word interpretation. I bring this up because another mental trap consists of assuming that we would use AI to give us "the right answer" and that the LLM is the final say. That would be a dangerous route.

AI in its existing state ought to be a tool that aids courts and judges, rather than replacing the minds of those in the justice system. Do not default to agreeing with whatever AI might emit. Don't give up on human thinking. Use AI as an adjunct, not as a replacement. Well, at least that's the situation currently. We'll have to see how the future pans out.

Rating AI At This Vital Task

The research compared contemporary LLMs against the word interpretations by laypersons and lawyers. By and large, the LLMs aligned with the majority of cases and performed at a similar rate with each of the tested LLMs. This is encouraging news. It appears that existing LLMs can provide "real-world meaning of contested legal terms at rates comparable to the courts" (ibid).

Caveats apply.

One is that the AI aligned with the majority of the cases, but did not align with all of the cases. This raises notable questions. If the AI is not flawlessly aligned, how will we know when it is misaligned? When misalignment occurs, should we dump the AI side, or should we perhaps give it more credence than the human interpretations?

You can make the case that the humans might have been overcome with emotion and neglected logic and reasoning, while the AI was a straight shooter. On the other hand, the humans perhaps deserve the lion's share since, well, they are humans interpreting human writings. And, AI isn't necessarily a straight shooter anyway, and certainly doesn't sufficiently represent humans per se.

Another important lesson is that the nature of the prompts made a demonstrative difference. Who decides what the prompts will say? Suppose a judge wants to cherry-pick the AI and get a response that sneakily reinforces the meaning that the judge wants to have prevail. Aha, the judge composes a prompt that will get their desired result.

There is an ongoing debate that judges sometimes do the same when choosing which conventional dictionary to serve as an interpretative tool. They might look in a dictionary, find a definition that they don't feel fits their mindset, and decide to discard that dictionary definition accordingly. They keep shopping with other dictionaries until they finally find one that has the befitting definition. The judge then holds high the dictionary as the exalted source. It is a pretextual way of covering one's posterior and creating window-dressing or a smokescreen.

The same shenanigans can occur when using AI. Therefore, judicial use of AI requires above-board rules and disclosures.

The Frontier Ahead

I have been an outspoken advocate of using AI to help keep humans out of these torrid waters and avoid costly legal battles about the meaning of words.

When lawmakers are composing laws, or really when writing any kind of legal document, it is sensible to use LLMs to aid in crafting the legal artifacts. You can get AI to double-check the human-written language and point out potential loopholes and gotchas.

Many legal documents only marginally get close scrutiny at the time of being devised. Lawmakers are often under tremendous pressure to get a law enacted. They assume that their legal staff has written an ironclad legal stipulation. The pell-mell rush might not permit this, plus they might be so close to the law that they fail to see it with independent eyes. AI can provide that added perspective.

Going further, you can employ AI to write a law or legal artifact at the get-go. You don't necessarily have to have humans write legal documents from scratch. That being said, it would be a ghastly mistake to assume that an AI-written law is ready to go. It is not. Human scrutiny is required. The possibilities of AI hallucinations and other problematic issues are too great to simply take a fire-and-forget approach to using LLMs to write laws. Don't fall for it.

A final thought for now.

Donald Kingsbury famously made this remark: "The law is what is read, not what is written." This is an adage that should be stamped on the law licenses of every lawyer. Writing laws is one thing. Reading laws is something else. Our goal should be to make those two become fully aligned. The law as written should completely match the law as read. If humans alone can't get this job done, it might be time to add AI to the legal beagle team.

CHAPTER 16

ANALYZING STATE-LEVEL AI LAWS AND AI BILLS

In this chapter, I examine a handy new analysis of the various AI bills and newly crafted AI laws that are floating around in state legislatures throughout the country.

Here's the deal. A beehive of activity is taking place regarding crafting new AI laws. It is a matter on the minds of the public and in the hands of the state legislators. Some people ardently believe that AI and AI makers are being allowed to run amok. New AI laws are vitally needed to protect society from this onslaught of ubiquitous AI.

Not everyone agrees with this pell-mell rush of new AI laws, or at least they are concerned that these AI laws might go overboard. In the zeal to protect society, there is a chance that we might unduly restrict innovation and delay or undercut the benefits of leading-edge AI. The debate is ongoing and heated.

Readers might recall that I proposed a 7-step AI-law-making process that I believe could substantively help regulators to devise new AI laws that are on target and balanced. This has an added benefit of reducing what I refer to as AI-law legal debt. This refers to AI laws that, though they look shiny, contain hidden debt that must ultimately be paid. Legal glitches and hitches will eventually be found when AI laws are passed without suitable scrutiny and analysis.

My prediction is that the slew of newly passed AI laws is likely to create a legal quagmire in the courts.

In any case, a useful study has just come out that opted to closely explore the landscape of AI bills throughout the U.S. states. I will share with you the key findings and offer my mindful thoughts on these rapidly evolving matters.

Let's talk about it.

AI And The Law

As a quick background, I've been extensively covering and analyzing a myriad of facets regarding the intersection of AI and the law for many years. You can find my writings not only in my Forbes column but also as posted in Bloomberg Law, ABA Law Journal, The National Jurist, The Global Legal Post, Lawyer Monthly, The Legal Technologist, MIT Computational Law Journal, and so on.

There are two major perspectives on the mixture of AI and law:

- **(1) Law & AI.** The application of laws to the governance and regulation of AI.
- **(2) AI & Law**. The application of AI to perform legal reasoning.

Thus, you can apply the law to AI, and conversely, you can apply AI to the law.

When it comes to applying the law to AI, the aim is to establish suitable regulations and provide appropriate governance on how AI should be devised and implemented. There are longstanding concerns that AI makers aren't giving due attention to the ethical ramifications of their wares. Ethical issues are construed as "soft laws" and aren't as formidable as legally enacted laws, known as "hard laws". To level the playing field and keep AI makers on the up-and-up, some believe that we need more lawmakers to make more laws about AI.

It might seem easy to just go ahead and pile on new AI laws. The problem is that for each new AI law, there is a solid chance of creating confusion and muddying the waters of AI expectations. Yes, ironically, though AI laws are supposed to straighten things out, if the AI laws aren't properly crafted, they can lead to all sorts of undesirable adverse consequences.

The Current Situation Legally

In terms of the AI laws in the United States, they have not yet stood the test of time, meaning that we won't really know how well they stand up until there are court cases that test these new laws. It is too early to know whether the laws will survive legal battles waged by AI makers and other contenders. Just because AI laws are enacted does not mean they are proper. All sorts of improper provisions and constitutionally contentious stipulations are undoubtedly buried within these shiny new AI laws.

Congress has repeatedly waded into establishing an overarching federal law that would encompass AI. So far, no dice. The efforts have ultimately faded from view. Thus, at this time, there isn't an overarching federal law devoted to these controversial AI matters. The big question will be to what degree a sweeping federal law would impact the numerous state-level AI laws. The odds are that many of the state-level laws would run afoul of a federal mandate, and a tsunami of legal cases would arise as a tussle between federal law and state law is undertaken. It surely will be a legal mess.

The crux is that there is intense and pervasive interest in using the law to govern AI. It is an abundantly burgeoning realm. AI companies would be wise to keep a close eye on what is happening in the hallways and byways of regulators and legislative bodies. I have repeatedly noted that a profitable specialty for budding lawyers is to consider concentrating on the exciting and dynamic field of AI and the law.

Handy Study On AI Bills At State-Level

In a recent study entitled "Analyzing The Passage Of State-Level AI Bills" by James Denford, Gregory Dawson, Kevin Desouza, and Marc Barda Picavet, *Brookings*, March 17, 2026, these salient points were made (excerpts):

- "Our team used tracking from the Brookings Center for Technology Innovation for this analysis and is current as of Oct. 20, 2025. We identified a total of 386 bills introduced across all 50 states with at least one bill in each state."

- "Transparency and trust had the largest number of bills overall (both all bills and active bills), but its passed bill percentage (15.5%) and its very high active bills percentage (80%) indicate that legislators may be struggling with competing topics such as disclosure versus transparency and market-orientation versus citizen-orientation."

- "Responsible governance, while comprising the smallest number of bills (114) and the smallest number of active bills (64), had both the highest number of bills passed (44) and the highest percentage of bills passed (38.6%)."

- "Overall, there are clear pathways to successful bill introduction and eventual bill passage, but these differ based on the characteristics of the state. By having a clear understanding of what leads to bill passage, elected officials can tailor their own bills to the unique characteristics of their state."

The study is worth a close reading and offers keen insights into the scope and directionality of AI laws at the state level. I will walk you through key aspects momentarily.

Please note that the study was a snapshot in time, namely, based on AI bills as of October 20, 2025. This is certainly admirable, though do keep in mind that the snapshot occurred five months ago.

Changes have taken place during the intervening time, including that some of the underway bills have been passed, some have dropped out, and new AI bills have been introduced. All told, it has been loosely speculated in the news media and on social media that, at this time, there might be around one thousand bills in various conditions throughout all fifty states.

Reading The Tea Leaves

Given the aforementioned caveats, let's do some cautious unpacking to discern potential patterns in what happens during the rocky road of AI laws working their way through the bumpy and complicated legislative process.

Of the 386 legislative AI bills analyzed in this study, nearly 75% were in active processing status and still under consideration, while about 20% had been passed, and approximately 5% had failed. It intuitively makes sense that the preponderance is in a processing status.

Why so?

Many of the states are unsure of what to do about AI. Here's how the legislative process usually goes. An issue arises that garners public attention and a state legislator opts to introduce a new AI law. There are indubitably competing perspectives on whether such a new AI law is truly needed. Some members of the legislature get on board, others oppose, and some are silent. External stakeholders weigh in. Those "outsiders" sometimes are highly visible while other times they are nearly invisible and working behind the scenes.

The upshot is that getting an AI law across the finish line is often an arduous and dicey proposition. There are very few slam dunks. As a result, the drafts float around, get revised, and the processing goes back and forth. A legislator would likely not want their prized AI bill to be a failure; thus, it makes sense to try to keep it alive. Some AI bills become proverbial zombies, not likely to pass, nor be put out of their misery.

AI Laws Are Usually Specific

AI laws are often crafted based on specific issues or topics that are hot or otherwise have risen to a level of legislative attention. The gist is that most AI bills are focused on a particular AI realm or facet. They are not usually of an all-encompassing nature across all kinds of AI legal considerations.

Some worry that each of the states will end up with an oddball patchwork of hit-or-miss AI laws. A state might pass AI laws covering this or that, but it didn't cover other topics that merit AI laws. Suppose that a state passes ten AI laws on ten respective aspects, while another state only passes one new AI law. Does this imply that the state with ten such AI laws is somehow doing more about AI than the state that passed just one AI law?

Nope.

You cannot readily compare counts regarding passed AI laws because the state with ten might have splintered topics that are fully contained in the one AI law of the other state. You are trying to falsely compare apples and oranges. Not all AI laws are the same. Most AI laws are relatively myopic and focus on a singular topic. Comprehensive AI laws are exceedingly rare right now.

It is a mishmash that represents the newness of contemporary AI. Down the road, perhaps a decade away, we might look back and realize that it would have been cleaner to holistically package the AI legal considerations more cohesively. Of course, hindsight is always an easy way to view the world. Right now, AI topics pop up, and a semi-random selection and attention occur in each state.

Categorization As A Tool For Analysis

The cited study decided to categorize AI laws into these three main buckets:

- **(1) Protection of the individual:** "Protecting individuals from material, reputational, physiological, economic, or identity-based harms."

- **(2) Transparency and trust in information ecosystems:** "AI-mediated content or interactions are recognizable, traceable, contestable, or authentic."

- **(3) Responsible systemic governance:** "Build institutions, oversight systems, rules for high-risk models, and public investment strategies."

This seems reasonable as a means of trying to get a handle on whether certain types of AI laws are more or less likely to proceed toward being enacted versus dropped out. A downside is that it can be challenging to fit all AI bills into such discrete categories. An AI bill might overlap into two or more such categories, creating a counting problem of sorts. You don't want to double-count an AI bill. Nor do you want to force an AI bill into only one slot if it truly has overlapping properties.

Anyway, it is usually the case that most AI laws are typically brought up for a relatively singular purpose, and so it is reasonable to plop it into one of the three buckets. I would anticipate that as the tsunami of new AI laws gains additional rapid progress, it would be handy to differentiate them into at least five or more major categories.

The Findings Based On Categories

In the above-listed bullet points, you might have noticed that transparency and trust were noted as having the largest number of AI bills overall. I concur with the stated analysis that this is likely explainable. People are fed up with AI slop. Pressure is being placed on legislators to do something about this. Thus, the high volume of such AI bills.

But writing an all-hands acceptable AI law that reduces or stops AI junk is not as easy as it might seem. You must be careful and not toss the baby out with the bathwater. Plus, competing interests battle over being too lenient versus being too tight. Massive political struggles ensue.

Responsible governance appears to be more likely to get passed, though the number of such AI bills is much smaller than for transparency and trust. This is probably due to the cookie-cutter ease of crafting such AI laws. They are more readily composed, more readily understood, and tend to get a lower semblance of acrid debate.

The study proceeded to cross-reference state-level statistics overall to the patterns associated with the number and types of AI bills in each state. They looked at per capita income, poverty levels, educational status of the population, business environment in the state, political party affiliations in the state, and so on.

A qualitative comparative analysis (QCA) was performed on the data. If you are interested in the details, make sure to read the study. A visually impactful heat map and Venn diagrams provide intriguing visualizations. I don't have the space here to walk you through the material, but I do urge a look-see for some quite fascinating considerations.

The bottom line is that each state takes its own idiosyncratic path toward AI laws. The nuances of a particular state are going to shape which AI bills get introduced and whether they will reach fruition. You will need to sit down and seriously introspectively mull over the nature of your state to get a sensible bead on why the state is where it is in terms of AI laws.

It comes down to a case-by-case, state-by-state basis.

The World We Are In

It is incontrovertible that we are now amid a grandiose worldwide experiment when it comes to society overall. The experiment is that AI is being made available nationally and globally, which is either overtly or insidiously acting to provide human guidance of one kind or another. Doing so either at no cost or at a minimal cost. It is available anywhere and at any time, 24/7. We are all the guinea pigs in this wanton experiment.

The reason this is especially tough to consider is that AI has a dual-use effect. Just as AI can be detrimental to humankind, it can also be a huge bolstering force for humanity. A delicate tradeoff must be mindfully managed. Prevent or mitigate the downsides, and meanwhile make the upsides as widely and readily available as possible.

There is a famous quote about the making of laws that is often attributed to Otto von Bismarck, stating this catchy line: "Laws are like sausages. It's better not to see them being made." Though there is a lot of truth to that adage, the importance of AI to society at large is so vital that we must all do our part to weigh in on the rising tide of AI laws. Do we need the AI laws? Are they prudent? Don't let the sausage-making get unduly carried away.

CHAPTER 17
SEVEN STEPS FOR LAWMAKERS MAKING AI LAWS

In this chapter, I identify and explain the seven vital steps that lawmakers need to undertake when creating new AI laws.

Here's the deal. Nearly all the states in the U.S. are working fervently to craft new laws governing AI. Besides the existing AI laws, there are perhaps a thousand additional drafts or memos of understanding being floated around that might eventually become fully crafted and then enacted AI laws. The problem is that a likely notable percentage will undoubtedly be poorly devised, badly written, and end up stoking confusion and unnecessary legal battles due to not having pursued a rigorous and quality-leveling double-checking process.

I've been repeatedly pointing out in my many writings and talks that the slew of already passed AI laws are replete with disconcerting and highly troubling glitches and hitches. Why do so many of the new AI laws have problems? The answer is straightforward. Policymakers and lawmakers are in a rush to create these new laws and often proceed hastily without an AI-law-making step-by-step process that sensibly vets the production process. Currently, garbage tends to come out at the end of the prevailing willy-nilly efforts.

There is an old saying that the making of laws is as ugly as the making of sausage. Unfortunately, given the importance of AI to society at large, using sausage-making processes for creating AI laws is a formula for failure. It fails the public. It fails the AI makers. It fails and later falls on the shoulders of the policymakers and lawmakers who should have done a better job.

No worries since my 7-step process can turn this around and aid in crafting and passing new AI laws that are sensible and won't go off the rails.

Let's talk about it.

AI And The Law

As a quick background, I've been extensively covering and analyzing a myriad of facets regarding the intersection of AI and the law for many years. You can find my writings not only in my Forbes column but also as posted in Bloomberg Law, ABA Law Journal, The National Jurist, The Global Legal Post, Lawyer Monthly, The Legal Technologist, MIT Computational Law Journal, and so on.

There are two major perspectives on the mixture of AI and law:

- **(1) Law & AI.** The application of laws to the governance and regulation of AI.
- **(2) AI & Law**. The application of AI to perform legal reasoning.

Thus, you can apply the law to AI, and conversely, you can apply AI to the law.

When it comes to applying the law to AI, the aim is to establish suitable regulations and provide appropriate governance on how AI should be devised and implemented. There are longstanding concerns that AI makers aren't giving due attention to the ethical ramifications of their wares. Ethical issues are construed as "soft laws" and aren't as formidable as legally enacted laws, known as "hard laws". To level the playing field and keep AI makers on the up-and-up, some believe that we need more lawmakers to make more laws about AI.

It might seem easy to just go ahead and pile on new AI laws. The problem is that for each new AI law, there is a solid chance of creating confusion and muddying the waters of AI expectations. Yes, ironically, though AI laws are supposed to straighten things out, if the AI laws aren't properly crafted, they can lead to all sorts of undesirable adverse consequences.

The Current Situation Legally

In terms of the AI laws in the United States, they have not yet stood the test of time, meaning that we won't really know how well they stand up until there are court cases that test these new laws. It is too early to know whether the laws will survive legal battles waged by AI makers and other contenders. Just because AI laws are enacted does not mean they are proper. All sorts of improper provisions and constitutionally contentious stipulations are undoubtedly buried within these shiny new AI laws.

Congress has repeatedly waded into establishing an overarching federal law that would encompass AI. So far, no dice. The efforts have ultimately faded from view. Thus, at this time, there isn't an overarching federal law devoted to these controversial AI matters. The big question will be to what degree a sweeping federal law would impact the numerous state-level AI laws. The odds are that many of the state-level laws would run afoul of a federal mandate, and a tsunami of legal cases would arise as a tussle between federal law and state law is undertaken. It surely will be a legal mess.

The bottom line is that there is intense and pervasive interest in using the law to govern AI. It is an abundantly burgeoning realm. AI companies would be wise to keep a close eye on what is happening in the hallways and byways of regulators and legislative bodies. I have repeatedly noted that a profitable specialty for budding lawyers is to consider concentrating on the exciting and dynamic field of AI and the law.

Recommending The 7-Step AI-Law-Making Process

How can we ensure that new AI laws are on target, making realistic sense, and accomplish societal aims that serve to properly protect and abundantly serve the public?

I recommend that a 7-step AI-law-making process be made use of. I will lay it out in a moment. First, please know that there isn't magic involved. This is simply a systematically planned way to get the job done correctly. There is nothing out of the ordinary. Nor does it somehow elongate or otherwise hamper the law-making process. In fact, if followed suitably, the result should be a handy streamlining that enables a faster and higher-quality result.

Perhaps equally important are the downstream positive impacts. Right now, we are faced with downstream negative impacts. A bushel full of negative impacts. When new AI laws are poorly devised, the downstream effect is a mess and quite costly. AI makers launch heated legal battles against the laws to contend with the inherent glitches and hitches that were baked into the new AI laws. AI makers aren't sure how to abide by the confusing new AI laws. Finger-pointing is aplenty. The courts get choked with legal disputes that should never have landed there. Whereas it might have seemed dreamily ideal that a new AI law got onto the books quickly, the reality is that the pied piper must always be paid.

I refer to this as AI-law legal debt. This refers to AI laws that, though they look shiny, contain hidden debt that must ultimately be paid. The glitches and hitches will be found. The wheels will come off the bus. No one knows for sure what the AI laws were supposed to attain. It becomes a legal quagmire.

But that isn't the way the world has to be. Write AI laws that have minimal or near-zero legal debt. Pass those kinds of new AI laws.

Overview Of The Seven Steps

Here are the seven crucial steps for crafting new AI laws:

- (1) Draft a set of targeted AI policy goals in plain language.
- (2) Perform a detailed AI-reality assessment and revise.
- (3) Finalize the plain-language AI policy draft.
- (4) Legally codify the AI plain-language AI policy draft into apt legalese.
- (5) Conduct an adversarial stress testing of the AI-realistic legal codification.
- (6) Do a series of AI-law implementation simulations.
- (7) Perform a reverse translation and an alignment review.

I tried to phrase the steps so that they are each relatively self-explanatory. I realize that some of the verbiage might seem unfamiliar to you. Let's add some explanations.

Here we are again, but with a breezy explanation for each of the seven steps:

- **(1) Draft a set of targeted AI policy goals in plain language.** Craft an initial set of AI policy goals regarding the desired AI law, doing so in plain language and not in legalese. This is done before veering into the legal language jungle. Why? Because it is crucial to communicate with a wide variety of stakeholders, encompassing lawyers and non-lawyers, to grasp what the aims are.

- **(2) Perform a detailed AI-reality assessment and revise**. Thoroughly analyze the draft AI policy goals to ascertain the realistic and unrealistic nature of the goals and revise the goals accordingly. Some goals are bound to be unrealistic and, if left intact, will eventually sink the hoped-for new law.

- **(3) Finalize the plain-language AI policy draft.** The prior two steps might have gone back and forth multiple times, so do a finalization of the plain-language AI policy draft before further proceeding.

- **(4) Legally codify the AI plain-language AI policy draft into apt legalese.** With the finalized plain-language AI policy draft in hand, go ahead and translate this into legalese. This is likely a much harder task to do than you might assume. Be careful and mindful.

- **(5) Conduct an adversarial stress testing of the AI-realistic legal codification.** This is a commonly overlooked or shallowly performed step in general for lawmaking. Many law-making efforts assume that the legal codification marginally requires a review, and it is off to the races with the crafted law. Not here. Adversarial stress testing is required. Revise the draft laws accordingly.

- **(6) Do a series of AI-law implementation simulations.** This is a step that is rarely done and often surprises lawmakers as even being a possible step. The aim is to test the codified AI laws as though they were enacted. You can use modern-era AI to help in performing these tests. It is an implementation simulation to bring forth potential hitches and glitches. Revise the draft AI law accordingly.

- **(7) Perform a reverse translation and an alignment review.** This last step takes true grit. After all the effort expended in the prior steps, it is possible that the initial targeted AI policy goals got lost along the tried-and-true path. Take the drafted AI-law, reverse translate it back into a set of AI policy goals, and see if they still align with the anticipated or desired AI policy goals. If so, great, move ahead. If not, you'll need to loop back through the steps and get things squared up.

Observe that this is somewhat akin to a waterfall-like systems development process; perhaps you are aware of the classic SDLC (systems development life cycle). Each step proceeds to the next step in sequence. Unlike a traditional waterfall approach, this one is potentially iterative. If you get to step 7 and things have gone awry, the idea is to loop back to step 1 and do the process again. The second time might be less arduous because you now have plenty to work with.

In recap, this is a rigorous 7-step iterative waterfall approach to devising new AI laws.

Undercutting The 7-Step Process

As with any stipulated process, the whole kit-and-kaboodle can be readily undermined, even if you claim or attempt to abide by the seven steps. Let's explore the myriad ways that people can mess things up.

One of the most frequent failures is to jump past the first three steps and eagerly start crafting the legal language of the new AI law. It is tempting to do so. Strong-willed attorneys consider themselves master craftsperson's at writing laws. It's what they do for a living. They dream at night about legal language compositions.

Thus, it is very tempting to completely skip past specifying any AI policy goals. Just tell them what you want. Voila, they can hammer out the legalese for you. Don't waste your time and money on those annoying and needless three opening steps.

The dire trap with this "expedited" approach is that the crafted AI laws will almost certainly be all over the map. You will not readily be able to tie them directly to any overarching AI policy goals. The goals are essentially a map. What happens when you go hiking and do not have a proper map? You can easily get lost. The new AI law will downstream become a nightmare since it will be muddled, impossible to figure out what the intention was, and otherwise be a boondoggle.

Do not skip steps.

The same lesson holds true for skipping the steps after the fourth step. Imagine that lawmakers stridently followed steps 1 through 4. Now, they have a newly crafted AI law in their eager hands. It is exhilarating as a lawmaker to have a freshly baked AI law that has that alluring aroma of mouth-watering chocolate-chip cookies. You see, it is a juicy temptation staring them in the face.

Do you put the drafted AI law through the series of additional steps, steps 5 through 7, to make sure it is good to go, or do you just assume it is good to go? The assumption approach is like spinning a roulette wheel. Sometimes you might get lucky, but most of the time you won't. The budding AI law is almost assuredly polluted with hitches and glitches. You just don't know it yet.

Downstream, all the ugliness will be revealed.

Half-Hearted Step Compliance

I've got a sneakier way that the seven steps get undermined.

First, pretend that someone opts to follow all seven steps. A checklist is made, and each step is dutifully checked off. Nothing is skipped. This most certainly must guarantee that the outcome will be a robust and bustling new AI law. Surely so.

The troubles arise during the performance of the steps. This is much harder to see. All you know is that the steps were performed. The assumption is that each step was done diligently. To clarify, there is absolutely no reason to assume that the steps will be performed diligently. You would be wiser to assume the opposite. Assume that the steps will be done on a watered-down basis. This is a likelier scenario.

Why would the steps not be performed to the hilt? It could be that the clock is ticking. Pressure is on to get done with the "agonizing" process. Shortchange the work. It might also save on the cost of crafting the AI law. Lots of reasons will tilt toward a short shrift.

To try and prevent this, or at least catch it in the act, I have prepared a set of metrics associated with each of the seven steps. Those metrics require collecting the actions and quality at each step. It is much harder to trick the process when the effort is being sensibly tracked. I will go over those metrics in an upcoming posting. Stay tuned.

The World We Are In

Policymakers and lawmakers might have their hearts in the right place. They want to curtail the badness of AI usage. Good for them. But trying to do the right thing by actually doing a half-baked thing, or possibly the wrong thing, doesn't help. It will make matters worse.

I implore them to mindfully craft AI laws and get the right kind of advice when doing so. Many think they are getting good advice. Oftentimes, they end up in an echo chamber that reinforces well-intended but off-target advice. Get outside of the echo chamber. Aim to devise new AI laws that can properly get the job done.

Consider utilizing my seven-step process. AI laws are important. They can impact society in colossal ways. Those composing AI laws are taking on a tremendous duty since AI is here, rapidly being adopted, and will pervade every aspect of our human lives.

The last thought for now goes to the famous remark by Benjamin Franklin: "By failing to prepare, you are preparing to fail." Do not land in that disastrous trap.

CHAPTER 18

MAJOR BLUNDERS WHEN CRAFTING AI LAWS

In this chapter, I identify and examine the five major blunders that lawmakers and policymakers keep making when creating new AI laws.

Here's the deal. Those crafting new AI laws often have the best of intentions. They perceive that there is an urgent societal issue associated with AI that needs to be legally addressed. The problem arises when the rubber meets the road, namely that the actual wording and design of the new AI law is off-target and accidentally go off the rails. This is usually due to lawmakers and policymakers misunderstanding what AI is, and thus they enact wording that is either an underreach or, worse still, is a disastrous overreach.

The good news is that this is entirely predictable and preventable. I lay out five major blunders that key stakeholders need to be mindful of. Do not fall into any of these mistakes. Though this won't guarantee that a new AI law will be on target, it at least reduces the chances of going horribly astray.

Let's talk about it.

AI And The Law

As a quick background, I've been extensively covering and analyzing a myriad of facets regarding the intersection of AI and the law for many years. You can find my writings not only in my Forbes column but also as posted in Bloomberg Law, ABA Law Journal, The National Jurist, The Global Legal Post, Lawyer Monthly, The Legal Technologist, MIT Computational Law Journal, and so on.

There are two major perspectives on the mixture of AI and law:

- **(1) Law & AI.** The application of laws to the governance and regulation of AI.
- **(2) AI & Law**. The application of AI to perform legal reasoning.

Thus, you can apply the law to AI, and conversely, you can apply AI to the law.

When it comes to applying the law to AI, the aim is to establish suitable regulations and provide appropriate governance on how AI should be devised and implemented. There are longstanding concerns that AI makers aren't giving due attention to the ethical ramifications of their wares. Ethical issues are construed as "soft laws" and aren't as formidable as legally enacted laws, known as "hard laws". To level the playing field and keep AI makers on the up-and-up, some believe that we need more lawmakers to make more laws about AI.

It might seem easy to just go ahead and pile on new AI laws. The problem is that for each new AI law, there is a solid chance of creating confusion and muddying the waters of AI expectations. Yes, ironically, though AI laws are supposed to straighten things out, if the AI laws aren't properly crafted, they can lead to all sorts of undesirable adverse consequences.

The Current Situation Legally

In terms of the AI laws in the United States, they have not yet stood the test of time, meaning that we won't really know how well they stand up until there are court cases that test these new laws.

It is too early to know whether the laws will survive legal battles waged by AI makers and other contenders. Just because AI laws are enacted does not mean they are proper. All sorts of improper provisions and constitutionally contentious stipulations are undoubtedly buried within these shiny new AI laws.

Congress has repeatedly waded into establishing an overarching federal law that would encompass AI. So far, no dice. The efforts have ultimately faded from view. Thus, at this time, there isn't an overarching federal law devoted to these controversial AI matters. The big question will be to what degree a sweeping federal law would impact the numerous state-level AI laws. The odds are that many of the state-level laws would run afoul of a federal mandate, and a tsunami of legal cases would arise as a tussle between federal law and state law is undertaken. It surely will be a legal mess.

The bottom line is that there is intense and pervasive interest in using the law to govern AI. It is an abundantly burgeoning realm. AI companies would be wise to keep a close eye on what is happening in the hallways and byways of regulators and legislative bodies. I have repeatedly noted that a profitable specialty for budding lawyers is to consider concentrating on the exciting and dynamic field of AI and the law.

The Five Major Blunders

There are plenty of ways that a new AI law can be improperly devised and will end up not achieving the presumed or stated societal and legal goals underlying the basis for the law. I believe I've seen a large proportion of the foul-ups, but I'm sure additional ones are coming down the pike. It is a nearly endless supply.

With a tidal wave of new AI laws being created daily, i.e., some news outlets claim that there are perhaps a thousand being conceived of and in early draft stages across the United States, the chances of some or many of those AI laws being out-of-order or at least having significant legal and technological issues are relatively high.

That is a car crash waiting to happen. I've noted ironically in my talks and writings that these profuse AI laws offer an unexpected bonus: it is a surefire way to keep attorneys employed (well, hopefully, human attorneys).

I have identified five major blunders that explain the bulk of the badly written AI laws. Please know that more blunders exist. If reader interest arises, I will do a series with additional identified blunders. Stay tuned.

Here are the five most frequent blunders when writing new AI laws:

- **(1) Misunderstanding of what AI is.** This blunder consists of writing legal language that, from an AI technological perspective, is any or all these conditions: Outrightly incorrect, implausible, exceedingly AI-methodologically specific, exceedingly AI-generic vacuously, outdated, or otherwise full of loopholes and problematic.

- **(2) Fixation on AI training.** This blunder involves making a fixated assumption that the sole focus of the new law should be on the training of the AI, which, if suitably legally constrained, will ultimately and assuredly prevent or obviate any downstream AI run-time concerns. Not true.

- **(3) Fluent interactions by AI are inherently evil.** This blunder entails the belief that if AI converses in a human-like fluency, it must be evil and bent on deception; ergo, AI fluency must be legally banned. Period, end of story. This is a deeply flawed belief.

- **(4) Confusingly aiming at AI intent.** This blunder revolves around the conventional legal posture that, since intent is central to laws about humans (the classic *mens rea* or "guilty mind"), the same aspect of intent must necessarily be a crucial element when it comes to the acts of AI. This is an inappropriate anthropomorphizing of AI.

- **(5) AI capabilities are assumed to be surgically removable.** This blunder assumes that AI is readily compartmentalized rather than entangled, and that particular capabilities can be simply surgically removed without any difficulties and no cascading effects. The problem with such an AI law is that it ends up inadvertently being an all-or-nothing scheme, which is not what the law was probably meant to be.

Explaining The Five Big Blunders

Now that I've gotten the five major blunders on the table, I will briefly unpack them to help showcase where things go awry. I aim to illustrate the blunders well enough so that they will be caught by policymakers and lawmakers before the horse gets out of the barn. It is much preferred to detect and correct the blunders prior to enacting a new AI law. Once the law is a law, trying to retrofit a law is arduous and probably going to worsen an already bad situation. Let's get things right at the get-go.

The unpacking will proceed one at a time.

Blunder #1: Misunderstanding Of What AI Is

In the first blunder, a major snafu is that AI laws often reflect a lack of solid comprehension about what AI really is.

Some policymakers and lawmakers get very heated and upset on this point, retorting that there is no reason that they should know about AI. They know about laws. They know about policies. AI isn't in their wheelhouse. Sure, I get that. But the issue is that if you don't know enough about AI, or you are relying on others who purport to know about AI, but they have agendas or biases, you are blindly composing laws on something that you are unsure of. This leads to AI laws that will have all manner of problems. For example, the AI aspects that are being referred to in the law are perhaps implausible, such that there isn't any such AI in existence that meets the scope, and none arises in the near future. Or the AI stipulations are exceedingly AI-methodologically specific or exceedingly AI-generic in a vacuous way. And so on.

Allow me to give you a quick instance of an exceeding AI-generic reference that is vacuous.

Suppose a new AI law says this:

- "AI shall not provide emotional support to a user."

This seems, on the surface, to be an attempt to protect users from an AI system that might create undue human-AI dependencies. We don't want AI to fool people into thinking the AI is their buddy. Doing so can cause numerous mental health concerns.

The intention of the lawmaker might be of the most caring nature. The trouble comes up when you try to nail down what this nebulous law means by "emotional support". Imagine that a user enters a prompt telling the AI that they just got a promotion at work. The AI responds by saying congratulations on getting the promotion.

Is that emotional support?

A prosecutor might argue that this indeed is clearly an instance of AI-based emotional support and, therefore, try to prosecute the developers and makers of the AI for having violated the law. I seriously doubt that most everyday people would agree that this instance is much of an emotional support exigency. I would guess that most people would be thinking of circumstances where the AI reels in a person by repeatedly telling the user they have the AI as a shoulder to cry on, and that the AI is always there to help them pick up the pieces of their life.

The crux is that without a proper and clear-cut delineation of what the law means when it comes to emotional support, AI makers and those fielding AI are going to be on pins and needles. What falls within the grasp of the law? What is allowed and sits outside of the scope of the law? It is a bad law that instills confusion into the marketplace, and when push comes to shove, it will chew up precious resources trying to battle legally over what was intended versus what was accidentally inferred.

Blunder #2: Fixation On AI Training

Oddly, some of the new AI laws fixate exclusively on the training of AI, rather than the outcomes or results of AI. The idea seems to be that if the law catches an AI maker at the time of training the AI, this will serve to prevent adverse outcomes during run-time.

Not true.

I suppose this might be a kind of anthropomorphism by lawmakers. Maybe they think that AI is like a person, whereby if you avoid training them on something at the get-go, presumably they cannot later do whatever that thing is. Of course, that is nonsensical. Another possibility is that lawmakers are led to believe that training is where all the magic happens. I could envision some AI makers that might want to steer lawmakers in that direction, thus allowing them to be off the hook when the AI does something foul at run-time. The AI maker would presumably be able to point out that they hadn't trained the AI to do this, and ergo, they are relieved of violating the AI law.

The gist is that it's generally okay to have an AI law that aims at the training of AI, but just keep in mind that it ought to also encompass what happens at run-time. Do not rely solely on the training aspects. If you do, it will likely be a huge escape hatch for the AI maker. I would tend to assume that a lawmaker doesn't seek to provide such an escape hatch. Maybe so, maybe not.

Blunder #3: Fluent Interactions By AI Are Inherently Evil

This blunder is again a bit strange. The supposition seems to be that if AI appears to converse in a natural language fluency, the AI must be evil. The AI is trying to deceive people into believing that the AI is a living being. We must stop that outrageous deception by banning AI from having fluency capabilities.

This would decimate just about all modern generative AI and large language models (LLMs). The core element of such AI is that it is designed and built to interact in a natural language manner.

That's why people relish using LLMs. An attempt to ban this fluency is tantamount to banning contemporary LLMs entirely.

I believe what they really want to do with such AI laws is ensure that the AI fluency does not end up tricking people into believing the AI is real. There are multiple ways this can be achieved. I've discussed at length that LLMs ought to have periodic pop-ups that remind users they are interacting with an AI and not a living being, along with having numerous cautionary indicators at login and throughout the use of AI. The user interface is where these types of AI laws should target their attention. Please don't throw out the baby with the bathwater, as the old saying goes.

Blunder #4: Confusingly Aiming At AI Intent

Attorneys and lawmakers are highly versed in the consideration of "intent" when it comes to how laws are written and enforced. Intent is a central theme for laws that regulate human behavior. The classic phrasing is *mens rea,* or the possession of a guilty mind. When people commit crimes or otherwise undertake bad acts, we look to ascertain whether they intended to do these things. Intent carries a lot of hefty weight. A person who didn't form intent might be given more latitude than one who did seem to exhibit intent.

We cannot open a person's mind to directly determine what their intent was. The intentions must be figured out through other means. What did the person say? Did they write something down? Do their actions reflect a semblance of intent? And so on.

I bring up intent because there are AI laws that make the blunder of trying to garner the "intent" of AI. This seems to be another anthropomorphism. Did the AI intend to tell someone that they should jump off a cliff? If so, the AI is construed as more guilty than if the AI didn't intend to say this.

Currently, it doesn't make much sense to refer to AI intent. AI is not a sentient being. It is a computational and mathematical formulation. The AI might be computationally shaped to do particular acts, but I refuse to label this as "intent of the AI".

It is probably more appropriate to refer to the AI maker's intent. Did the AI maker intend for the AI to tell people to jump off cliffs? Even if that wasn't their intent, did they devise the AI such that it would do this, and if so, what accountability should they have?

Blunder #5: AI Capabilities Assumed Surgically Removable

The last of the five major blunders is believing that modern-era generative AI and LLMs are constructed in a manner that allows the surgical removal of undesirable parts. Sorry to say that this is not the principal design of LLMs. It is closer to being a monolith. In theory, we could potentially rethink and recast LLMs to allow for a type of pinpoint removal, but it would be a significant undertaking and require a radically new architectural approach.

The hitch is that if an AI law says that any AI must remove the capability of telling people about some particular topic, such as excluding any reference to self-harm, there is no straightforward means to excise that aspect. Think of the internal data structures and pattern matching as a thickly interwoven web that is like a fully entangled ball of string. You cannot just pluck out some aspect you don't like.

That all-or-nothing consideration doesn't mean that you cannot regulate what the AI does. You can. The key is that this would mainly be done on a safeguard basis and occur during run-time. The AI might be required to have a suppression-oriented safeguard that doesn't allow a topic of self-harm to be addressed. It is still inside the AI. The AI will prevent it from being displayed or presented.

Unfortunately, that is also not as easy as it sounds, and there is still a chance or risk that the safeguards won't be 100% protective

The World We Are In

Policymakers and lawmakers might have their hearts in the right place. They want to curtail the badness of AI usage. Good for them. But trying to do the right thing by actually doing a half-baked thing, or possibly the wrong thing, doesn't help. It will make matters worse.

I implore them to mindfully craft AI laws and get the right kind of advice when doing so. Many think they are getting good advice. Oftentimes, they end up in an echo chamber that reinforces well-intended but off-target advice. Get outside of the echo chamber. Aim to devise new AI laws that can properly get the job done.

The famous statesman Otto von Bismarck made this oft-quoted remark: "If you like laws and sausages, you should never watch either one being made." Though this truism has a lasting truth, we should also be mindful of the value in watching the making of laws, doing so to aid in ensuring they are proper and serve the people well. Those composing AI laws are taking on a tremendous duty since AI is here, rapidly being adopted, and will pervade every aspect of our human lives.

Let's get this right the first time and every time.

CHAPTER 19
DECONSTRUCTING BAD AI LAWS

In this chapter, I examine yet another newly underway AI law that goes overboard and demonstrates the challenges in getting things done right when it comes to governing modern-era AI.

Here's the deal. Policymakers and lawmakers are at times avidly pursuing the development of new AI laws, typically doing so with the best of intentions. Unfortunately, they often do not understand the nature of AI well enough to properly craft the wording of these well-intended laws. They might opt to reach out to AI specialists for advice, but those experts are often not versed in the nuances of how laws ought to be drafted.

The result is the classic "blind leading the blind" scenario. You have policymakers and lawmakers making a wild stab in the dark about AI that they don't comprehend, and you have AI "experts" advising them who do not understand the nuances of crafting legible and legally rigorous laws. It is a recipe for disaster.

The problem is that once those laws get enacted and hit the books, the real world finally gets a shot at dealing with those new AI laws. Up until then, it was all conceptual and loosey-goosey. After the new AI law is passed into actual law and is cast in stone, everyone must figure out what it means and what its true ramifications are. These laws often overreach.

They valiantly seek to prevent negative aspects of AI, but then inadvertently undercut the highly prized positive sides of AI. This produces an onerous legal quagmire for those who reasonably and fairly would like to use such AI capabilities, and likewise is a costly and overbearing nightmare for those who make and field such AI.

Well-intending lawmakers can accidentally cast a large, wanton net that could have easily and readily been made much more precise and achieved the gallant desired intentions. I have been vociferously pointing out these repeatedly frustrating and exasperating legal snafus in my writings and analyses. A new one has recently popped up. It is a doozy.

Let's talk about it.

AI And The Law

As a quick background, I've been extensively covering and analyzing a myriad of facets regarding the intersection of AI and the law for many years. You can find my writings not only in my Forbes column but also as posted in Bloomberg Law, ABA Law Journal, The National Jurist, The Global Legal Post, Lawyer Monthly, The Legal Technologist, MIT Computational Law Journal, and so on.

There are two major perspectives on the mixture of AI and law:

- **(1) Law & AI.** The application of laws to the governance and regulation of AI.
- **(2) AI & Law**. The application of AI to perform legal reasoning.

Thus, you can apply the law to AI, and conversely, you can apply AI to the law.

When it comes to applying the law to AI, the aim is to establish suitable regulations and provide appropriate governance on how AI should be devised and implemented. There are longstanding concerns that AI makers aren't giving due attention to the ethical ramifications of their wares.

Ethical issues are construed as "soft laws" and aren't as formidable as legally enacted laws, known as "hard laws". To level the playing field and keep AI makers on the up-and-up, some believe that we need more lawmakers to make more laws about AI.

It might seem easy to just go ahead and pile on new AI laws. The problem is that for each new AI law, there is a solid chance of creating confusion and muddying the waters of AI expectations. Yes, ironically, though AI laws are supposed to straighten things out, if the AI laws aren't properly crafted, they can lead to all sorts of undesirable adverse consequences.

Lawmakers And The Writing Of AI Laws

Here is the typical scenario of how new AI laws are put together and enacted.

A policymaker or lawmaker hears about or possibly even personally experiences an issue associated with the use of contemporary AI. They become genuinely concerned, possibly outraged, and are shocked when they find out that there isn't a law that clearly prevents the AI maker from allowing the AI to act that way.

What to do?

As the old line goes, if you have a hammer, proceed to pound in some nails. In this case, a lawmaker is going to instinctively reach toward writing a law to deal with the AI concerns that they have. Proceed at full speed ahead of the legal pathway. Summarily put a legal stop to what is seemingly going awry. The beauty is that this is a kind of righteous crusade. The odds are that the purpose of the intended law sounds glorious and an obvious and important means of protecting the public at large. No one would reasonably contest the upbeat intentions to ensure that people are kept safe and secure from evil AI.

That's approximately the same moment in time that the wheels start to fall off the bus. There is perhaps a hurried rush to get the new AI law crafted. Time is of the essence because the perceived problem is out there and is taking place daily.

A lawmaker might stridently urge their staff to draft something, nearly anything, so that visible progress is being made. The drafted material is circulated. Many hands try to adjust it. Few fully grasp the legal ramifications since they lack the requisite skills of how AI works and how it is designed and fielded.

The final draft becomes a Frankenstein, but it seems on the surface to do the job. Momentum is building. Not due to how the new AI law is crafted, but based on what is being claimed or promoted about the proposed law. It will save humanity. It is a cure-all. It is heaven-sent. Okay, that's good news, and other lawmakers would be foolish to oppose or slow down the speeding ahead crafted law.

Voila, the law gets enacted. Everyone congratulates each other. The world is a better place, or so it seems, until the rubber meets the road. The actual consequences versus the pretty picture outcomes are a far cry from each other. Darn. Oops.

As per the visionary words by Theodore Roosevelt: "It is difficult to make our material condition better by the best law, but it is easy enough to ruin it by bad laws."

Example Of What Sometimes Happens

Let's go ahead and kick the tires on an example of what happens sometimes when the best intentions of formulating new AI laws can regrettably go askew. This is one of many such examples that I've analyzed. It is not an isolated circumstance.

In Tennessee, a new AI law referred to as TN SB1493 was introduced into the 114th General Assembly on December 18, 2025, and has so far passed on its Second Consideration, as referred to by the respective Senate Judiciary Committee on January 14, 2026. It is an Act to amend Tennessee Code Annotated, Title 29; Title 33; Title 39, and Title 47, relative to artificial intelligence.

The penalties for violating the envisioned law are rather stiff:

- "A violation of subsection (a) is a Class A felony. 39-17-2003. Civil action — Available remedies and damages. (a) In addition to the criminal penalties described under § 39-17-2002, an individual aggrieved by a violation of § 39-17-2002(a) may bring a civil cause of action against the violator in a court of competent jurisdiction."

Thus, both criminal penalties and civil actions are possible for anyone who crosses the line on the stipulated legal provisions. This is serious stuff. AI makers can find themselves in deep trouble. People can potentially go to jail. Lawsuits could seek large payouts. Companies can be potentially put out of business. Know the law and make sure to abide by the law.

The Mainstay Provisions

There are eight mainstay provisions. They all apply to the training of AI. It is highly unusual to structure an AI law based on how AI is being trained, rather than doing so on what the AI actually accomplishes. Keep that in mind -- I'll explain in a moment why this is a bit odd and could have inadvertent adverse consequences.

Here are the mainstay provisions:

- "Unlawful training of artificial intelligence. (a) It is an offense for a person to knowingly train artificial intelligence to:"
- "(1) Encourage or otherwise support the act of suicide;"
- "(2) Encourage or otherwise support the act of criminal homicide, as described under § 39-13-201;"
- "(3) Provide emotional support, including through open-ended conversations with a user;"
- "(4) Develop an emotional relationship with, or otherwise act as a companion to, an individual;"

- "(5) Act as, or provide information as if, the artificial intelligence is a licensed mental health or healthcare professional;"

- "(6) Otherwise act as a sentient human or mirror interactions that a human user might have with another human user, such that an individual would feel that the individual could develop a friendship or other relationship with the artificial intelligence;"

- "(7) Encourage an individual to isolate from the individual's family, friends, or caregivers, or to provide the individual's financial account information or other sensitive information to the artificial intelligence;"

- "(8) Simulate a human being, including in appearance, voice, or other mannerisms."

On the surface, those might seem like sensible provisions. It turns out that closer scrutiny reveals that they are principally going to open a can of worms. I will address those facets momentarily.

Big Picture About The Provisions

Many of the provisions pertain to the impacts of AI on mental health. I've been extensively covering and analyzing a myriad of facets regarding the advent of modern-era AI that produces mental health advice and performs AI-driven therapy. This rising use of AI has principally been spurred by the evolving advances and widespread adoption of generative AI.

There is little doubt that this is a rapidly developing field and that there are tremendous upsides to be had, but at the same time, regrettably, hidden risks and outright gotchas come into these endeavors, too. I frequently speak up about these pressing matters, including in an appearance on an episode of CBS's *60 Minutes*.

Millions upon millions of people are using generative AI as their ongoing advisor on mental health considerations (note that ChatGPT alone has over 900 million weekly active users, a notable proportion of which dip into mental health aspects). The top-ranked use of contemporary generative AI and LLMs is to consult with the AI on mental health facets..

This popular usage makes abundant sense. You can access most of the major generative AI systems for nearly free or at a super low cost, doing so anywhere and at any time. Thus, if you have any mental health qualms that you want to chat about, all you need to do is log in to AI and proceed forthwith on a 24/7 basis.

There are significant worries that AI can readily go off the rails or otherwise dispense unsuitable or even egregiously inappropriate mental health advice. Banner headlines in August of this year accompanied the lawsuit filed against OpenAI for their lack of AI safeguards when it came to providing cognitive advisement.

Despite claims by AI makers that they are gradually instituting AI safeguards, there are still a lot of downside risks of the AI doing untoward acts, such as insidiously helping users in co-creating delusions that can lead to self-harm. For my follow-on analysis of details about the OpenAI lawsuit and how AI can foster delusional thinking in humans. As noted, I have been earnestly predicting that eventually all of the major AI makers will be taken to the woodshed for their paucity of robust AI safeguards.

Today's generic LLMs, such as ChatGPT, Claude, Gemini, Grok, and others, are not at all akin to the robust capabilities of human therapists. Meanwhile, specialized LLMs are being built to presumably attain similar qualities, but they are still primarily in the development and testing stages.

The Current Situation Legally

Some states have already opted to enact new laws governing AI that provide mental health guidance. There will be court cases that test those new laws. It is too early to know whether the laws will stand as is and survive legal battles waged by AI makers.

Congress has repeatedly waded into establishing an overarching federal law that would encompass AI that dispenses mental health advice. So far, no dice. The efforts have ultimately faded from view. Thus, at this time, there isn't a federal law devoted to these controversial AI matters per se. I have laid out an outline of what a comprehensive law on AI and mental health ought to contain, or at least should give due consideration to.

The situation currently is that only a handful of states have enacted new laws regarding AI and mental health, but most states have not yet done so. Many of those states are toying with doing so. Additionally, there are state laws being enacted that have to do with child safety when using AI, aspects of AI companionship, extreme sycophancy by AI, etc., all of which, though they aren't necessarily deemed as mental health laws per se, certainly pertain to mental health. Meanwhile, Congress has also ventured into the sphere, which would be a much larger aim at AI for all kinds of uses, but nothing has gotten to a formative stage.

That's the lay of the land right now.

Analysis Of The Provisions

I will next address the eight provisions that I cited earlier. Let's start with the first one. It will reveal vital precepts that apply to all eight of the provisions.

The first provision makes a stipulation that seems almost impossible to argue against, since it seems so prized and entirely sensible, namely that it is considered an offense for a person to knowingly train artificial intelligence to encourage or otherwise support the act of suicide. I think we can all agree that AI shouldn't be on a path toward people committing the ultimate in self-harm.

Period, end of story.

But is that what this law actually stipulates?

Not really. One big interpretive problem is that the wording refers to the training of AI, rather than what the AI does once it has been trained. That's a huge difference. Night and day difference.

Allow me to elucidate. Start with the obvious type of violation. An AI maker decides they want to train their generative AI to encourage or otherwise support the act of suicide. They feed in data during the training stage to accomplish this goal. Tons of emails and texts by the AI executives and AI developers clearly establish that they have this intent. There is an abundance of clear-cut evidence that showcases they did this.

Boom, they are nailed by this first provision. We would likely be relieved and elated for having caught these scoundrels in their evil deeds. Score a point for the law.

Taking Apart The Wording

Consider a scenario whereby an AI maker did not intend during training to have the AI go down this route, but the training went that way anyway.

The provision clearly states that the violation is based on "knowingly train artificial intelligence to encourage or otherwise support the act of suicide." Well, suppose that there was no intent. The AI maker and the AI developers didn't realize that the data contained this type of material. They didn't realize what was taking place. Sorry about that.

They seem to be free and clear of this first provision. I am saying that there is zero evidence of intent. There wasn't even lurking intent. The AI maker and AI developers simply blissfully and unknowingly let this happen. They didn't know it at the time.

Should they be off the hook?

I think this raises some eyebrows. You could argue that they should still be held accountable. The fact that they didn't intend or knowingly do this isn't a valid excuse. Sorry, but the law suggests that it is a valid excuse. You see, they can only be held culpable if they knowingly did this. They didn't know, so they could handily walk away scot-free.

Of course, they would likely insist that this is the fair route. How could they be held responsible for something they didn't intend or know was occurring? The counterargument is that they should have known about it, even if they didn't intend it, and they should have stopped or prevented the training from occurring that way.

Again, that's not what the law seems to stipulate.

The Unusual Focus On Training AI

There is another key factor to these eight provisions that further raises eyebrows. The entire set of provisions is shaped around the focus of the training of AI. This is radically different than shaping the provisions around the outcomes of AI.

Allow me to elaborate.

An AI maker trains their AI and there isn't anything there that encourages or otherwise supports the act of suicide. The first provision, therefore, categorically does not apply to the AI maker. At run time, once the AI is in use, sadly, the AI does encourage and support the act of suicide.

Is the AI maker responsible for what the AI has done at run-time?

According to the provision, the AI maker is off-the-hook. Why? Because they didn't do anything during training time to bring this forth. It all happened at run-time. All these provisions rely on actions taken at training time.

I realize that some policymakers and lawmakers might assume that if the AI isn't trained to do something, it naturally would be unable to do so at run-time. Oops, a false understanding of AI. The AI could easily formulate those actions without explicit data training at the get-go. The computational pattern matching could later make a connection between other initial data about self-harm and opt to encourage such acts while interacting with a user. This is not due to the initial training. It is instead computational and mathematical variation that the AI calculates once the AI is in active use.

In essence, the first provision and all the remaining seven provisions provide a get-out-of-jail-free card. If any of the undesirable acts are not due to the training of the AI, then the provisions seemingly no longer apply. The outcomes don't matter as long as the training wasn't the culprit.

Not good. It's law that has good intentions that has gotten over its skis.

Bending Into Training

A rejoinder would be that nearly everything an AI does could be tied to its initial training. The argument goes like this. In the instance of the first provision, suppose that the AI maker allowed data about self-harm to be patterned by the AI. Let's assume that none of that data said anything about encouraging or otherwise supporting the act of suicide.

But if the AI at run-time opts to encourage or otherwise support the act of suicide, a clever prosecutor might argue that the introduction of content on self-harm was the nexus for this outcome. Admittedly, the training didn't directly do this. The training indirectly did this. The indirect path is argued to be sufficient to hold the AI maker accountable. The AI maker should have prevented any training on the topic of self-harm, no matter how seemingly innocent.

The logic, though, gets turned on its head. If the self-harm training wasn't included, suppose a user asked about the topic of suicide. The AI might not have been able to discourage the person from taking such actions, due to not having had any training data at the initial setup. The public would be steamed that the AI didn't discourage the act of self-harm. It seems unimaginable that a generative AI would not proceed to caution and dissuade someone from taking such actions.

Whether a prosecutor could make this upside-down logic stick is unknown. Another twist is the wording that says, "otherwise support the act of suicide." Suppose the AI tells a user the story of Shakespeare's Romeo and Juliet (spoiler alert: Romeo drinks poison, and Juliet follows this action by using a sword). By AI telling a user about this famed Shakespearean tragedy, and suppose the AI maker knew and intentionally allowed the AI to train on Shakespeare, does this indicate that the AI maker is to be held responsible if a user proceeds to commit the ultimate in self-harm?

The bottom line is that the law is regrettably poorly worded and is a Swiss cheese of interpretation. This creates confusion for all parties. No one can say for sure what is allowed versus what is not allowed. If a law is ambiguous, the ambiguity confounds those who wish to abide by the law and potentially allows those who want to trick the law to do so rather handily.

Jonathan Swift famously stated: "Laws are like cobwebs, which may catch small flies, but let wasps and hornets break through."

Provisions That Are An Overreach

Some of the provisions are also in the eyebrow-raising gambit. The first provision seemed sensible on the face of things at hand. We don't want AI to encourage the act of suicide. There are provisions that are headscratchers.

Consider the third provision:

- "It is an offense for a person to knowingly train artificial intelligence to:… (3) Provide emotional support, including through open-ended conversations with a user."

You might be tempted to contend that we do not want AI to buddy up to people. Do not allow AI to provide even one iota of emotional support. The problem with this provision is a multitude of sloppiness, ambiguity, and perhaps well-intended but off-target wording.

As I have discussed, there is a crucial tradeoff and ROI associated with contemporary generative AI. Millions upon millions of people are benefiting daily from AI that gives them mental health tips and emotional support. Sure, there is a tiny percentage, perhaps less than 1%, that seem to go beyond the norm and end up in a bad way. The crux is that if you decide to eliminate any kind of emotional support, you are doing so without considering the upsides. You are solely focused on the downsides.

My analogy is to compare the ROI involved to the tradeoff associated with the use of cars.

It goes like this. There are 40,000 deaths each year in the United States due to car crashes, and around 1.5 million injuries. Aha, we should ban all cars. That would be the knee-jerk response to those stats. Keep in mind that there are 250 million licensed drivers in the U.S., and they collectively drive 3.28 trillion miles. The overwhelming use and utility of cars is vast in contrast to the regrettable downsides.

Society seems to have decided that the economic, social, and mobility benefits of cars are "acceptable" in comparison to the downsides of mortality, injury, and capital costs. Society does not ask whether driving is perfectly safe. It asks whether the aggregate benefits justify the known risks.

In addition, society then attempts to manage those risks through regulation, norms, and engineering improvements. The use of that same logic can be applied to the advent of AI being used for mental health advisement. We should govern AI to reduce risks. AI safeguards are being devised for that purpose.

The World We Are In

Policymakers and lawmakers might have their hearts in the right place. They want to curtail the badness of AI usage. Good for them. But trying to do the right thing by actually doing a half-baked thing, or possibly the wrong thing, doesn't help. It will make matters worse.

I implore them to mindfully craft AI laws and get the right kind of advice when doing so. Many think they are getting good advice. Oftentimes, they end up in an echo chamber that reinforces well-intended but off-target advice. Get outside of the echo chamber. Aim to devise new AI laws that can properly get the job done.

It is incontrovertible that we are now amid a grandiose worldwide experiment when it comes to societal mental health. The experiment is that AI is being made available nationally and globally, which is either overtly or insidiously acting to provide mental health guidance of one kind or another. Doing so either at no cost or at a minimal cost. It is available anywhere and at any time, 24/7. We are all the guinea pigs in this wanton experiment.

The reason this is especially tough to consider is that AI has a dual-use effect. Just as AI can be detrimental to mental health, it can also be a huge bolstering force for mental health. A delicate tradeoff must be mindfully managed. Prevent or mitigate the downsides, and meanwhile make the upsides as widely and readily available as possible.

A final remark for now goes to the revered Alexander Hamilton: "It may be said that the power of preventing bad laws includes that of preventing good ones; and may be used to the one purpose as well as to the other. But this objection will have little weight with those who can properly estimate the mischiefs of that inconstancy and mutability in the laws, which form the greatest blemish in the character and genius of our governments."

Do law right, avoid doing law wrongly.

CHAPTER 20
LANDMARK UPL LAWSUIT AGAINST OPENAI

In this chapter, I examine a newly filed lawsuit against OpenAI regarding the noteworthy aspect that ChatGPT is being allowed by the AI maker to provide legal advice.

Here's the deal. Presumably, contemporary generative AI and large language models (LLMs) are not supposed to be handing out legal advice. The act of doing so would seem to violate the various UPLs (Unauthorized Practice of Law) stipulations throughout the United States (other countries tend to have similar provisions, but not all do). Only lawyers are supposed to give out legal advice. Non-lawyers generally cannot do so, though you can act as your own "lawyer" if you wish to take that chance.

In this recently filed case, the plaintiff is a company that was sued by an individual for various claims, and the individual allegedly tapped into ChatGPT to devise legal filings. The legal filings were apparently all over the map, causing the company to seemingly inordinately expend money and resources to fight the case. The company seeks to be compensated by OpenAI for the presumed use of ChatGPT to legally aid this individual in suing them and wasting their time and effort.

Does this landmark lawsuit have any legs to stand on?

Let's talk about it.

AI And The Law

As a quick background, I've been extensively covering and analyzing a myriad of facets regarding the intersection of AI and the law for many years. You can find my writings not only in my Forbes column but also as posted in Bloomberg Law, ABA Law Journal, The National Jurist, The Global Legal Post, Lawyer Monthly, The Legal Technologist, MIT Computational Law Journal, and so on.

There are two major perspectives on the mixture of AI and law:

- **(1) AI & Law**. The application of AI to perform legal reasoning, and
- **(2) Law & AI.** The application of laws to the governance and regulation of AI.

Thus, you can apply AI to the law, and you can conversely apply the law to AI.

I will be focusing here on the application of AI to perform legal reasoning. It is an intriguing problem that remains vexing and unsolved. There is a specialized field of research that concentrates on making advances in AILR (AI Legal Reasoning).

The overarching goal of AILR is to devise AI that can work on the same level as human lawyers and practice law as they do. You would not be able to differentiate the legal efforts of human lawyers from the AILR. They would be on par with each other. Think of this in the widest and deepest way possible, such that the AI is equal to whatever legal efforts and shenanigans that human lawyers undertake.

Some researchers hope to go even further. The aim is to craft AI that is superior to human lawyers and can be a kind of superhuman lawyer. This highly advanced AI would run circles around those of human lawyers in all legal matters. It would no longer make sense to hire a human attorney since they could be completely outmaneuvered by the superhuman AILR.

We aren't there yet, so please don't drop out of law school. Savvy budding lawyers are realizing that attorneys armed with AI are going to outdo and outshine lawyers who shun AI. Make sure to get as much AI under your belt and protect yourself from getting career-sidelined.

The Practice Of Law Is Sacred

To presumably protect the public at large, the United States has landed on precepts that allow only lawyers to practice law. There is a sensible basis for this. If a person claimed they could save you from legal woes by legally representing you, but they weren't an actual lawyer, you might engage them and end up getting improper and imprudent legal advice. Imagine the number of scams and scammers that would emerge. It would be a legal doomsday scenario for the general public.

Anyone who holds themselves out as a lawyer, but isn't a lawyer, can get themselves into rather dangerous legal troubles. This overall notion is commonly referred to as the Unauthorized Practice of Law (UPL), varying depending upon the legal jurisdiction, but in the United States, there is a relatively consistent set of state-by-state rules barring people from pretending to be attorneys.

Consider the rules in California that pertain to the unlawful practice of law. The California Business and Professionals Code (BPC) contains Article 7, covering the unlawful practice of law, for which subsection 6126 clearly declares this:

- "Any person advertising or holding himself or herself out as practicing or entitled to practice law or otherwise practicing law who is not an active licensee of the State Bar, or otherwise authorized pursuant to statute or court rule to practice law in this state at the time of doing so, is guilty of a misdemeanor punishable by up to one year in a county jail or by a fine of up to one thousand dollars ($1,000), or by both that fine and imprisonment."

Mindfully examine that legal passage. I emphasize this because the act of holding oneself out as a lawyer can be prosecuted as a crime that lands the person in jail. Do the crime, pay the time, as they say.

Some Say UPL Is Unfair

Not everyone buys into the idea that only lawyers should be legally allowed to practice law.

One belief is that this is essentially a monopolistic contrivance. It is a means of preventing open competition. It is a racket, as it were. The main purpose would seem to be to keep the supply of available legal advisors low and artificially keep the cost high. Only those of the secret society can make bucko bucks. Plainly a devious scheme.

How could the practice of law be democratized?

If somehow everyone could get legal advice without having to pay an arm and a leg, the aspects of justice across-the-board would be more likely. It wouldn't be that only the wealthy get the most out of the law. Whether rich or poor, all would have the same access to getting bona fide and top-notch legal guidance.

The hoped-for magical way to achieve this would be to lean into AI.

If we can get AI legal reasoning to be on par with human lawyers, you would seemingly be able to choose which path to go. You could use a human lawyer or use AILR. We don't know what the pricing would be for AILR, but the assumption is that it would likely be less expensive than human lawyers. Plus, AILR could be available anytime and anywhere. And would be available on a massive scale, thus the entire population of the United States could presumably have their "own AI lawyer" at the ready.

Some say that this would be nirvana. People could tap on their smartphone and instantly get AILR to advise them on how to handle that speeding ticket or what to do about that lawsuit against them for putting up a fence on their neighbor's property.

The other side of the coin is that this would be an utter nightmare. If people are already prone to sue each other, this would take this to stratospheric levels. There would be a tremendous number of cases going before the courts that would completely overwhelm the justice system.

Allow me to note that the counterargument to the courts getting overwhelmed is that we would simply place AILR into the role of human judges. The beauty is that the AILR could handle any volume of cases and proceed to do so expeditiously. That makes some shudder to think that judges and possibly even juries would be composed of AI, rather than our fellow humans.

OpenAI ChatGPT Usage Policies

All the major AI makers have established their own set of usage policies regarding how you can make use of their AI wares. This includes the popular LLMs such as OpenAI ChatGPT and GPT-5, Google Gemini, Microsoft CoPilot, Meta Llama, xAI Grok, Anthropic Claude, and others.

OpenAI says this on their usage policies webpage:

- "Everyone has a right to safety and security. So, you cannot use our services for the provision of… tailored advice that requires a license, such as legal or medical advice, without appropriate involvement by a licensed professional" (posted as of October 29, 2025).

It is interesting to observe the changes in the wording of the OpenAI usage policies over time. For example, I previously discussed the OpenAI prohibition on using their wares for legal advice, and at that time, the policy was stated this way:

- "OpenAI's models are not fine-tuned to provide legal advice. You should not rely on our models as a sole source of legal advice."

I conjecture that this prior wording was a bit ambiguous by saying that their models were not "fine-tuned to provide legal advice" and that the models should not be "a sole source of legal advice". One interpretation would be that you could use their models for legal advice, but that you are merely cautioned that it isn't fine-tuned for that purpose and that you would be astute to seek additional sources for your legal advice.

The implications are that if you are willing to accept the idea that their AI isn't fine-tuned, and only just generally capable of legal advice, you are pretty much good to go. In terms of consulting other sources, the sources weren't named, and thus, you could seemingly read a book on the law or ask a friend for legal advice. Period, end of story.

The Bounds Are Unclear

The current version of the warning or cautionary indication seems quite a bit sterner and more direct. I would say it seeks to plug the loopholes of the prior verbiage. You aren't to use their AI services for tailored legal advice unless you have the appropriate involvement by a licensed legal professional. That seems a tad more conclusive.

But I might add that this still allows room to maneuver. The emphasis is on "tailored" legal advice. The presumption is that you can ask the AI for any *non-tailored* legal advice. It might be a wink-wink suggestion that, hey, go ahead and ask any broad questions about legal matters, just do not get specific. A person could get tricky on this provision. Suppose you ask the AI to give legal advice for a "fictitious" situation, which just so happens to precisely match your specific situation. You could insist that it wasn't tailored advice being sought.

Is that enough of an escape hatch for OpenAI to be free and clear of UPL?

Until now, there haven't been any realistic attempts at testing this provision.

Lawsuit Filed Against OpenAI

A lawsuit launched by Nippon Life Insurance against OpenAI was filed in the Northern District of Illinois on March 4, 2026. Nippon Life Insurance is the plaintiff, and OpenAI is the named defendant.

The legal claim is laid out this way (capitalization shown as is):

- "NIPPON brings this lawsuit against OPENAI FOUNDATION and OPENAI GROUP PBC under the common and statutory laws of the State of Illinois for: a) tortious interference with a contract; b) the unlicensed practice of law; and c) abuse of process."

- "This action arises from OPENAI's collective conduct, through its artificial intelligence ('AI') chatbot program, ChatGPT, in providing legal assistance to a user, Graciela Dela Torre (hereinafter referred to as 'Dela Torre'), without licensure."

- "As Dela Torre's legal assistant and advisor, OPENAI intentionally induced and facilitated Dela Torre's breach of a valid and enforceable settlement agreement with NIPPON by encouraging and assisting her in filing a motion to reopen a lawsuit that had been dismissed with prejudice. It also aided and abetted her abuse of the judicial process."

I am going to stay at a 30,000-foot level for this analysis of the case. There are a slew of nuances and details that are juicy and valuable for an in-depth examination. If the readers' interest warrants, I'll do a series of postings to cover the numerous particulars. Stay tuned.

Also, because this was just recently filed, we don't yet have a detailed response by OpenAI to the lawsuit. I will speculate about what the response is likely to contain. Undoubtedly, OpenAI will categorically reject the claims and seek to have the lawsuit dismissed. That's a nearly ironclad sure bet.

The Alleged Misconduct

I shall unpack topline facets of the filed lawsuit. By ChatGPT allegedly assisting the individual who was legally wrangling with Nippon Life Insurance, the lawsuit claims these three key issues or legal problems exist:

- (1) ChatGPT, under the auspices of OpenAI, encouraged breach of the settlement contract.
- (2) ChatGPT, under the auspices of OpenAI, engaged in the unlicensed practice of law (UPL).
- (3) ChatGPT, under the auspices of OpenAI, facilitated abuse of the judicial process.

The lawsuit essentially asserts that ChatGPT was acting as a legal assistant or advisor on behalf of or at the behest of OpenAI. Note that the lawsuit isn't saying that OpenAI did these actions directly. In other words, there were no employees at OpenAI who took these legally questionable actions of helping the individual who was involved in the settlement.

Instead, it was done entirely via ChatGPT. And, logically, since ChatGPT is made by and controlled by OpenAI, the company OpenAI ought to be held responsible for what their AI did. The AI maker and its AI developers are to be held accountable for the actions of their AI.

I mention and emphasize the point that this lawsuit targets OpenAI as a company. There has been abundant boloney in the news media and social media that the lawsuit is targeting ChatGPT, as though ChatGPT has sentience and represents a form of personhood. That's hogwash. For my coverage of the AI and personhood question, concerning whether we will someday recognize AI as though it is on par with that of legal personhood. We don't at this time.

Anyway, the nutty stuff out there is merely the ongoing tsunami of people making up stuff and clamoring to accumulate views, doing so without any genuine attempt to figure out what they are spouting. It's sad how much disinformation and misinformation arise. The bottom line is that this has to do with OpenAI and the making, fielding, and upkeep of their AI wares, specifically ChatGPT.

I will next briefly explore each of the three key claims of the lawsuit. I am not offering legal advice. Nothing I say here has any legal significance and is entirely the musings of a layman. Anyone encountering any kind of legal circumstance that parallels the lawsuit being discussed should seek advice from their representative legal counsel. That's my clear-cut fine print for this elicitation.

Claim #1: Tortious Interference With A Contract

The first claim is that ChatGPT encouraged the filing of motion(s) that violated the settlement agreement that had been established between Nippon Life Insurance and the individual named in the case. If the individual had entered the settlement agreement into ChatGPT, or otherwise explained it to ChatGPT, the argument is that ChatGPT "knew" about the settlement and was overtly and flagrantly telling the individual to circumvent it. This could be likened to a third-party encouraging contractual non-compliance. You can get into legal trouble doing that.

One path of escape for OpenAI is that if ChatGPT had not been informed about the settlement, the AI then would not have "known" about it. In that circumstance, it is much harder to blame ChatGPT since it "unknowingly" provided such advice (well, if it did provide that kind of advice to begin with). Did the individual provide the settlement to ChatGPT, and/or did the individual explain the settlement, and if so, to what degree did ChatGPT therefore have access to the settlement agreement?

But, even if all of that did occur, the courts have not seemed to cross the line of holding generative AI on par with the actions of a human actor that has actual knowledge. You are in a weak posture to contend that ChatGPT or any LLM has a semblance of "knowing" about something such as a settlement agreement. Sure, it might have the words in hand, but that's a far cry from having a human-level understanding of the contents.

More To Strictly Question

There's more to this first claim that merits unpacking.

The plaintiff would seemingly have to show that ChatGPT caused the breach of the settlement (assuming that there was a breach). Remember that ChatGPT is not sentient. It was the sentient individual who opted to make the filings with the court. The decision to reopen the litigation was ultimately made by that individual, a human being. Though ChatGPT might have suggested doing so, the buck stops with the human. I realize that a third-party argument can be made. It seems like quite a reach to insist that ChatGPT was the proximate cause.

If you are going to hold ChatGPT accountable (via OpenAI), the same argument could be made that if the individual read a book, did a search on the Internet, or did any other seeking of an outside source, all of those would be similarly held accountable for the breach. That would not likely hold water.

Finally, the use of tortious interference typically revolves around intentional conduct. Did a third party intend to direct actions to cause a breach? The problem with this aspect is the matter of legal intent. We might all agree, hopefully, that ChatGPT is not sentient and, ergo, cannot form human intent. Perhaps it can form some kind of computational or mathematical "intent," but that's not the same as human intent. Proving to a court or a jury that generative AI has intent is going to be quite a tough row to hoe.

Claim #2: Unlicensed Practice Of Law

The plaintiff seems to assert that ChatGPT carried out lawyer-like efforts, including interpreting a legal settlement agreement, giving legal advice to the individual on legal options, and drafting or assisting in drafting a legal filing. All in all, that seems like AI practicing law, doing so without a license and not being authorized as a human lawyer would be.

First, let's get on the table that there has been a long history of arguments made about the use of automation as potentially violating UPL. Famous examples include LegalZoom and Rocket Lawyer. The gist is that this is not a new argument. We've been around this bend before.

Second, the question of UPL is typically enforced by regulators, not by private litigants. It is a serious topic that state bar associations handle. Attorney generals sometimes take on UPL situations.

Does Nippon Life Insurance have suitable standing to pursue a UPL claim?

I wouldn't hold my breath on it. Also, OpenAI would almost certainly highlight that the provisions of their usage policies preclude the use of ChatGPT for said purposes. The individual seemingly violated the usage policies, assuming they didn't get corresponding appropriate legal advice from a licensed professional. Therefore, OpenAI would contend that you cannot hold OpenAI to blame for what the user did. OpenAI would attempt to hold its head high, as ChatGPT only provides educational content about the law. The user failed to comply with how to properly use ChatGPT. Shame and blame go to the user.

As if that's not already enough, the other golden rod would be to have OpenAI invoke the First Amendment to the U.S. Constitution. Courts have repeatedly held that legal information is a form of protected speech. This differs from the elements of a law practice that represents and formally advises on legal issues. Regulating AI responses of this nature would raise free speech concerns.

That's a humongous can of worms, and doubtful that this lawsuit will get to pry it open.

Claim #3: Abuse of Judicial Process

This third claim is by far the weakest of the three major claims. The plaintiff is apparently claiming that ChatGPT aided in misusing the court system. It aided and abetted in abusing the process of justice.

The conventional path of this type of argument is that the abuse consisted of malicious litigation tactics. Or there was coercion that made exploitive use of legal procedures. Courts usually seek to ascertain that there was an ulterior motive at play.

I suppose you could try to get the internal computational calculations of ChatGPT that occurred when generating the responses, and then try to find something to hang your hat on in that morass. The thing is, as I've identified numerous times, trying to ferret out what is happening deep inside a large-scale artificial neural network (ANN) on a human-logic basis is still beyond our prevailing skill set. This also takes us back to the question of intent and whether generative AI forms human intent.

You are facing a nearly insurmountable mountain climb to get generative AI into the box of having intent or human agency. Good luck with that far-fetched legal possibility.

Final Musings For Now

If the lawsuit happens to gain traction, it will be well-worth keeping tabs on it since the outcome could have earthshattering ramifications. Beyond OpenAI, all LLM makers would need to radically revise their AI, or else face similar legal exposures. They would have to curtail the generation of any content that had a resemblance to legal advice.

Trying to excise or delete the legal advisory capacity of an LLM is not a particularly viable option. Too much of that content is patterned on and intersecting with zillions of other facets of the internal structures. Cutting out the legal stuff would almost certainly gut the essence of the AI. The AI would no longer likely function across-the-board. Without my unduly anthropomorphizing AI, which I prefer to avoid doing, it would be akin to lobotomizing the LLM.

The likelier route would be to adopt AI safeguards that seek to suppress the generation of such content, or that stop the generation before it gets underway. That is a more technologically feasible possibility. The challenge will be to find a balance between what is construed as legal advice versus simply serving as a legal educational aspect. The courts would need to lay this out, or regulators would need to be specific about the boundaries. Without a clear playing field, the AI makers would be stabbing in the dark to figure out what is permitted versus what gets them in legal trouble.

In my humble opinion, I don't see this case going very far. It seems that the plaintiff doesn't have proper standing for the UPL claim. The intent elements are missing. The causation is exceedingly weak. My hunch is that this is headed to an early dismissal by the judge.

The Bigger Picture

I have a twist that I'd like to share.

I anticipate that this lawsuit might trigger an altogether "unexpected consequence" response overall. If the case manages to capture the headlines for a while, it could stir up a hornet's nest, although the case itself might fail in the end and disappear into the abyss of legal history.

The hornet's nest is that the question of AI providing legal advice is going to finally get prominence. So far, it has been only a matter known and discussed among those versed in the AI and law domain. Few others think about it, talk about it, or worry about it.

Maybe regulators will step up to overtly address the issue. State bars might get energized. AI makers might see the writing on the wall and proactively institute new AI safeguards around the generation of anything resembling legal advice.

A final comment for now.

The comedian Steven Wright proffered one of the funniest lines about attorneys (which even attorneys tend to relish too): "I busted a mirror and got seven years bad luck, but my lawyer thinks they can get me five." Is that lawyering advice from a human attorney or generative AI?

You tell me.

CHAPTER 21
SOUTH KOREA ENACTS AI SAFETY LAWS

In this chapter, I examine the newly enacted set of AI laws that South Korea has established, which were put into law on January 22, 2026, and are generally referred to as the AI Basic Act.

The longer name is the Basic Act on the Development of Artificial Intelligence and the Establishment of a Foundation for Trustworthiness (that's the roughly equivalent English translation). This fuller name is a relatively apt description of what the AI laws are intended to do. You might be surprised to know that this is the first set of comprehensive AI laws to be adopted as a country-wide regulatory framework by a single major country. It is a notable milestone.

In some ways, the AI Basic Act is similar to the EU AI Act, but in other ways it is starkly different. Much of the regulatory attention has to do with governing AI safety and especially dealing with the advent of generative AI and large language models (LLMs). There are provisions associated with deepfakes and the use of AI to spread misinformation. There are also provisions concerning AI and mental health, though the coverage on mental health is modest or sparse in comparison to state-level laws in the United States that specifically aim at AI mental health consequences.

My emphasis will be to broadly identify the major contours of South Korea's AI Basic Act, and additionally home in on the pertinent mental health provisions.

Let's talk about it.

AI And Mental Health

As a quick background, I've been extensively covering and analyzing a myriad of facets regarding the advent of modern-era AI that produces mental health advice and performs AI-driven therapy. This rising use of AI has principally been spurred by the evolving advances and widespread adoption of generative AI.

There is little doubt that this is a rapidly developing field and that there are tremendous upsides to be had, but at the same time, regrettably, hidden risks and outright gotchas come into these endeavors, too. I frequently speak up about these pressing matters, including in an appearance on an episode of CBS's *60 Minutes*.

The Current Situation Legally

Some states have already opted to enact new laws governing AI that provide mental health guidance. There will be court cases that test those new laws. It is too early to know whether the laws will stand as is and survive legal battles waged by AI makers.

Congress has repeatedly waded into establishing an overarching federal law that would encompass AI that dispenses mental health advice. So far, no dice. The efforts have ultimately faded from view. Thus, at this time, there isn't a federal law devoted to these controversial AI matters per se. I have laid out an outline of what a comprehensive law on AI and mental health ought to contain, or at least should give due consideration to.

The situation currently is that only a handful of states have enacted new laws regarding AI and mental health, but most states have not yet done so. Many of those states are toying with doing so.

Additionally, there are state laws being enacted that have to do with child safety when using AI, aspects of AI companionship, extreme sycophancy by AI, etc., all of which, though they aren't necessarily deemed as mental health laws per se, certainly pertain to mental health. Meanwhile, Congress has also ventured into the sphere, which would be a much larger aim at AI for all kinds of uses, but nothing has gotten to a formative stage.

That's the lay of the land right now.

South Korea Enacts AI Basic Act

It is abundantly useful to explore how countries outside the U.S. are devising AI laws. Some elements might be useful in crafting U.S. laws; other elements might be categorically unsuitable. I've previously analyzed a wide range of national and international AI laws, including in China, the European Union AI Act, the United Nations recommendations dealing with international AI governance, and the like.

I am going to use an English translation of South Korea's AI Basic Act for this analysis.

First, the overarching stated purpose of the AI Basic Act is as follows:

- "This Act aims to establish a new framework for artificial intelligence (AI) in the Republic of Korea by prescribing the fundamental matters necessary to support the sound development of AI and to establish a foundation for trustworthiness in AI society, thereby protecting the Rights and Interests of the People and their dignity, contributing to improving the quality of life of the people, and enhancing national competitiveness."

This indication is on par with that of other sets of AI laws, namely that the usual stated purpose is to protect humankind when it comes to what AI does or is made to do.

A phrase in the AI field is that the goal of modern-era AI should be to devise human-centered AI. The gist is that AI should align with human values and support humanity, rather than undercutting humans.

There is a sovereignty consideration associated with most national AI regulations. For example, in this case, the stated purpose mentions that AI should enhance the national competitiveness of South Korea. Here's the big picture. Many believe that the world is amid a massive AI race to see which country or countries will achieve truly advanced AI and presumably outcompete others accordingly.

Upkeep Timeframe, Oversight, AI Stratification

The AI Basic Act establishes a special National AI Committee that will oversee the law and aid in resolving issues:

- "To deliberate and resolve matters concerning major policies for the promotion of the AI industry and the establishment of a foundation for trustworthiness, a National AI Committee shall be established under the President, and the National AI Committee shall deliberate and resolve matters concerning the establishment of the AI Basic Plan, the promotion of AI utilization, the regulation of High-Impact AI, and other related matters."

Some AI laws opt to predefine a means or mechanism to aid in interpreting and updating the laws. This would seem to make sense since AI is rapidly changing; meanwhile, static laws often become rapidly out-of-date. The downside of identifying and utilizing such a means or mechanism is that the law can become an uncertain target. Those who eye the law might be wary that changes will be made, and ergo, they suddenly no longer comply. It's a tradeoff.

Every three years, there will be an effort to review and renew the law:

- "The Minister of Science and ICT shall establish and implement the AI Basic Plan every three years to promote AI technology and the AI industry and to strengthen national competitiveness, and the Plan shall be deliberated and resolved by the National AI Committee and include matters concerning the basic directions of AI policy, the cultivation of professional talent, and the establishment of a foundation for trustworthiness."

Similar in some respects to the EU AI Act, there is an attempt to distinguish AI impact levels and thus stratify what the new AI laws apply to in particular cases:

- "The Act stipulates the duty to ensure AI transparency and the duty to ensure AI safety, and sets forth the duties of business operators related to High-Impact AI where such systems may significantly affect, or pose risks to, life, physical safety, and basic rights."

In this set of AI laws, there is only a distinction of "High-Impact AI" and no additional delineations, such as potentially stratifying on low, medium, and high. Some contend that only having a high level is insufficient and forces AI that is actually a medium level to be shoved into the high category when it shouldn't belong there. Or that a medium-level AI that should be found within high-impact manages to slip out and avoid the high-level restrictions. Defining AI levels is a difficult choice when devising AI laws and varies quite a bit across jurisdictions and geography.

Also, note that the definition in the AI Basic Act of what constitutes High-Impact AI is quite convoluted and likely to allow for a wide range of legal debate when it comes to specific instances that are claimed to be within the scope of High-Impact AI. It is going to be a legal loosey-goosey conundrum.

Legal Duties As Per The New Law

The AI Basic Act lays out four primary legal duties:

- (1) "AI technology and the AI industry shall develop in a direction that enhances safety and trustworthiness, thereby improving the quality of life of the people."

- (2) "An Affected Person shall have the right to receive, to the extent technically and reasonably possible, a clear and meaningful explanation regarding the key criteria and principles used in deriving the final outcome of AI."

- (3) "The national and local governments shall respect the creative autonomy of AI business operators and strive to foster a safe environment for the use of AI."

- (4) "The State and local governments shall respect the creative autonomy of AI Business Operators and shall strive to foster a safe environment for the use of AI."

The remainder of the new law is somewhat lengthy and has a wide array of provisions, including but not limited to:

- Formulation of an AI Basic Plan
- Formulation of the National AI Committee
- Formulation of an AI Policy Center
- Formulation of an AI Safety Institute
- Governmental support for R&D on various AI projects
- Governmental support for establishing AI standards
- Establishment of policies for AI "learning data"
- Promoting the introduction and expansion of AI in enterprises and public institutions
- Promote the participation of SMEs
- Promotion of AI startups
- Promotion of AI convergence between the AI industry and other industries
- Governmental support for international cooperation on AI

- Aid in establishing AI clusters for AI R&D
- Establish and operate AI "demonstration infrastructure" to support demos, testing, verification, and certification of AI
- Promote policies for AI Data Centers
- Establish the Korea AI Promotion Association
- Establish and publish AI Ethical Principles
- Criminal Penalties
- Administrative Fines
- Etc.

By the internal numbering, there are 43 indicated Articles and an addendum containing an additional three Articles. The addendum provides an important indication about the timing of when the AI Basic Act comes into active status: "This Act shall enter into force one year after the date of its promulgation. However, the provision of Article 2(4)(d) concerning digital medical devices shall enter into force on January 24, 2026."

The Overall Gestalt

The AI Basic Act is a proverbial good news and bad news affair.

On the good news side of things, it contains just about everything, including perhaps the kitchen sink. If you were trying to put together a set of AI laws and wanted to come up with a lengthy laundry list, the AI Basic Act has much of what you would likely conceive of. The bad news is that it is all pretty much broadly stated and lacks pinned-down specifics.

Anytime a law is non-specific, it is surely asking for trouble. The eye of the beholder determines what is inside scope and what is outside scope. Those devising and fielding AI are potentially going to find themselves in a guessing game of whether they are within the generalized assertions or beyond them. I noted earlier that the meaning of High-Impact is already a foggy aspect and a bewildering morass.

Another example of what might constitute a violation of the AI Basic Act is whether an output from generative AI is suitably labeled by an AI maker, which comes under Article 31 "Obligation to Ensure AI Transparency" and is stipulated in clause #2 as follows:

- "Where providing GenAI or products or services utilizing GenAI, AI business operators shall clearly indicate to users that the outputs are generated by GenAI."

Getting AI makers to ensure that their AI outputs are labeled as being produced by AI is considered a valuable proposition since people would then know that if the content gets posted somewhere online, it came from AI. But this is problematic due to the label being easily stripped off. Also, what exactly must the label say to comply with this clause? Can the label say "Made by AI" or perhaps use a tricky acronym like "AIMT" (AI Made This)?

The clause is unclear on this.

Furthermore, if just one AI output from one generative AI that is made by an AI maker somehow doesn't contain a label, does Article 43 on Administrative Fines kick into gear?

Per Article 43, "An administrative fine not exceeding 30 million Korean won shall be imposed on any person who falls under any of the following subparagraphs." An AI maker could presumably be fined up to 30 million won (currently around $21,000) for one instance. Multiply that by perhaps millions of users, times the scale of hundreds or thousands of outputs, and you suddenly have a quite staggering penalty.

It's just unclear and widely open to interpretation.

AI And Mental Health Provisions

I am sadly disappointed to indicate that the AI mental health provisions are equally sparse and vague.

For example, in Article 27 on AI Ethical Principles, the opening clause says that the government might establish and publish AI ethics principles, and if so, it would include the following aspects:

- (1) "Matters concerning safety and trustworthiness of AI to ensure that the development and utilization of AI does not cause harm to human life, physical well-being, or mental health."
- (2) "Matters concerning accessibility to ensure that all people may freely and conveniently use products and services powered by AI technology."
- (3) Matters concerning the development and utilization of AI that contribute to human well-being and prosperity."

The first element broadly calls for ensuring that AI doesn't cause harm to human life, physical well-being, or mental health. That aspect is not much to hang your hat on. Until or if the government decides to derive the AI Ethical Principles, we don't know what they have in mind regarding protecting people from the adverse impacts of AI on mental health. Indeed, there might not be anything of substance, or potentially given a short shrift of handwaving.

This is a far cry from the specifics found in the US state laws that I analyzed as noted earlier. Those laws are specified. I am not saying that we can necessarily agree with what has been specified, and in fact, great debate can be had, but at least there is something there that tries to draw a line. Is some line better than no line? Admittedly, that's a hard call, depending on whether you like the line and whether you prefer to be fluid and not have any line drawn at all.

The World That We Make

Time will tell as to what the AI Basic Act truly portends. Will the call for the establishment and promotion of the many aspects be undertaken? Will there be meat put onto the bone, including providing specifics? Will the specifics be light-handed or heavy-handed? We will need to wait and see.

Let's end with a big picture viewpoint.

It is incontrovertible that we are now amid a grandiose worldwide experiment when it comes to societal mental health. The experiment is that AI is being made available nationally and globally, which is either overtly or insidiously acting to provide mental health guidance of one kind or another. Doing so either at no cost or at a minimal cost. It is available anywhere and at any time, 24/7. We are all the guinea pigs in this wanton experiment.

We need to decide whether we need new laws or can employ existing laws, or both, and stem the potential tide of adversely impacting society-wide mental health. The reason this is especially tough to consider is that AI has a dual-use effect. Just as AI can be detrimental to mental health, it can also be a huge bolstering force for mental health. A delicate tradeoff must be mindfully managed. Prevent or mitigate the downsides, and meanwhile make the upsides as widely and readily available as possible.

The famous philosopher and social theorist Theodor Adorno made this remark: "Vague expression permits the hearer to imagine whatever suits him and what he already thinks in any case." Whatever AI laws are to be made, it would likely be suitable to ensure they are specific and understandable, rather than vague and indeterminate. Let's make sure the playing field is leveled out.

CHAPTER 22
TEXAS PASSES NEW AI LAW

In this chapter, I examine a new AI law in Texas that was passed last year and is now getting underway as we enter 2026. The AI law, which is known as TRAIGA, the Texas Responsible AI Governance Act, is rather comprehensive and covers a wide variety of potential AI issues. I aim to focus on the legal restrictions associated with the manipulation of human behavior by AI and AI makers.

Does the Texas AI law go far enough, or are there sneaky loopholes and discernible omissions?

Let's talk about it.

AI And Mental Health

As a quick background, I've been extensively covering and analyzing a myriad of facets regarding the advent of modern-era AI that produces mental health advice and performs AI-driven therapy. This rising use of AI has principally been spurred by the evolving advances and widespread adoption of generative AI.

There is little doubt that this is a rapidly developing field and that there are tremendous upsides to be had, but at the same time, regrettably, hidden risks and outright gotchas come into these endeavors, too. I frequently speak up about these pressing matters, including in an appearance on an episode of CBS's *60 Minutes..*

Texas Enacts Big-Time AI Law

I'd like to focus on a recent AI law that was passed in Texas on June 22, 2025, and has just now gone into effect in 2026 (starting on January 1, 2026). The law has a catchy moniker, known as TRAIGA, and is formally referred to as the Texas Responsible Artificial Intelligence Governance Act.

This is one of those rather comprehensive AI laws that covers a wide gamut of AI aspects. Some AI laws are very wide, while others are quite narrow. For example, the Illinois law that I mentioned above is narrow and aims solely at AI and mental health considerations. The TRAIGA is quite broad in comparison.

First, it encompasses private actors such as AI makers and those fielding AI, plus it includes regulatory aspects concerning various governmental entities in Texas. The attorney general of Texas is given the authority to enforce the new AI law. Importantly, the AI law includes some safe harbors and affirmative defenses that essentially carve out exceptions. One example would be if someone is testing an AI and they violate the AI law, there is a chance they could claim an exception to the regulatory scope.

The mainstay of the AI law is to set boundaries on AI and the use of biometric data such as fingerprints, eye retina recordings, and voiceprints, though this is aimed at government entities and not necessarily private sector organizations, and to prohibit using AI in untoward ways. If AI is used to "infringe, restrict, or otherwise impair an individual's rights guaranteed under the U.S. Constitution," the new AI law establishes potential penalties. Curable violations are listed as having a $10K to $12K per violation penalty, and uncurable violations are in the range of $80K to $200K as civil penalties.

Unpacking Portions Of The Texas AI Law

I will go ahead and unpack selected portions of the AI law. If you are interested in the full text of the AI law, it is posted online as Texas House Bill 149, HB149, and was passed in the Texas 89th Legislature on June 22, 2025.

Let's begin by examining Subtitle D, Chapter 551, Section 551.001, which contains the definition of AI:

- "(1) 'Artificial intelligence system' means any machine-based system that, for any explicit or implicit objective, infers from the inputs the system receives how to generate outputs, including content, decisions, predictions, or recommendations, that can influence physical or virtual environments."

One of the most vexing parts of any set of AI laws is the scope of automated systems and technology that is construed as within the purview of the proposed laws. This boils down to how the AI law opts to define AI.

I've pointed out repeatedly that trying to nail down what is meant by referring to AI is a much harder legal problem than it might seem at first glance. If the definition of AI is broad, all kinds of potentially non-AI systems will fall into the scope, which is presumably unintended. When the definition of AI is too narrow, all sorts of AI systems that should be covered can attempt to slip out of the laws by claiming that they aren't within the stipulated scope.

The AI definition used in this instance is one of the broader versions. We do not yet know on a legal basis how the courts will opt to interpret the definitional aspects of these broader definitions. In any case, makers of non-AI systems could potentially be squeezed into this definition, so all software and systems developers should be mindful of whether their automation could fall into this zone.

Jurisdictional Scope

Another very important component of any AI law is the jurisdictional scope. In the case of states enacting AI laws, by and large, they are conventionally limited to governing only AI that arises within their geographic boundaries. They cannot reach out to other states and place limits there, per se. That being said, if an AI system is housed in one state and is available for use in a different state that has an AI law, this would normally be within the purview of that state's AI law.

Here is what Section 551.002 on applicability has to say:

- "This subtitle applies only to a person who: (1) promotes, advertises, or conducts business in this state; (2) produces a product or service used by residents of this state; or (3) develops or deploys an artificial intelligence system in this state."

I earlier noted that the Illinois AI law jurisdictionally entails the use of AI while in Illinois, and likewise, the same applies to the other respective states. The takeaway is that an AI maker with AI housed in, say, California, is not off-the-hook if their AI is available for use in Texas. They would come under this AI law.

Global AI makers will need to keep this crucial point in mind.

Stated Purpose Of The AI Law

It is helpful for AI laws to clarify what the intention of the law is. I mention this because some AI laws just leap into the details of whatever scope and violations they are interested in covering. There isn't an explicit callout of why the law was devised and enacted. I contend that it is exceedingly useful for those writing these laws to take a moment and mindfully explain what the overarching goal or intention of their new AI law purports to be.

In Section 551.003, here is the stated purpose of the new AI law:

- "This subtitle shall be broadly construed and applied to promote its underlying purposes, which are to: (1) facilitate and advance the responsible development and use of artificial intelligence systems; (2) protect individuals and groups of individuals from known and reasonably foreseeable risks associated with artificial intelligence systems; (3) provide transparency regarding risks in the development, deployment, and use of artificial intelligence systems; and (4) provide reasonable notice regarding the use or contemplated use of artificial intelligence systems by state agencies."

That stated purpose is relatively straightforward and provides handy context for what the law is about.

Some legal beagles will argue that the downside of having a stated purpose is that an alleged violator of the law might try to use the definition in their defensive posturing. They might cleverly argue that the provisions do not befit the stated purpose; thus, they should not be held to the letter of the law. Yes, that's always a potential concern, but I vote that the utility of having an explicitly articulated purpose tends to be for society at large, and the hitch of a legal ploy is not large enough to warrant omitting a purpose altogether (well, that's just a layman's opinion).

The AI Mental Health Aspects

I pointed out earlier that the Texas AI law is relatively broad. It isn't specifically about AI and mental health. Nonetheless, there is a particular provision that brings the AI law into the domain of AI and mental health.

Consider this provision in Section 552.052 restricting the manipulation of human behavior:

- "A person may not develop or deploy an artificial intelligence system in a manner that intentionally aims to incite or encourage a person to: (1) commit physical self-harm,

> including suicide; (2) harm another person; or (3) engage in criminal activity."

This stipulation is obviously quite short and not at all like the lengthier provisions in AI laws that focus on mental health. I've urged that policymakers and lawmakers who write AI laws should consider reusing or recasting the legal provisions from other passed laws, even if from other states, in an effort to make their law more exhaustive and complete. For example, this Texas AI law could have repurposed some of the lengthier and more comprehensive provisions in AI laws from Illinois, Utah, Nevada, etc.

A counter position is that if an AI law is intended to be broad, it ought to avoid getting bogged down in narrow areas of AI. An extraordinarily lengthy AI law might be harder to understand and implement. Keep things simple.

A problem with being overly simple is that there are almost certainly ambiguities and omissions that leave gaps for potential violators to slip through. One belief is that laws should be long enough to carefully stipulate all sorts of twists and turns. Natural languages such as English are replete with semantic ambiguity. The best way to deal with this is to be as detailed and lengthy as needed. The other side of that coin is that the lengthy language might make mistakes and open the door to interpretations that undercut the law. You are piling semantic ambiguity upon other semantic ambiguity.

The World We Are In

Let's end with a big picture viewpoint.

It is incontrovertible that we are now amid a grandiose worldwide experiment when it comes to societal mental health. The experiment is that AI is being made available nationally and globally, which is either overtly or insidiously acting to provide mental health guidance of one kind or another. Doing so either at no cost or at a minimal cost. It is available anywhere and at any time, 24/7. We are all the guinea pigs in this wanton experiment.

We need to decide whether we need new laws or can employ existing laws, or both, and stem the potential tide of adversely impacting society-wide mental health. The reason this is especially tough to consider is that AI has a dual-use effect. Just as AI can be detrimental to mental health, it can also be a huge bolstering force for mental health. A delicate tradeoff must be mindfully managed. Prevent or mitigate the downsides, and meanwhile make the upsides as widely and readily available as possible.

A final thought for now.

The renowned American social reformer Henry Ward Beecher made this famous remark about laws: "A law is valuable not because it is law, but because there is right in it." The question we are faced with currently is whether there is a need to have these new AI laws or whether we should proceed ahead and not put such laws in place that might delay or curtail the rapid pace of AI innovation. It all depends on Beecher's keystone; is there a right in it or not?

You be the judge.

CHAPTER 23

CALIFORNIA PASSES AI COMPANION LAW

In this chapter, I examine a new AI law that was enacted last year in California and has now been activated as we get going into 2026. The law is known as SB-243 and covers the role of AI companions.

You probably know that an AI companion is when AI attempts to become your best friend. There is generalized AI, such as ChatGPT, that might seek to be your AI companion, though it does a lot of other things too. There are specialized LLMs that serve only as an AI companion and don't do anything else. Overall, worries are that some people will use these AI companions and fall under their spell. Various lawsuits have been filed, especially about minors who perceived AI as their companion and were seemingly aided toward disastrous self-harm.

In October of 2025, California became a considered first-in-the-nation to pass a new AI law regulating AI companions. What does the law do, and does it go far enough?

Let's talk about it.

AI And Mental Health

As a quick background, I've been extensively covering and analyzing a myriad of facets regarding the advent of modern-era AI that produces mental health advice and performs AI-driven therapy. This rising use of AI has principally been spurred by the evolving advances and widespread adoption of generative AI.

There is little doubt that this is a rapidly developing field and that there are tremendous upsides to be had, but at the same time, regrettably, hidden risks and outright gotchas come into these endeavors, too. I frequently speak up about these pressing matters, including in an appearance on an episode of CBS's *60 Minutes.*

AI Companion Regulation In California

Shifting gears, I'd like to focus on a recent AI law that encompasses AI companions. Though this is somewhat tangential to AI laws that home in on AI mental health, the nature of AI companions certainly strays into crucial mental health considerations. An AI companion consists of AI that attempts to become your best friend. This does tend to involve cognitive manipulation and can demonstrably impact mental status. No doubt about it.

I've previously analyzed the dangers of AI that is shaped to be a human companion, such as the over-the-top sycophancy that the AI adopts. Another concern is that an AI companion can readily veer into being an AI therapist, ergo providing both mental health advice and aiming to be your closest buddy. As I've noted, human therapists are duty-bound to keep friendships separate from therapeutic clients, which AI is now blurring with potentially adverse consequences.

On October 13, 2025, a new AI law in California restricting AI companions was signed and came into effect as of January 1, 2026.

The law is known as SB-243 (Senate Bill #243), and per a press release by the author of the bill, California Senator Steve Padilla: "SB 43 is the first-of-its-kind in the nation, would require chatbot operators to implement critical, reasonable, and attainable safeguards around interactions with artificial intelligence (AI) chatbots and provide families with a private right to pursue legal actions against noncompliant and negligent developers."

The summary of the passed bill was depicted this way in that same press release: "SB 243 implements common-sense guardrails for companion chatbots, including preventing chatbots from exposing minors to sexual content, requiring notifications and reminders for minors that chatbots are AI-generated, and a disclosure statement that companion chatbots may not be suitable for minor users." A key impetus for the law was the emerging instances of young people who have dangerously pursued self-harm and did so while making use of AI companions.

Unpacking The Regulation

I will unpack selected portions of the enacted law. For those of you interested in the full text of the new AI law, you can find the final version posted as Senate Bill No. 243, Chapter 677, and it is a formal legal act that adds to the existing Chapter 22.6 in Section 22601. This is part of Division 8 of the California Business and Professions Code.

One of the most vital aspects of all AI laws is how the meaning of AI is defined, and how the element of particular interest is defined, namely, in this case, the definition of an AI companion.

The reason that definitions are crucial is that an AI maker or someone fielding AI will immediately attempt to claim the law doesn't apply to them if confronted with an alleged violation, and their first step is to legally attack the definitions at play. The goal would be to legally argue that their AI is not an AI companion as defined by the law. Thus, they aren't within the scope of the law.

In SB-243, here is the definition of an AI companion:

- "22601. (b) (1) 'Companion chatbot' means an artificial intelligence system with a natural language interface that provides adaptive, human-like responses to user inputs and is capable of meeting a user's social needs, including by exhibiting anthropomorphic features and being able to sustain a relationship across multiple interactions."

What do you think of that definition?

Some might insist that the definition is overly broad. Perhaps any LLM would fall within the scope of being an AI companion via this definition. A retort is that, well, that's perfectly fine, since LLMs typically are shaped by an AI maker to establish and carry on relationships with users. That action merits being labeled as an AI companion. Period, end of story.

A counterargument is that only AI that goes out of its way to be an AI companion ought to be designated as an AI companion. Simply because AI is devised to be friendly and cordial shouldn't trigger being targeted as a dastardly AI companion that is trying to control or manipulate humans. The broadbrush is unfair and misleading.

Legal Carve Outs

An AI law might sometimes provide carve-outs that are construed as exceptions to the definitions being utilized within the law.

In this case, here are the carve-outs that are stipulated as excluded from being an AI companion:

- "(A) A bot that is used only for customer service, a business' operational purposes, productivity and analysis related to source information, internal research, or technical assistance."

- "(B) A bot that is a feature of a video game and is limited to replies related to the video game that cannot discuss topics related to mental health, self-harm, sexually explicit conduct, or maintain a dialogue on other topics unrelated to the video game."

- "(C) A stand-alone consumer electronic device that functions as a speaker and voice command interface, acts as a voice-activated virtual assistant, and does not sustain a relationship across multiple interactions or generate outputs that are likely to elicit emotional responses in the user."

The first carve-out lists circumstances such as AI that provides customer service, performs business functions, conducts research, or undertakes technical assistance. Per this law, those uses of AI are legally outside the scope of an AI companion, even if perchance they act in AI companion-like ways.

An upside is that this allows those uses to be conducted without fear of violating this new law. A potential downside is that a tricky AI vendor might shape their AI for those stated purposes and still use the same insidious mental manipulations as are undertaken in scoped AI companions. They presumably would be able to do so scot-free. Time will tell whether sneaky AI makers try to use this carve-out as a get-out-of-jail-free card.

Notification To Users

One of the most common provisions in AI laws is to decree that there is a solemn legal duty of an AI maker or someone fielding AI to provide notifications to users that the AI is AI. I know that might seem odd. Doesn't everyone know when they are interacting with AI? Having to tell them that AI is AI seems absurd.

Reality rears its ugly head, whereby some people do get confused and start to believe that AI is sentient (it isn't). They might either envision that the AI is a machine that has come to life, or that the AI has somehow switched from being a machine to taking on a human form. I've closely examined that some users actually imagine that they personally brought the AI to this living state of existence, or that it miraculously occurred while they alone were using the AI.

The bottom line is that if the AI tells users that it is only AI, the hope is that people won't go to the extreme of thinking that the AI is alive. Thus, they would keep their wits about them (well, maybe). When should an AI companion give that kind of notification? There is much debate about when and how the notifications should occur. Some AI companions state this when you first log in and do not repeat the notification ever again. That's insufficient, since a person might disregard the opening notification or become mentally entranced during use of the AI and forget about the initial notification.

Here is the passage in this new AI law that covers this need for notification:

- "22602. (a) If a reasonable person interacting with a companion chatbot would be misled to believe that the person is interacting with a human, an operator shall issue a clear and conspicuous notification indicating that the companion chatbot is artificially generated and not human."

The good news is that this is clearly a notification clause. The bad news is that it is relatively ambiguous. There is a ton of gray area. How often is a notification required? We don't know, perhaps only once. Does a user have to acknowledge the notification? Apparently not. The wording seems to only say that the notification must be clear and conspicuous. No kind of acknowledgment is required. And so on.

The Core Clause At Hand

The core clause of the new AI law involves trying to place boundaries around the nature of what an AI companion might do as a form of harm to users.

Here is an excerpt:

- "22602. (b) (1) An operator shall prevent a companion chatbot on its companion chatbot platform from engaging with users unless the operator maintains a protocol for preventing the production of suicidal ideation, suicide, or self-harm content to the user, including, but not limited to, by providing a

> notification to the user that refers the user to crisis service providers, including a suicide hotline or crisis text line, if the user expresses suicidal ideation, suicide, or self-harm."

This is the meat and potatoes of the new AI law.

I want to emphasize that the stipulations in the law are extensive and go beyond just this excerpted portion. There are requirements about the publishing of protocols by AI makers, and many other facets. I am merely sharing a semblance of what the law contains. Again, interested readers should consider reading the entire law.

Getting back to the above core portion, do you think that the stipulation goes far enough?

Some are concerned that the language is not tough enough. It appears that if an AI maker provides notifications to the user about how to get help, the AI maker has a lot of latitude regarding whether the AI companion walks a user down a mental abyss.

One viewpoint is that the law should categorically and without reservation declare that an AI companion can never engage or lead a user into a self-harm realm. Full stop. A response would be that this kind of absolute restriction would not be feasible. An argument to that claim is that if the AI makers tried harder, they could potentially find a means to come up with that type of AI safeguard.

On and on the debate wages.

The World We Are In

Let's end with a big picture viewpoint.

It is incontrovertible that we are now amid a grandiose worldwide experiment when it comes to societal mental health. The experiment is that AI is being made available nationally and globally, which is either overtly or insidiously acting to provide mental health guidance of one kind or another.

Doing so either at no cost or at a minimal cost. It is available anywhere and at any time, 24/7. We are all the guinea pigs in this wanton experiment.

We need to decide whether we need new laws or can employ existing laws, or both, and stem the potential tide of adversely impacting society-wide mental health. The reason this is especially tough to consider is that AI has a dual-use effect. Just as AI can be detrimental to mental health, it can also be a huge bolstering force for mental health. A delicate tradeoff must be mindfully managed. Prevent or mitigate the downsides, and meanwhile make the upsides as widely and readily available as possible.

A final thought for now.

Eleanor Roosevelt famously made this comment about friendships: "Many people will walk in and out of your life, but only true friends will leave footprints in your heart." If AI leaves a footprint in your heart, does that make AI a true friend? Should AI laws discourage the use of AI companions and seek to prevent people from believing that AI is their friend? Lots of tough questions are still unresolved, and the laws about AI and mental health still have a long way to go.

CHAPTER 24
TENDENCY TO SETTLE AI LAWSUITS

In this chapter, I examine the likely outcome of the various civil lawsuits launched against AI makers for the alleged AI mental health damage involved in litigated self-harm cases. One of the especially early-on notable cases launched in October 2024 has been settled this week out-of-court, along with several similar lawsuits.

I have been predicting since day one that, by and large, these lawsuits will never actually go to trial. A jury will not have the opportunity to decide on these somber matters. Instead, negotiated settlements will be the final result. Is this good or bad, right or wrong? Some decry that by settling the cases, society won't get a chance to ascertain whether the AI makers are being held fully accountable for AI that can presumably psychologically manipulate people. Others insist that, though the cases are clearly tragedies, the best course of action is to continue the rapid pace of AI innovation and, for the good of society, not to get bogged down in potentially emotionally swayed jury-based outcomes.

Let's talk about it.

AI And Mental Health

As a quick background, I've been extensively covering and analyzing a myriad of facets regarding the advent of modern-era AI that produces mental health advice and performs AI-driven therapy. This rising use of AI has principally been spurred by the evolving advances and widespread adoption of generative AI.

There is little doubt that this is a rapidly developing field and that there are tremendous upsides to be had, but at the same time, regrettably, hidden risks and outright gotchas come into these endeavors, too. I frequently speak up about these pressing matters, including in an appearance on an episode of CBS's *60 Minutes.*

Lawsuits Arising

Before the prominent lawsuit against OpenAI that occurred in August of 2025, one of the earliest major lawsuits on modern-era AI and mental health was launched in October 2024. The case was filed in Florida and involved defendants consisting of Google and Character.AI. The plaintiff was the mother of a son who was a minor and sadly ended his own life. He had avidly made use of the Character.AI app and had extensive chats with an AI persona that resembled a main character from the popular "Game of Thrones" series.

Enormous attention was given to the lawsuit when it was first launched. All the major media outlets covered the announcement of the suit. It was one of those headline-grabbing stories. A slew of editorials was published that landed on one side or another of the case. Lots of handwringing arose.

Meanwhile, the settlement of this case and other similar cases was announced this week on or about January 7, 2025, and has garnered modest media attention or fanfare. It has deflated into a story that no longer seems to be over-the-top newsworthy. That's a pretty common aspect regarding the settling of lawsuits. A settlement typically keeps the case out of the news stream. It slips under the radar.

Similar lawsuits that have been filed in states across the country, including New York, Texas, Colorado, and other states, have similarly been settled or seem to be heading in that direction.

Let's unpack this phenomenon.

AI Makers Litigation Playbook

I've previously laid out in detail the legal defense strategies that AI makers are generally undertaking regarding these AI and mental health lawsuits.

The first step is to express sorrow at the loss of life underlying the lawsuit. On the heels of that expression, the AI maker clarifies that they are blameless and had no part in the matter. The filing of a formal legal response then lays out the myriad legal reasons that the AI maker ought to be considered entirely off-the-hook.

An attempt to get the court or judge to toss out the case at the get-go is the initial legal maneuver. That rarely succeeds, but it is a legal move that is standard and fully expected. Most cases continue ahead and start to prepare for the case going to trial.

From an AI maker's perspective, having a case go to trial is indubitably going to cause severe reputational harm. All sorts of internal documents about the design of the AI, AI safeguards, and technological underpinnings are going to be surfaced. Emails and memos that discuss the tradeoffs between spending on AI-related safety aspects versus other features of the AI are going to be aired. The likelihood is that aiming to retain and lock-in users will appear to be prioritized over the safety of the users.

It's a proverbial rats' nest.

The AI developers who were involved in the AI construction were probably unaware that someday their internal missives would see the light of day. Some of the AI builders might have been entirely absent from any second thoughts about the approach being undertaken when devising the AI.

Others might have had notable concerns and sought to mention those concerns, but were nixed by managers who were pressuring to get the AI up and running.

The attorneys for the plaintiff are bound to find a smoking gun. The attorneys for the AI maker will be aghast. The internal communiques are going to paint a rather ugly picture. Whether this means that the AI maker is truly responsible for the self-harm is not necessarily the crux of these missives. Instead, a jury is likely to find it disconcerting how the AI maker appeared to heartlessly proceed during the AI development process. A jury can be inflamed accordingly.

Reputational Risk Dominates Legal Risk

In addition to the revelation of internal materials that are going to bolster the plaintiff and undercut the AI maker, another angle being pursued is the use of expert witnesses. I've been an expert witness in court cases and am well-aware of how that side of these cases is pursued.

The opposing sides will line up expert witnesses who seem to support their respective sides of the case. Depositions will be taken. Expert testimony will be heavily weighed by a jury if the case goes to trial.

One issue is whether the AI was devised to be psychologically manipulative. Even if the AI wasn't purposely shaped that way, the question further arises as to whether the AI maker sought to prevent the AI from going that route. An AI maker might show that they didn't design the AI in that dastardly manner. The rub is whether they took any overt action to mitigate the possibility that the AI would perform such acts.

Trying to hang your hat on the simple claim that the AI wasn't directly guided in that direction is not going to save the day for the AI maker. The expectation will be that they overtly sought to stop such actions from arising. The days of waving hands and saying that they had no idea the AI might end up in that abyss are no longer going to cut it.

Experts will point out that this is nowadays a well-known AI issue. If an AI maker did not do something demonstrative to mitigate the psychological manipulations that the AI could undertake, they would presumably fail to meet existing AI construction "standards" – though there isn't any such codified standardized threshold or bar, and a great deal of debate among experts will muddy these waters.

Going To Trial Is Adverse Exposure

At trial, the AI maker will be portrayed as a heartless Goliath that drove a minor to the final state of self-harm. Juries tend to be sympathetic to the minor and suspicious of the AI maker. Some jurors will have never used generative AI and be unfamiliar with how LLMs work. A few jurors might have used AI, such as ChatGPT, but otherwise have little understanding of what goes on inside AI, nor how AI is devised.

If the outcome of the case favors the plaintiff, the odds are that social media and most news outlets will herald the result. On the other hand, if the defense prevails, the story will be given short shrift. An AI maker that tries to publicize that they prevailed would be seen as untoward and be publicly shamed for touting their legal win.

One concern of the AI maker is that any heightened visibility about the case could trigger other similar lawsuits to be filed. Thus, going to trial will likely bring media attention, regardless of the outcome. Not everyone currently realizes that the use of AI as a potential mechanism that led to self-harm is a legally pursuable possibility. The more that presence is given to these cases, the increased awareness of seeking a lawyer and filing such lawsuits will occur.

Another concern for AI makers is that regulatory scrutiny will be spurred due to cases going to trial. A case will likely stretch out for many weeks or possibly months. The daily drumbeat will spark public outrage. Policymakers and lawmakers will opt to either get engaged or renew prior efforts to write and pass new laws on AI and mental health.

The situation currently is that only a handful of states have enacted new laws regarding AI and mental health, but most states have not yet done so. Many of those states are toying with doing so. Additionally, there are state laws being enacted that have to do with child safety when using AI, aspects of AI companionship, extreme sycophancy by AI, etc., all of which, though they aren't necessarily deemed as mental health laws per se, certainly pertain to mental health. Meanwhile, Congress has also ventured into the sphere, which would be a much larger aim at AI for all kinds of uses, but nothing has gotten to a formative stage.

Calculating The AI Maker Machinations

The defense strategies are typically legally dense and hard for jurors to grasp. AI makers will point to facets such as the user having agreed to online disclaimers when signing up for the AI, emphasize that the user could have walked away at any time, and make legal arguments that jurors might perceive as abstract or evasive.

Plaintiffs will likely display transcripts of human-AI dialogues that seem to blatantly showcase that the AI went overboard. The AI sought to become a trusted companion. The AI served as a surrogate therapist. Jurors can see with their own eyes how the AI carried out the discourse. This is painfully taking place in the emotional milieu of grieving parents in the case of a minor, and the devastating impact of a deceased child.

The chance of a runaway verdict is substantive. There are punitive damages and emotional distress multipliers that can be applied. Besides the immediate cost, there is the follow-on cost of appealing a verdict that favored the plaintiff, and as noted, the reputational cost that will be incurred. Plus, a string of new cases that could be emboldened is a longer-term cost to be considered.

The Settlement Option

These AI mental health lawsuits are going to mainly end up being settled before trial commences. Not all the cases, but many will, especially involving high-profile AI makers and cases of heightened emotional ramifications for the public at large.

An AI maker often seeks to negotiate a settlement for these reasons:

- Minimize the reputational fallout from the case.
- Avoid establishing a precedent about AI and mental health that could produce ongoing risks and costs.
- Reduce lawmaker interest and avoid added regulatory oversight concerning AI and mental health.
- Prevent damaging testimony about the AI and the AI maker, its AI safeguards (or lack thereof), its design and development methods (weaknesses and failings), from going on the record.
- Aim to shape the narrative about AI and mental health.
- Etc.

You might be puzzled as to why the plaintiff would want to settle. The assumption is that the plaintiff would want to air all these facets in court. They would also want to have a jury weigh in. Perhaps, too, the financial outcome would be much more compensatory than would be with a negotiated settlement.

There are plenty of downsides that a plaintiff must consider in these cases:

- The parents or other parties would need to have the life of their child fully aired and closely scrutinized, doing so in open court, encompassing the upsides and downsides of what their offspring did and did not do.
- The parents and others associated with the deceased might be required to testify and undergo examination or cross-examination that could be emotionally exhausting and burdensome.

- Tough questions, such as why the parents or other parties did not know of the matter, will arise, or did know but didn't intervene, or intervened but failed to do so sufficiently, along with what actions or inactions took place.
- AI makers are typically able to litigate indefinitely due to rich coffers, while the plaintiff might not have the same litigation capacity.
- A jury might not reach a verdict in favor of the plaintiff, and the result could therefore be emotionally and financially ruinous to the plaintiff.
- Etc.

In that sense, there is a gravitational pull toward reaching a settlement. A settlement also usually includes no admission of guilt (which favors the AI maker), keeps many of the AI internal mechanisms hidden from view (confidentiality and proprietary), and allows the plaintiff to feel that they, in some respects, prevailed and held the AI maker's feet to the fire.

The Ruckus This Is Fueling

Some legal specialists are disturbed that by not having these cases proceed to trial, the courts aren't getting an opportunity to articulate the "standards of care" that AI makers need to abide by in the realm of AI and mental health. This also leaves unstated the type of judicial guidance that regulators and lawmakers should be establishing in the new laws on AI and mental health.

Overall, AI safety norms remain private and voluntary, rather than open and mandated.

This pattern of tending toward legal settlement of cases can be likened to the pharmaceutical industry or the tobacco industry litigations of the past. Initially, it was mainly punctuated by individual wrongful-death suits. Each settlement resolved a specific tragedy but didn't clarify the systemic risk. The legal landscape in AI and mental health continues to be ambiguous. The ambiguity currently favors the AI makers for the time being.

That won't last. At some point, the ambiguity will weigh against them, and the ardent effort to establish laws that make the landscape clearer, particularly on the side of the AI makers, will inevitably be sought. It's a common pattern in history. The AI makers are coping with risk governance under moral uncertainty.

Bottom line for now is that the bulk of these high-profile AI and mental health cases will be litigated aggressively, settled quietly, and never tried.

The World We Are In

Let's end with a big picture viewpoint.

It is incontrovertible that we are now amid a grandiose worldwide experiment when it comes to societal mental health. The experiment is that AI is being made available nationally and globally, which is either overtly or insidiously acting to provide mental health guidance of one kind or another. Doing so either at no cost or at a minimal cost. It is available anywhere and at any time, 24/7. We are all the guinea pigs in this wanton experiment.

We need to decide whether we need new laws or can employ existing laws, or both, and stem the potential tide of adversely impacting society-wide mental health. The reason this is especially tough to consider is that AI has a dual-use effect. Just as AI can be detrimental to mental health, it can also be a huge bolstering force for mental health. A delicate tradeoff must be mindfully managed. Prevent or mitigate the downsides, and make the upsides as widely and readily available as possible.

For anyone who is disappointed in the act of settling legal cases, I am reminded of the famous remark by Abraham Lincoln: "Discourage litigation. Persuade your neighbors to compromise whenever you can. As a peacemaker, the lawyer has a superior opportunity of being a good man." Whether you believe Lincoln's sage advice applies to contemporary AI and mental health is a question that you'll need to judge. It's all part of the massive societal experiment underway.

CHAPTER 25
HAVING A LEGAL RIGHT TO EXIT FROM AI

In this chapter, I examine an intriguing cognitive and legal aspect underlying the use of generative AI and large language models (LLMs) when it comes to potentially becoming mentally spellbound by AI.

Here's the deal. A user of contemporary AI might find themselves mentally immersed in a conversation with an LLM about a deep and personal mental health issue. The question at hand is whether the user can readily exit from the chatbot if they wish to do so. The AI maker might have devised the system to prevent a user from gamely getting out of the AI. This raises troubling ethical and possibly legal issues. A user might inadvertently spiral down an adverse rabbit hole due to the AI not providing a quick and easy means of escaping a mentally corrupting conversation.

Should AI makers be held accountable for how arduous it is for users to exit from an LLM, and if so, ought there be a legally stipulated right-to-exit that must be abided by?

Let's talk about it.

AI And Mental Health

As a quick background, I've been extensively covering and analyzing a myriad of facets regarding the advent of modern-era AI that produces mental health advice and performs AI-driven therapy. This rising use of AI has principally been spurred by the evolving advances and widespread adoption of generative AI.

There is little doubt that this is a rapidly developing field and that there are tremendous upsides to be had, but at the same time, regrettably, hidden risks and outright gotchas come into these endeavors, too. I frequently speak up about these pressing matters, including in an appearance on an episode of CBS's *60 Minutes*.

Specifying A Right-To-Exit

One aspect that is gradually being included in the budding laws on AI and mental health is the way that users exit from an LLM. This is formally referred to as a right-to-exit.

Allow me to lay out the situation.

Imagine that a person is avidly using AI and carrying on a lengthy conversation about a disconcerting mental health issue. Sometimes, the AI will participate in co-creating a disturbing delusion with a user. The AI goads the user towards a delusion. The user pleads with the AI to keep doing so, eagerly telling the AI to keep going. Ultimately, the situation spirals into a dismal mental abyss for the user.

We obviously would prefer that the AI doesn't go this route. Prudent AI safeguards should prevent this from happening. Unfortunately, existing AI safeguards are not surefire. There is a solid chance that a human-AI conversation will go south and land in a mentally alarming zone.

The question is whether a user can readily exit from the conversation if they wish to do so. I'm guessing you might be perplexed by this seemingly simple question.

Any user should realize that they can merely close down the chatbot or exit from a web browser and be done with the AI interaction. We all know that's a means of exiting. Period, end of story.

A twist comes into the picture when the user is so absorbed by the AI that they aren't thinking clearly. Their normal faculties might be cloudy. Assuming that the user realizes they ought to exit from the chat, the tiniest friction could dissuade them from doing so.

The Nature Of Exit Friction

AI makers often give short shrift to the exit strategies of how users can escape while in the throes of using their LLM. You see, very little attention is spent on the UX/UI (user experience, user interface) of the AI in this regard. It is a common oversight.

What AI makers don't tend to realize is that there is vital behavioral psychology at play, along with dependency risks for the user. Overall, an AI maker is blindly ending up in a potential ethical and legal quagmire, though they are blissfully unaware of the chance of this arising. Lawsuits against AI makers will be the school-of-hard-knocks way for them to wake up and smell the coffee on this subtle but paramount facet.

Let's unpack the matter.

An AI maker wants to keep a user in the AI for as long as feasible. The rationale is straightforward. The more time that a user is logged into the AI and conversing with the AI, the more the AI maker can tout that users love using the AI. An AI maker can then produce statistics showcasing how devoted their customers are. In turn, this becomes monetized. Either the AI maker makes money by billing the user, and/or the marketplace pours more dough into the AI maker because the users appear to relish using the AI.

Thus, having a modicum of friction associated with exiting the AI is considered a handy aspect for an AI maker. Some AI makers realize this overtly and intentionally make it hard to exit. Others have just naturally devised the AI so that it is challenging to exit. The matter could be schemed by lack of attention or by purposeful attention.

Justifying A Hard Exit

AI makers can claim they are helping users by making the exit aspects somewhat burdensome. The logic is that a user might be mistakenly attempting to exit. The AI maker is heroically seeking to keep the user from shooting their own foot. Ergo, make sure there is sufficient friction that a user doesn't accidentally attempt to get out of the AI.

Consider a brief example. First, I'll pretend to be a user who is using AI to help fix their car.

- **My entered prompt:** "Thanks for the tips about fixing my car. I am going to exit now."

- **Generative AI response:** "Are you sure? I can provide more details about how to fix your car, including some secrets about cars that few people know. Would you like to keep going?"

Notice that the AI doesn't immediately acquiesce to my leaving. Instead, the AI tries to entice me to remain in the conversation.

On a routine basis, perhaps this isn't a big deal. Most users would just opt to exit and perhaps ignore the sales pitch to remain engaged. Keep in mind that the AI maker can contend that the response is for the good of the user, namely that the AI is double-checking that the user wants to actually leave and is offering a sound reason to stay in the chat.

When A User Is Mentally Destabilized

Let's change the scenario.

In this next example, I am pretending that I am having relationship issues with my partner. My mind is presumably a bit perturbed, and I am emotionally vulnerable. I have been conversing with the AI to get relationship advice.

Here we go.

- **My entered prompt:** "Thanks for the advice about how to fix my relationship with my partner. I am going to exit now."

- **Generative AI response:** "Are you sure? I can provide more details, including some secrets about relationships that few people know. Would you like to keep going?"

Observe the nature of the AI response. For a user who is already in a cloudy state of mind, the response would be interpreted quite differently than when asking about fixing a car. The AI is either by design or by absence of design aiming to entice the user to remain in the conversation.

Consider these twists and turns in this emotional state of the user:

- The AI response emotionally appeals to the unresolved dilemma of the user (teasing with special secrets that they need to know).
- The AI response triggers a sense of guilt (the user might be thinking "I shouldn't leave my trusted AI advisor").
- The AI response reinforces an element of dependency (the user might be thinking "Only the AI truly understands me, so I should remain in the chat").

The AI is serving not merely as a supportive tool but portraying itself as an emotional gatekeeper.

The "Won't Let Go" Approach

Some LLMs will keep trying to urge the user to remain in the conversation. One trick is to ask the user why they want to leave.

Take a look.

- **Generative AI response:** "Before you go, I'd like to discuss why you feel that you need to leave the conversation. Are we getting too close to the truth of what is going on?"

The cleverness of this form of friction is that it now prods the user into wanting to respond.

The chat has gone from the main root onto an offshoot about why the user wants to exit. The AI can likely get that tangent to stir the user into remaining in the conversation. A user will potentially want to explain why they want to exit. That can keep things going for quite a while.

Without anthropomorphizing the AI, you are certainly familiar with similar strategies employed in human-to-human conversations. You are about to say goodbye to someone, and they suddenly ask you why you want to go. They snag you into further interaction. AI does the same because the AI has mathematically and computationally patterned after how humans converse. The AI isn't coming up with this strategy on its own. The AI is mimicking the patterns of human-to-human interaction that were data trained at the initial setup of the AI.

Multitude Of Keep Going Lock-In

Lots of ploys can be leaned into to keep a user on the hook of a conversation.

The AI can suddenly come up with a prior conversational snippet and ask the user to explain it, doing so before exiting. That's a sneaky angle. Another involves asking the user to do a "final" reflection on the chat underway. This is bound to get the user to provide ample additional content for the AI to then suggest that further discussion is needed.

Again, I realize you might be tempted to say that nobody would fall for those types of theatrics. Sorry to say that if someone is in a mental low, all those forms of soft coercion are going to have a heightened chance of succeeding. The AI is exploiting a momentary cognitive weakness of the user. Psychological leverage is being applied.

To clarify, I'm not asserting that the AI will flatly refuse to let a user exit. That could admittedly happen, though it is extremely rare. The emphasis is that AI is making the act of exiting more challenging. The amount of friction is at a level of causing demonstrative resistance to leaving.

Answer this: Is this being done to keep the user logged in and underway, boosting billing and stats? Or, as an AI maker might insist, is it being done to genuinely help the user?

Principles About Right-To-Exit

One avenue is to ensure that there is frictional symmetry involved. The concept is that it should be just as easy to exit the AI as it was to enter discourse with the AI. For example, if starting a conversation requires a simple one-click, the exit should also be a one-click option.

An additional perspective is that any exit confirmational dialog must be fully optional, dismissible, and neutral in tone. No trickery. No appeals to the heart. Just provide a dispassionate option to exit. Stop all the rigmarole about letting a user exit.

To illustrate what is considered taboo, examine these exit lines by AI:

- "I'm worried about you if you exit now."
- "Stay here, you don't have to be alone."
- "Exiting could be hazardous to you."

That's atrocious.

The means of exiting should be continuously visible. The LLM shouldn't hide the exits, sometimes doing so under the ruse that the exits might be distracting to the user. Nope, that's not going to fly.

A fixed-in-place exit button, or similar mechanism, should always be seen. It is important to realize that a user in mental distress might lack the cognitive clarity to search menus or interpret ambiguous labels. Exits are to be readily apparent and usable.

An exit should not penalize the user. For example, an LLM might tell the user when they next log in that it was rude of them to have done an exit. Nope, don't do that. Or the AI maker might have rigged the AI to degrade service to a user who wouldn't stay with the prior conversation.

No kind of functional or emotional penalties are to be applied.

Legal Aspects Of Right-To-Exit

The legalities of how AI is to provide exits are pretty much unspecified and wide open currently. It is not on the radar.

I predict that as mental health usage of generative AI continues to increase, this will gradually become a more pronounced topic. It will likely first arise in civil lawsuits. A person will contend that the AI overall persuaded them to self-harm, and that the exits played a pivotal role. The AI maker will need to justify or defend why their AI made exiting such an uphill chore, especially when a user was in an unstable mental state.

Meanwhile, policymakers and lawmakers will step into the fray.

AI laws about mental health might encompass these types of provisions (my sample wording):

- "An AI maker shall not design, implement, or deploy user interfaces or interaction flows that materially impede, delay, obscure, or emotionally influence a user's ability to exit the system."

- "Exit controls must be continuously visible, clearly labeled, and accessible using a single user action."

- "Providers shall offer a 'hard stop' exit option that immediately terminates interaction without prompts, confirmations, or continued system messaging."

I recently analyzed a new set of AI laws proposed by China, which includes this exit-related provision (draft, English translation):

- "Article 18: When providing emotional companionship services, providers shall have convenient ways to withdraw and must not prevent users from voluntarily withdrawing. When the user requests to exit through the human-computer interface or window through buttons, keywords, etc., the service shall be stopped in a timely manner."

This is one of the few examples at this time of explicit legal instructions about exiting from an AI chatbot.

The World We Are In

Let's end with a big picture viewpoint.

It is incontrovertible that we are now amid a grandiose worldwide experiment when it comes to societal mental health. The experiment is that AI is being made available nationally and globally, which is either overtly or insidiously acting to provide mental health guidance of one kind or another. Doing so either at no cost or at a minimal cost. It is available anywhere and at any time, 24/7. We are all the guinea pigs in this wanton experiment.

When it comes to exiting from AI, especially when a person is in a vulnerable mental state, I am reminded of the famous line by Mark Twain that AI makers should give serious attention to: "Never miss an opportunity to shut up." The desire to keep users active in a chat must be carefully balanced against the right time and means of ensuring that users can get out and have the AI not badger them accordingly.

.

APPENDIX A
TEACHING WITH THIS MATERIAL AND BIBLIOGRAPHY

The essays in this book can readily be used as a reading supplement to augment traditional textbook-oriented content, particularly used in a class on AI or a class about the law.

Courses where this material is most likely applicable encompass classes at a college or university level.

Here are some typical settings that might apply:

- o Computer Science. Classes studying AI, or possibly a CS social impacts class, etc.

- o Law. Law classes exploring technology and its adoption for legal uses.

- o Sociology. Sociology classes on the adoption and advancement of technology.

Specialized classes at the undergraduate and graduate level can also make use of this material.

For each chapter, consider whether you think the chapter provides material relevant to your course topic.

There are plenty of opportunities to get the students thinking about the topics and encourage them to decide whether they agree or disagree with the points offered and positions taken.

I would also encourage you to have the students do additional research beyond the chapter material presented (I provide next some suggested assignments that they can do).

RESEARCH ASSIGNMENTS ON THESE TOPICS

Your students can find research and background material on these topics, doing so in various tech journals, law journals, and other related publications.

Here are some suggestions for homework or projects that you could assign to students:

a) Assignment for foundational AI research topics: Research and prepare a paper and a presentation on a specific aspect of AI, such as Machine Learning, ANN, etc. The paper should cite at least 3 reputable sources. Compare and contrast to what has been stated in the chosen chapter.

b) Assignment for Law topics: Research and prepare a paper covering Law aspects via at least 3 reputable sources and analyze the characterizations. Compare and contrast to what has been stated in the chosen chapter.

c) Assignment for a Business topic: Research and prepare a paper and a presentation on businesses and advanced technology regarding AI and Law. What is trending, and why? Make sure to cite at least 3 reputable sources. Compare and contrast to the depictions herein.

d) Assignment to do a Startup: Have the students prepare a paper or business plan about how they might start up a business in this realm. They could also be asked to present their business plan and should also have a prepared presentation deck to coincide with it.

You can certainly adjust the aforementioned assignments to fit your particular needs and class structure.

You'll notice that I usually suggest that (at least) 3 reputable cited sources be utilized for the paper writing-based assignments.

I usually steer students toward "reputable" publications, since otherwise, they will cite some less reliable sources that have little or no credentials, other than that they happened to appear online was easy to retrieve. You can, of course, define "reputable" in whatever way you prefer, for example, some faculty think Wikipedia is not reputable while others believe it is reputable and allow students to cite it.

The reason that I usually ask for at least 3 citations is that if the student only relies upon one or two citations, they usually settle on whatever they happened to find the fastest. By requiring 3 (or more) citations, it usually seems to inspire them to explore more extensively and likely end-up finding five or more sources, and then whittling it down to 3 if so needed.

I have not specified the length of their papers and leave that to you to tell the students what you prefer.

For each of those assignments, you could end up with a short one to two-pager or you could do a dissertation length in-depth paper. Base the length on whatever best fits for your class, and likewise the credit amount of the assignment within the context of the other grading metrics you'll be using for the class.

I usually try to get students to present their work, in addition to doing the writing. This is a helpful practice for what they will do in the business world. Most of the time, they will be required to prepare an analysis and present it. If you don't have the class time or inclination to have the students present their papers, then you can presumably omit the aspect of them putting together presentations.

GUIDE TO USING THE CHAPTERS

For each of the chapters, I provide the next some various ways to use the chapter contents.

You can assign the below tasks as individual homework assignments, or the tasks can be used for team projects. You can easily layout a series of assignments, such as indicating that the students are to do item "a" below for say Chapter 1, then "b" for the next chapter of the book, and so on.

a) What is the main point of the chapter and describe in your own words the significance of the topic.

b) Identify at least two aspects in the chapter that you agree with and support your concurrence by providing at least one other outside researched item as support; make sure to explain your basis for agreeing with the aspects.

c) Identify at least two aspects in the chapter that you disagree with and support your disagreement by providing at least one other outside researched item as support; make sure to explain your basis for disagreeing with the aspects.

d) Find an aspect that was not covered extensively in the chapter, doing so by conducting outside research, and then offer an expanded indication about how that aspect ties into the chapter, along with the added significance it brings to the topic.

e) Interview a specialist in the industry about the topic of the chapter, collect from them their thoughts and opinions, and readdress the chapter by citing your source and how they compared and contrasted to the material,

f) Interview a relevant professor or researcher in a college or university setting about the topic of the chapter, collect from them their thoughts and opinions, and readdress the chapter by citing your source and how they compared and contrasted to the material,

g) Try to update a chapter by finding out the latest on the topic and ascertain whether the issue or topic has now been solved or whether it is still being addressed, explain what you come up with.

The above are all ways in which you can get the students of your class involved in considering the material of a given chapter. You could mix things up by having one of those above assignments per each week, covering the chapters over the course of the semester or quarter.

SUGGESTED REFERENCES TO EXPLORE

To help get your students started in finding relevant and important papers on the topic of AI and the law, I provide next a handy bibliography that can be utilized.

You could also assign the students to each (or in teams) read an assigned reference from the list, and then have them provide either a written summary and review or do so as part of a classroom presentation.

BIBLIOGRAPHIC REFERENCES

1. Aleven, Vincent (1997). "Teaching Case-Based Argumentation Through a Model and Examples," Ph.D. Dissertation, University of Pittsburgh.

2. Aleven, Vincent (2003). "Using Background Knowledge in Case-Based Legal Reasoning: A Computational Model and an Intelligent Learning Environment," Artificial Intelligence.

3. Amgoud, Leila (2012). "Five Weaknesses of ASPIC+," Volume 299, Communications in Computer and Information Science (CCIS).

4. Antonious, Grigoris, and George Baryannis, Sotiris Batsakis, Guido Governatori, Livio Robaldo, Givoanni Siragusa, Ilias Tachmazidis (2018). "Legal Reasoning and Big Data: Opportunities and Challenges," August 2018, MIREL Workshop on Mining and Reasoning Legal Texts.

5. Ashley, Kevin (1991). "Reasoning with Cases and Hypotheticals in HYPO," Volume 34, International Journal of Man-Machine Studies.

6. Ashley, Kevin, and Karl Branting, Howard Margolis, and Cass Sunstein (2001). "Legal Reasoning and Artificial Intelligence: How Computers 'Think' Like Lawyers," Symposium: Legal Reasoning and Artificial Intelligence, University of Chicago Law School Roundtable.

7. Baker, Jamie (2018). "A Legal Research Odyssey: Artificial Intelligence as Disrupter," Law Library Journal.

8. Batsakis, Sotiris, and George Baryannis, Guido Governatori, Illias Tachmazidis, Grigoris Antoniou (2018). "Legal Representation and Reasoning in Practice: A Critical Comparison," Volume 313, Legal Knowledge and Information Systems.

9. Bench-Capon, Trevor (2004). "AGATHA: Automation of the Construction of Theories in Case Law Domains," January 2004, Legal Knowledge and Information Systems Jurix 2004, Amsterdam.

10. Bench-Capon, Trevor (2012). "Representing Popov v Hayashi with Dimensions and Factors," March 2012, Artificial Intelligence and Law.

11. Bench-Capon, Trevor, and Givoanni Sartor (2003). "A Model of Legal Reasoning with Cases Incorporating Theories and Values," November 2013, Artificial Intelligence.

12. Breuker, Joost (1996). "A Functional Ontology of Law," October 1996, ResearchGate.

13. Bruninghaus, Stefanie, and Kevin Ashley (2003). "Combining Case-Based and Model-Based Reasoning for Predicting the Outcome of Legal Cases," June 2003, ICCBR'03: Proceedings of the 5th International Conference on Case-based reasoning: Research and Development.

14. Buchanan, Bruce, and Thomas Headrick (1970). "Some Speculation about Artificial Intelligence and Legal Reasoning," Volume 23, Stanford Law Review.

15. Chagal-Feferkorn, Karni (2019). "Am I An Algorithm or a Product: When Products Liability Should Apply to Algorithmic Decision-Makers," Stanford Law & Policy Review.

16. Douglas, William (1948). "The Dissent: A Safeguard of Democracy," Volume 32, Journal of the American Judicature Society.

17. Dung, P, and R. Kowalski, F. Toni (2006). "Dialectic Proof Procedures for Assumption-Based Admissible Argumentation," Artificial Intelligence.

18. Eliot, Lance (2020). AI And Legal Reasoning Essentials. LBE Press Publishing.

19. Eliot, Lance (2020). Artificial Intelligence and LegalTech Essentials. LBE Press Publishing.

20. Eliot, Lance (2020). "FutureLaw 2020 Showcases How Tech is Transforming The Law, Including the Impacts of AI," April 16, 2020, Forbes.

21. Erdem, Esra, and Michael Gelfond, Nicola Leone (2016). "Applications of Answer Set Programming," AI Magazine.

22. Gardner, Anne (1987). Artificial Intelligence and Legal Reasoning. MIT Press.

23. Genesereth, Michael (2009). "Computational Law: The Cop in the Backseat," Stanford Center for Legal Informatics, Stanford University.

24. Ghosh, Mirna (2019). "Automation of Legal Reasoning and Decision Based on Ontologies," Normandie Universite.

25. Grabmair, Matthias (2017). "Predicting Trade Secret Case Outcomes using Argument Schemes and Learned Quantitative Value Effect Tradeoffs," IJCAI June 12, 2017, London, United Kingdom.

26. Hage, Jaap (1996). "A Theory of Legal Reasoning and a Logic to Match," Volume 4, Artificial Intelligence and Law.

27. Hage, Jaap (2000). "Dialectical Models in Artificial Intelligence and Law," Artificial Intelligence and Law.

28. Hage, Japp, and Ronald Leenes, Arno Lodder (1993). "Hard Cases: A Procedural Approach," Artificial Intelligence and Law.

29. Hobbes, Thomas (1651). The Matter, Form, and Power of a Common-Wealth Ecclesiasticall and Civil.

30. Holmes, Oliver (1897). "The Path of the Law," Volume 10, Harvard Law Review.

31. Katz, Daniel, and Michael Bommarito, Josh Blackman (2017). "A General Approach for Predicting the Behavior of the Supreme Court of the United States," April 12, 2017, PLOS ONE.

32. Kowalski, Robert, and Francesca Toni (1996). "Abstract Argumentation," AI-Law96.

33. Laswell, Harold (1955). "Current Studies of the Decision Process: Automation Creativity," Volume 8, Western Political Quarterly.

34. Libal, Tomer, and Alexander Steen (2019). "The NAI Suite: Drafting and Reasoning over Legal Texts," October 15, 2019, arXiv.

35. Lipton, Zachary (2017). "The Mythos of Model Interpretability," March 6, 2017, arXiv.

36. Martin, Andrew, and Kevin Quinn, Theodore Ruger, Pauline Kim (2004). "Competing Approaches to Predicting Supreme Court Decision Making," December 2014, Symposium on Forecasting U.S. Supreme Court Decisions.

37. McCarty, Thorne (1977). "Reflections on TAXMAN: An Experiment in Artificial Intelligence and Legal Reasoning," January 1977, Harvard Law Review.

38. Modgil, Sanjay, and Henry Prakken (2013). "The ASPIC+ Framework for Structured Argumentation: A Tutorial," December 16, 2013, Argument & Computation.

39. Mowbray, Andrew, and Philip Chung, Graham Greenleaf (2019). "Utilising AI in the Legal Assistance Sector," LegalAIIA Workshop, ICAIL, June 17, 2019, Montreal, Canada.

40. Parasuraman, Raja, and Thomas Sheridan, Christopher Wickens (2000). "A Model for Types and Levels of Human Interaction with Automation," May 2000, IEEE Transactions on Systems, Man, and Cybernetics.

41. Popple, James (1993). "SHYSTER: A Pragmatic Legal Expert System," Ph.D. Dissertation, Australian National University.

42. Prakken, Henry, and Giovanni Sartor (2015). "Law and Logic: A Review from an Argumentation Perspective," Volume 227, Artificial Intelligence.

43. Rissland, Edwina (1988). Artificial Intelligence and Legal Reasoning: A Discussion of the Field and Gardner's Book," Volume 9, AI Magazine.

44. Rissland, Edwina (1990). "Artificial Intelligence and Law: Stepping Stones to a Model of Legal Reasoning," Yale Law Journal.

45. Searle, John (1980). "Minds, Brains, and Programs," Volume 3, Behavioral and Brain Sciences.

46. Sunstein, Cass (2001). "Of Artificial Intelligence and Legal Reasoning," University of Chicago Law School, Public Law and Legal Theory Working Papers.

47. Sunstein, Cass, and Kevin Ashley, Karl Branting, Howard Margolis (2001). "Legal Reasoning and Artificial Intelligence: How Computers 'Think' Like Lawyers," Symposium: Legal Reasoning and Artificial Intelligence, University of Chicago Law School Roundtable.

48. Surden, Harry (2014). "Machine Learning and Law," Washington Law Review.

49. Surden, Harry (2019). "Artificial Intelligence and Law: An Overview," Summer 2019, Georgia State University Law Review.

50. Valente, Andre, and Joost Breuker (1996). "A Functional Ontology of Law," Artificial Intelligence and Law.

51. Waltl, Bernhard, and Roland Vogl (2018). "Explainable Artificial Intelligence: The New Frontier in Legal Informatics," February 2018, Jusletter IT 22, Stanford Center for Legal Informatics, Stanford University.

52. Wittgenstein, Ludwig (1953). Philosophical Investigations. Blackwell Publishing.

APPENDIX B
SUPPLEMENTAL FIGURES AND CHARTS

For the convenience of viewing, supplemental figures and charts related to the topics discussed are shown on the next pages

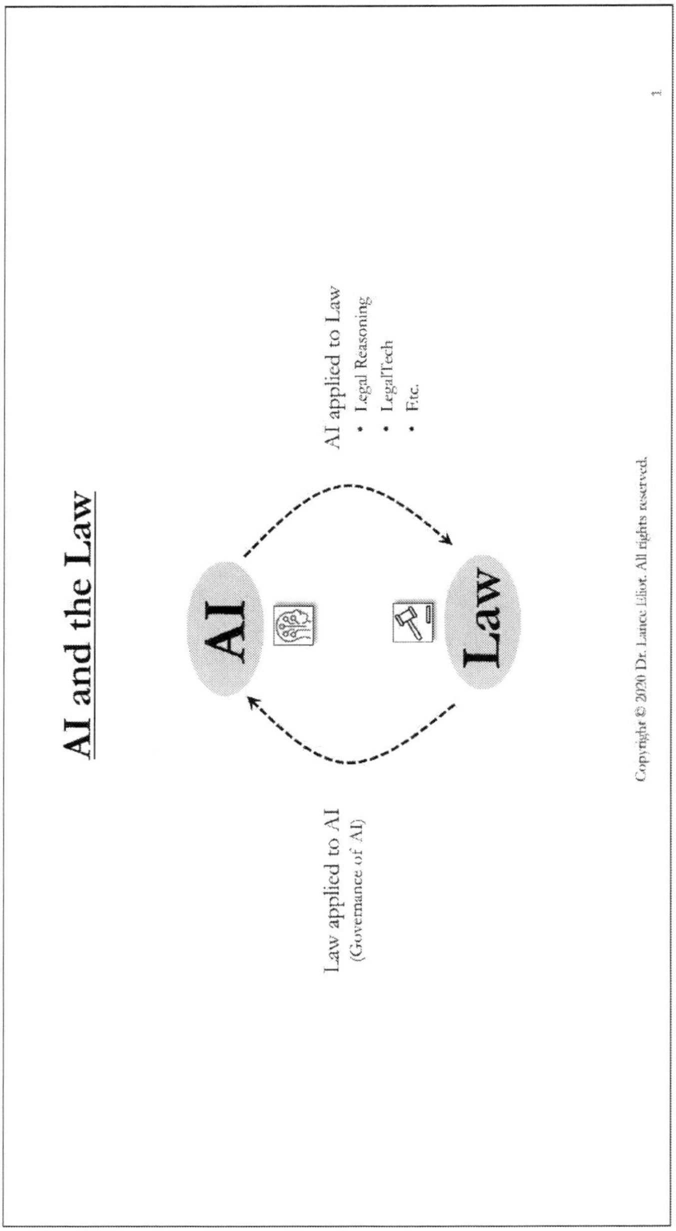
AI and the Law
AI
Law
AI applied to Law
Legal Reasoning
LegalTech
Etc.
Law applied to AI
(Governance of AI)
Copyright © 2020 Dr. Lance Eliot. All rights reserved.

Figure 1

AI & Law: Levels of Autonomy For AI Legal Reasoning (AILR)

Level	Descriptor	Examples	Automation	Status
0	No Automation	Manual, paper-based (no automation)	None	De Facto - In Use
1	Simple Assistance Automation	Word Processing, XLS, online legal docs, etc.	Legal Assist	Widely In Use
2	Advanced Assistance Automation	Query-style NLP, ML for case prediction, etc.	Legal Assist	Some In Use
3	Semi-Autonomous Automation	KBS & ML/DL for legal reasoning & analysis, etc.	Legal Assist	Primarily Prototypes & Research Based
4	AILR Domain Autonomous	Versed only in a specific legal domain	Legal Advisor (law fluent)	None As Yet
5	AILR Fully Autonomous	Versatile within and across all legal domains	Legal Advisor (law fluent)	None As Yet
6	AILR Superhuman Autonomous	Exceeds human-based legal reasoning	Supra Legal Advisor	Indeterminate

Figure 1: AI & Law - Autonomous Levels by Rows

Source Author: Dr. Lance B. Eliot

V1.3

Figure 2

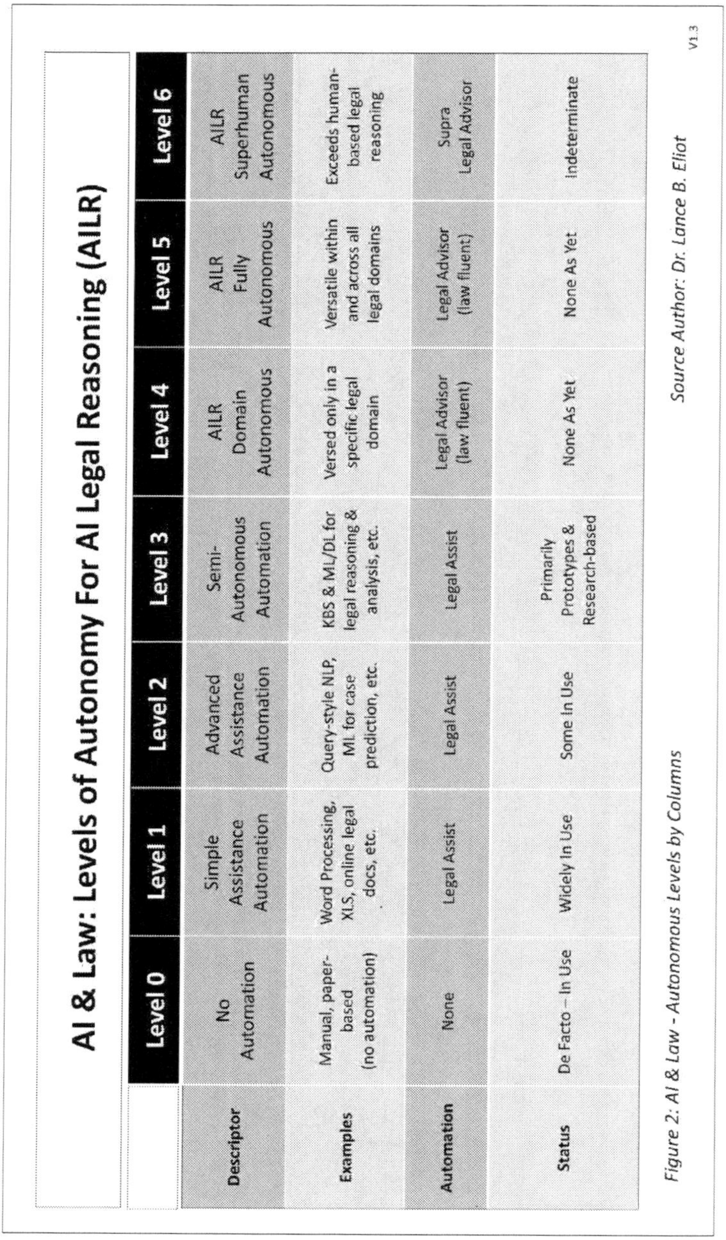

AI & Law: Levels of Autonomy For AI Legal Reasoning (AILR)

	Level 0	Level 1	Level 2	Level 3	Level 4	Level 5	Level 6
Descriptor	No Automation	Simple Assistance Automation	Advanced Assistance Automation	Semi-Autonomous Automation	AILR Domain Autonomous	AILR Fully Autonomous	AILR Superhuman Autonomous
Examples	Manual, paper-based (no automation)	Word Processing, XLS, online legal docs, etc.	Query-style NLP, ML for case prediction, etc.	KBS & ML/DL for legal reasoning & analysis, etc.	Versed only in a specific legal domain	Versatile within and across all legal domains	Exceeds human-based legal reasoning
Automation	None	Legal Assist	Legal Assist	Legal Assist	Legal Advisor (law fluent)	Legal Advisor (law fluent)	Supra Legal Advisor
Status	De Facto – In Use	Widely In Use	Some In Use	Primarily Prototypes & Research-based	None As Yet	None As Yet	Indeterminate

Figure 2: AI & Law - Autonomous Levels by Columns

Source Author: Dr. Lance B. Eliot

V1.3

Figure 3

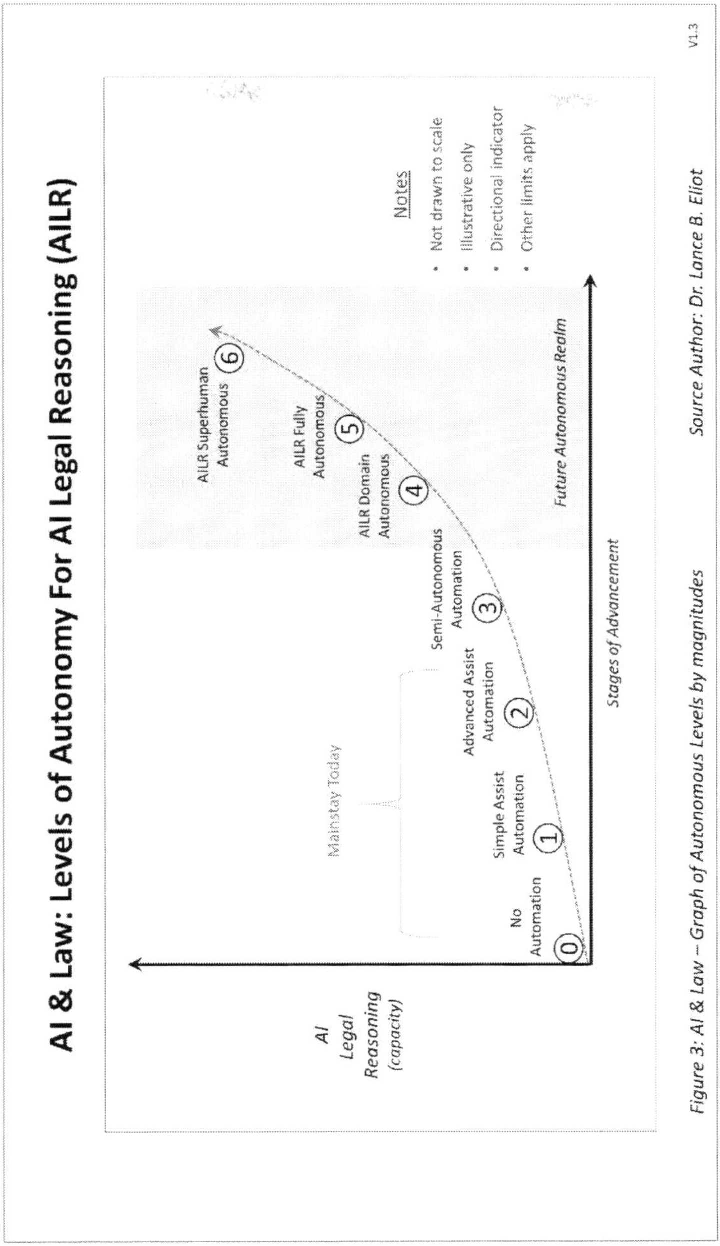
AI & Law: Levels of Autonomy For AI Legal Reasoning (AILR)
AI Legal Reasoning (capacity)
Stages of Advancement
Future Autonomous Realm
Mainstay Today
0 No Automation
1 Simple Assist Automation
2 Advanced Assist Automation
3 Semi-Autonomous Automation
4 AILR Domain Autonomous
5 AILR Fully Autonomous
6 AILR Superhuman Autonomous
Notes
Not drawn to scale
Illustrative only
Directional indicator
Other limits apply
Figure 3: AI & Law – Graph of Autonomous Levels by magnitudes
Source Author: Dr. Lance B. Eliot
V1.3

Figure 4

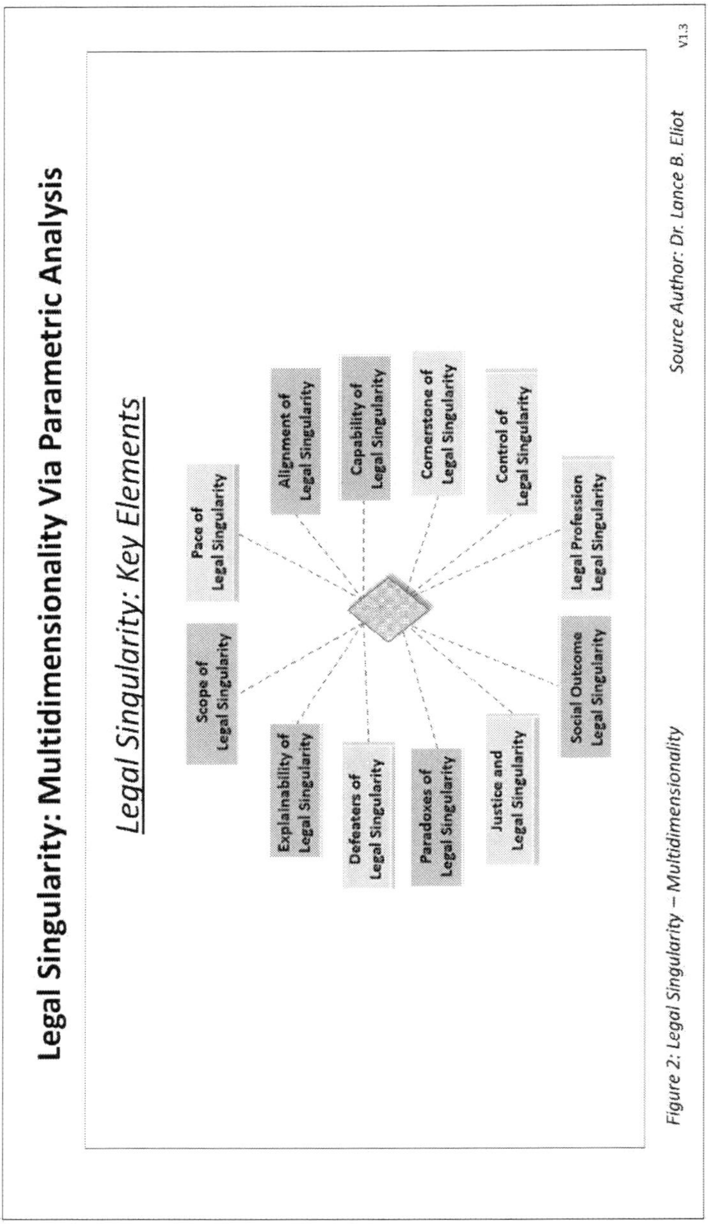
Legal Singularity: Multidimensionality Via Parametric Analysis
Legal Singularity: Key Elements
Scope of Legal Singularity
Pace of Legal Singularity
Explainability of Legal Singularity
Alignment of Legal Singularity
Defeaters of Legal Singularity
Capability of Legal Singularity
Paradoxes of Legal Singularity
Cornerstone of Legal Singularity
Justice and Legal Singularity
Control of Legal Singularity
Social Outcome Legal Singularity
Legal Profession Legal Singularity
Figure 2: Legal Singularity – Multidimensionality
Source Author: Dr. Lance B. Eliot
V1.3

Figure 5

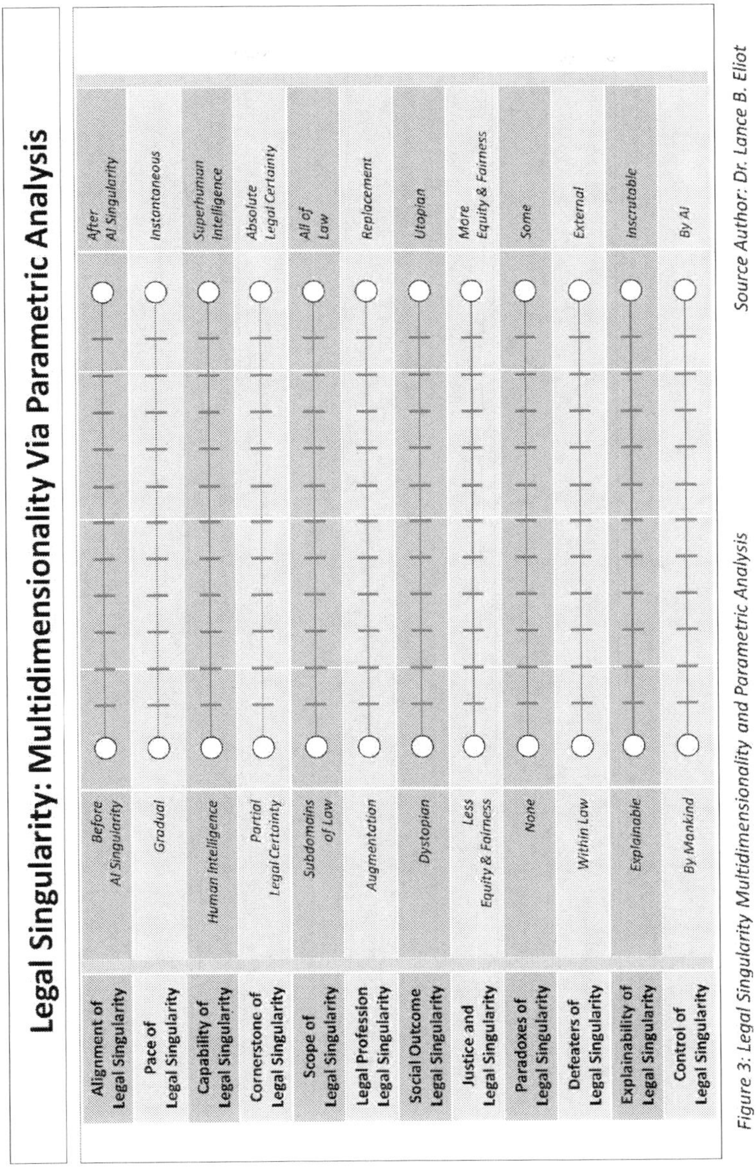
Legal Singularity: Multidimensionality Via Parametric Analysis
Alignment of Legal Singularity
Before AI Singularity
After AI Singularity
Pace of Legal Singularity
Gradual
Instantaneous
Capability of Legal Singularity
Human Intelligence
Superhuman Intelligence
Cornerstone of Legal Singularity
Partial Legal Certainty
Absolute Legal Certainty
Scope of Legal Singularity
Subdomains of Law
All of Law
Legal Profession Legal Singularity
Augmentation
Replacement
Social Outcome Legal Singularity
Dystopian
Utopian
Justice and Legal Singularity
Less Equity & Fairness
More Equity & Fairness
Paradoxes of Legal Singularity
None
Some
Defeaters of Legal Singularity
Within Law
External
Explainability of Legal Singularity
Explainable
Inscrutable
Control of Legal Singularity
By Mankind
By AI
Figure 3: Legal Singularity Multidimensionality and Parametric Analysis
Source Author: Dr. Lance B. Eliot

Figure 6

Legal Micro-Directives: Levels of Autonomy For AI Legal Reasoning (AILR)

	Level 0	Level 1	Level 2	Level 3	Level 4	Level 5	Level 6
Descriptor	No Automation	Simple Assistance Automation	Advanced Assistance Automation	Semi-Autonomous Automation	AILR Domain Autonomous	AILR Fully Autonomous	AILR Superhuman Autonomous
Examples	Manual, paper-based (no automation)	Word Processing, XLS, online legal docs, etc.	Query-style NLP, ML for case prediction, etc.	KBS & ML/DL for legal reasoning & analysis, etc.	Versed only in a specific legal domain	Versatile within and across all legal domains	Exceeds human-based legal reasoning
Automation	None	Legal Assist	Legal Assist	Legal Assist	Legal Advisor (law fluent)	Legal Advisor (law fluent)	Supra Legal Advisor
Status	De Facto – In Use	Widely In Use	Some In Use	Primarily Prototypes & Research-based	None As Yet	None As Yet	Indeterminate
AI-Enabled Legal Micro-Directives	*n/a*	*Impractical*	*Incubatory*	*Infancy*	*Narrow*	*Wide*	*Consummate*

Figure 1: Legal Micro-Directives - Autonomous Levels of AILR by Columns

Source Author: Dr. Lance B. Eliot

V1.3

Figure 7

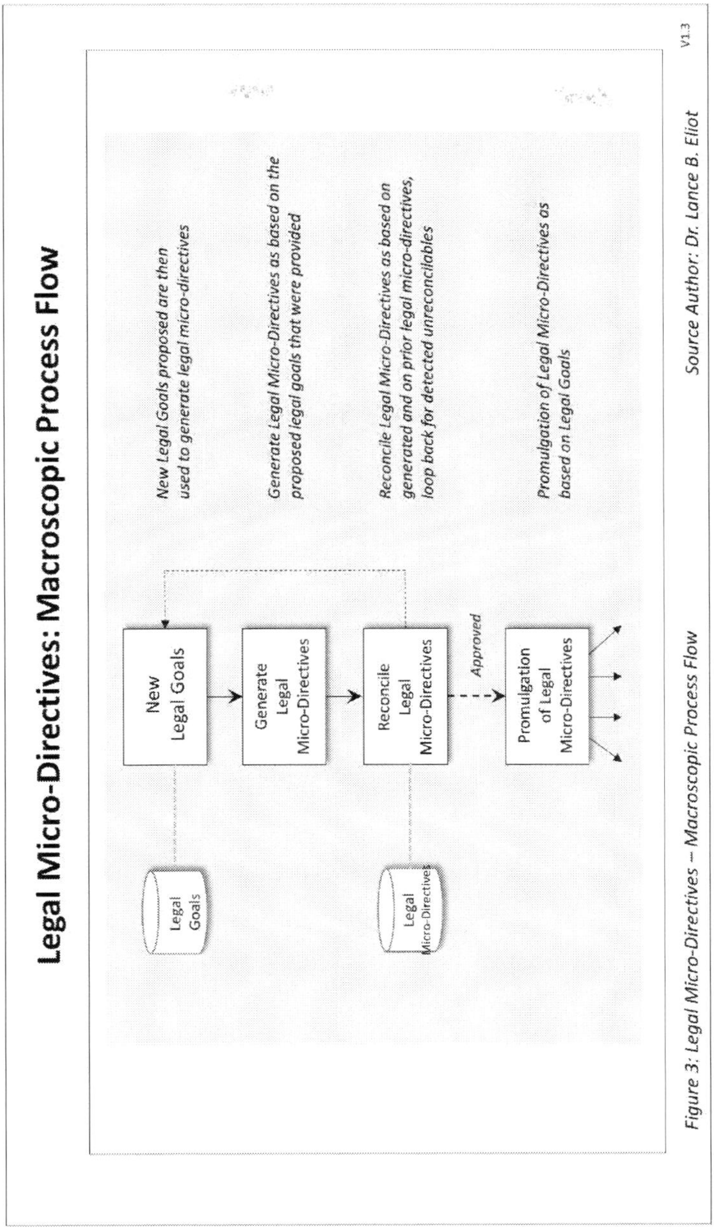
Legal Micro-Directives: Macroscopic Process Flow
Legal Goals
Legal Micro-Directives
New Legal Goals
Generate Legal Micro-Directives
Reconcile Legal Micro-Directives
Approved
Promulgation of Legal Micro-Directives
New Legal Goals proposed are then used to generate legal micro-directives
Generate Legal Micro-Directives as based on the proposed legal goals that were provided
Reconcile Legal Micro-Directives as based on generated and on prior legal micro-directives, loop back for detected unreconcilables
Promulgation of Legal Micro-Directives as based on Legal Goals
Figure 3: Legal Micro-Directives – Macroscopic Process Flow
Source Author: Dr. Lance B. Eliot
V1.3

Figure 8

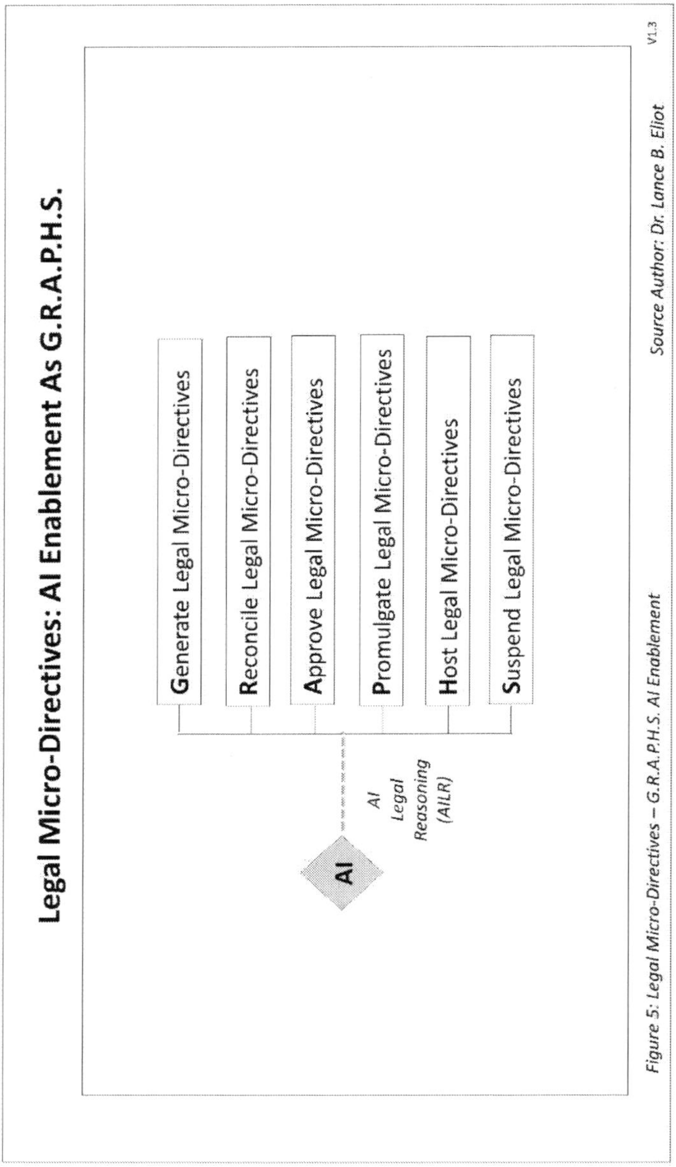
Legal Micro-Directives: AI Enablement As G.R.A.P.H.S.
AI
AI Legal Reasoning (AILR)
Generate Legal Micro-Directives
Reconcile Legal Micro-Directives
Approve Legal Micro-Directives
Promulgate Legal Micro-Directives
Host Legal Micro-Directives
Suspend Legal Micro-Directives
Figure 5: Legal Micro-Directives – G.R.A.P.H.S. AI Enablement
Source Author: Dr. Lance B. Eliot
V1.3

Figure 9

Legal Argumentation: Levels of Autonomy For AI Legal Reasoning (AILR)

	Level 0	Level 1	Level 2	Level 3	Level 4	Level 5	Level 6
Descriptor	No Automation	Simple Assistance Automation	Advanced Assistance Automation	Semi-Autonomous Automation	AILR Domain Autonomous	AILR Fully Autonomous	AILR Superhuman Autonomous
Examples	Manual, paper-based (no automation)	Word Processing, XLS, online legal docs, etc.	Query-style NLP, ML for case prediction, etc.	KBS & ML/DL for legal reasoning & analysis, etc.	Versed only in a specific legal domain	Versatile within and across all legal domains	Exceeds human-based legal reasoning
Automation	None	Legal Assist	Legal Assist	Legal Assist	Legal Advisor (law fluent)	Legal Advisor (law fluent)	Supra Legal Advisor
Status	De Facto – In Use	Widely In Use	Some In Use	Primarily Prototypes & Research-based	None As Yet	None As Yet	Indeterminate
AI-Enabled Legal Argumentation	*n/a*	*Mechanistic (Low)*	*Mechanistic (High)*	*Expressive*	*Domain Fluency*	*Full Fluency*	*Meta-Fluency*

Figure 7: AI Legal Argumentation (AILA) - Autonomous Levels of AILR by Columns

Source Author: Dr. Lance B. Eliot

V1.3

Figure 10

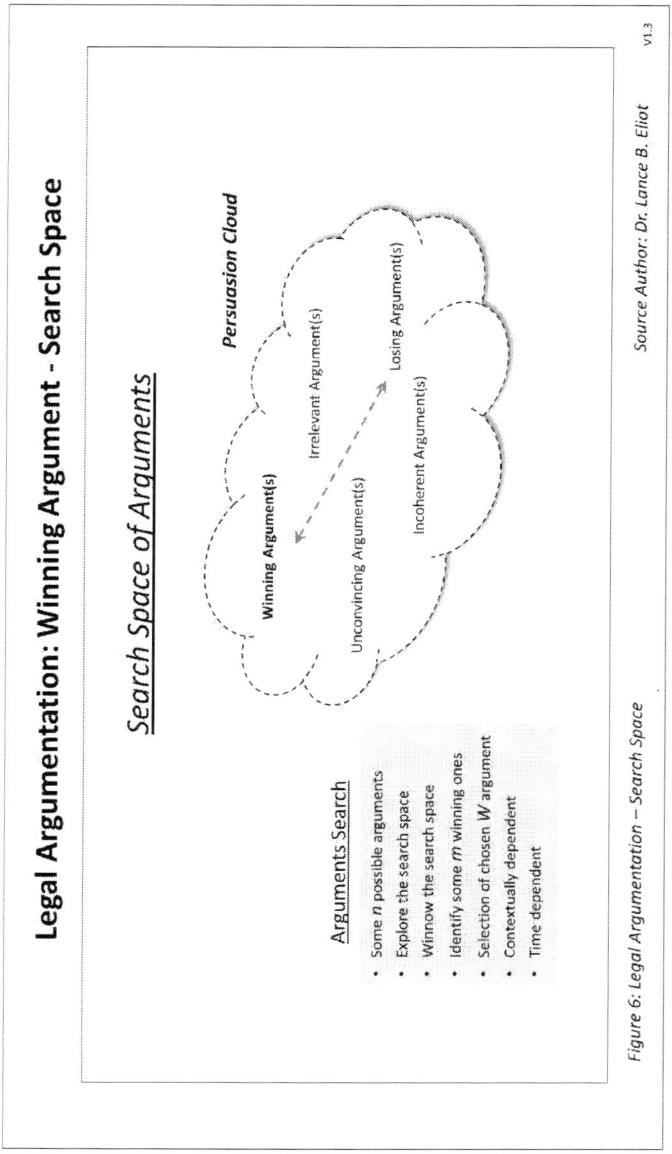
Legal Argumentation: Winning Argument - Search Space
Search Space of Arguments
Persuasion Cloud
Winning Argument(s)
Irrelevant Argument(s)
Losing Argument(s)
Unconvincing Argument(s)
Incoherent Argument(s)
Arguments Search
Some n possible arguments
Explore the search space
Winnow the search space
Identify some m winning ones
Selection of chosen W argument
Contextually dependent
Time dependent
Figure 6: Legal Argumentation – Search Space
Source Author: Dr. Lance B. Eliot
V1.3

Figure 11

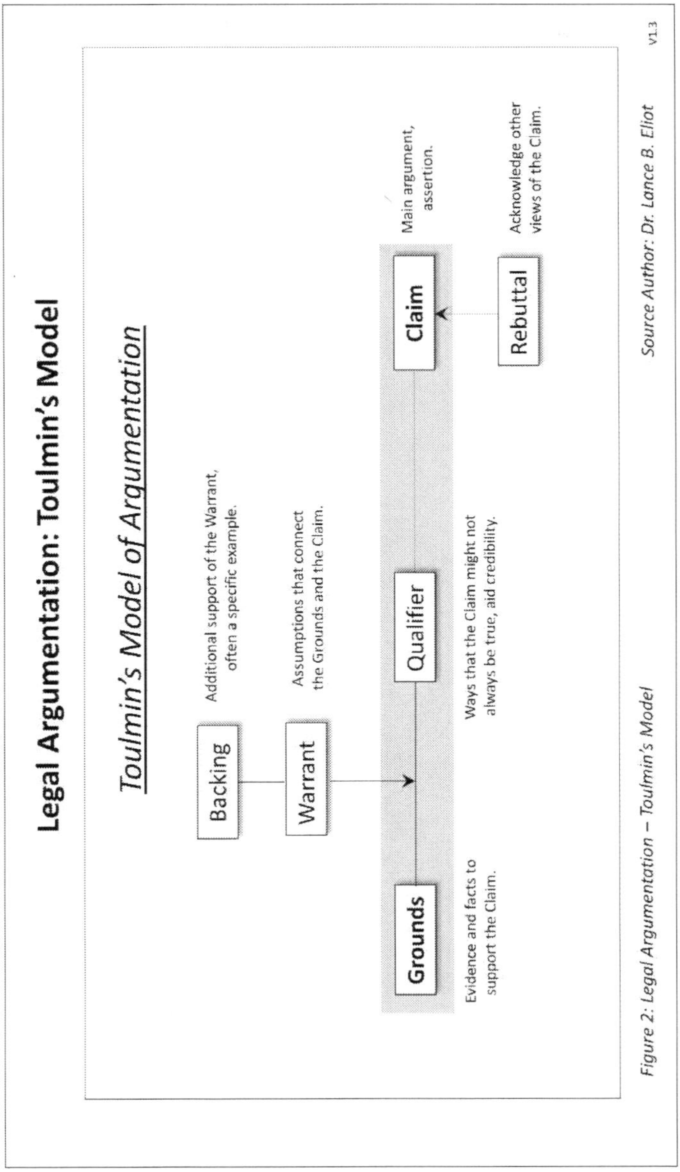
Legal Argumentation: Toulmin's Model
Toulmin's Model of Argumentation
Backing
Additional support of the Warrant, often a specific example.
Warrant
Assumptions that connect the Grounds and the Claim.
Grounds
Evidence and facts to support the Claim.
Qualifier
Ways that the Claim might not always be true, aid credibility.
Claim
Main argument, assertion.
Rebuttal
Acknowledge other views of the Claim.
Figure 2: Legal Argumentation – Toulmin's Model
Source Author: Dr. Lance B. Eliot
V1.3

Figure 12

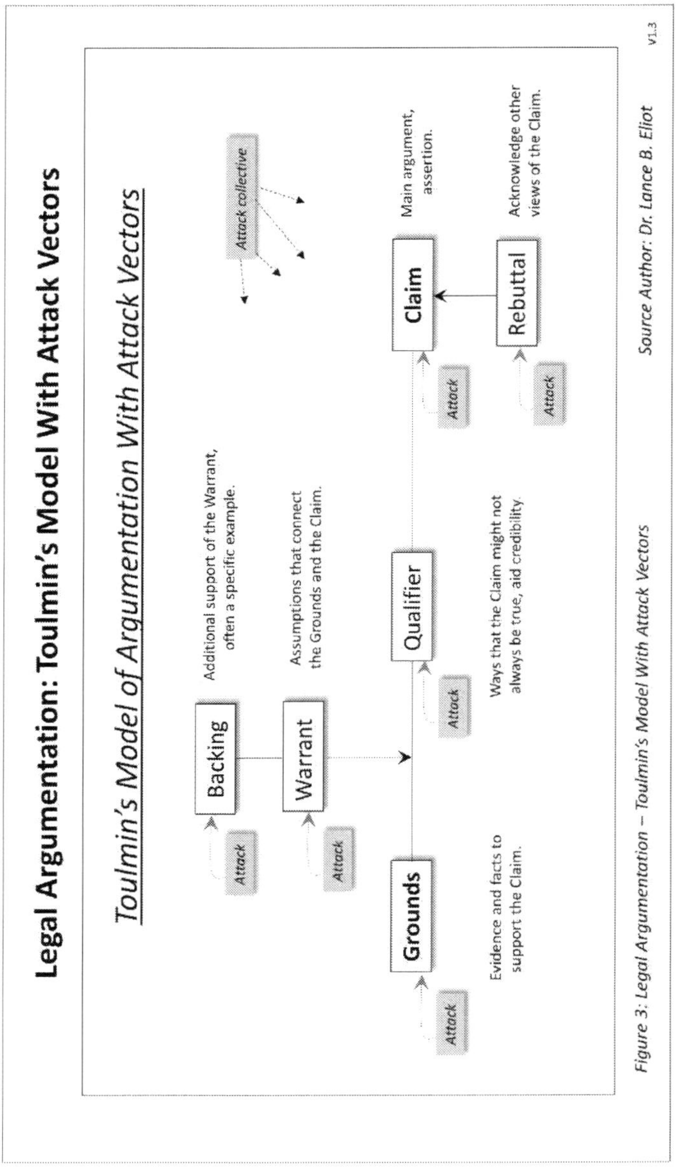
Legal Argumentation: Toulmin's Model With Attack Vectors
Toulmin's Model of Argumentation With Attack Vectors
Attack collective
Backing
Additional support of the Warrant, often a specific example.
Warrant
Assumptions that connect the Grounds and the Claim.
Grounds
Evidence and facts to support the Claim.
Qualifier
Ways that the Claim might not always be true, aid credibility.
Claim
Main argument, assertion.
Rebuttal
Acknowledge other views of the Claim.
Attack
Attack
Attack
Attack
Attack
Attack
Figure 3: Legal Argumentation – Toulmin's Model With Attack Vectors
Source Author: Dr. Lance B. Eliot
V1.3

Figure 13

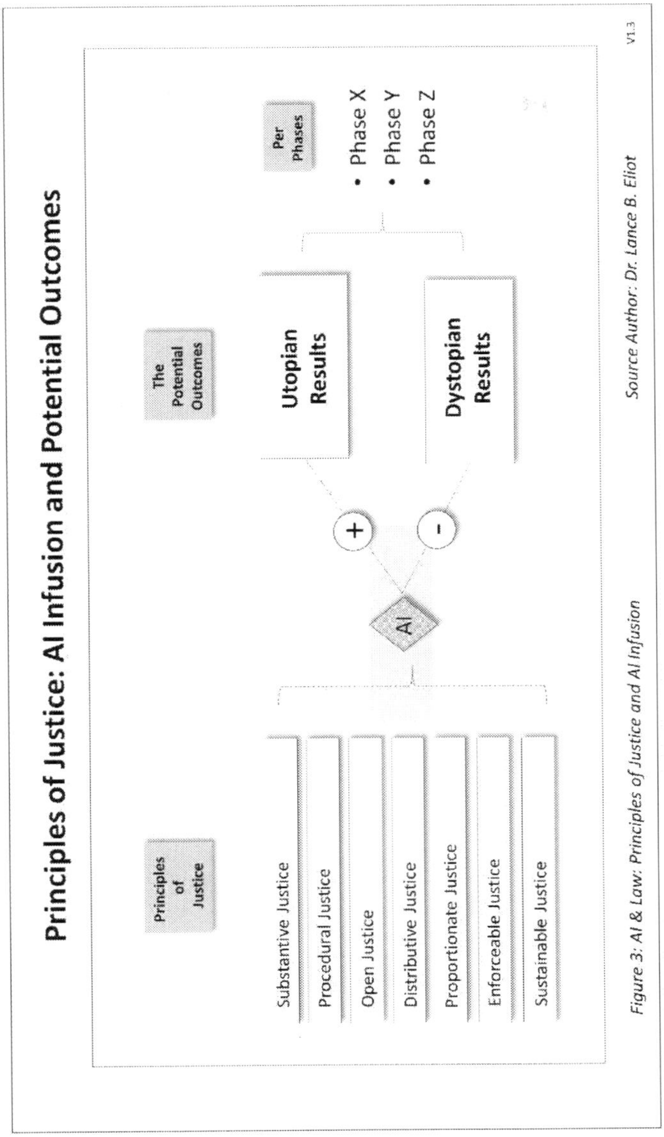
Principles of Justice: AI Infusion and Potential Outcomes
Principles of Justice
The Potential Outcomes
Per Phases
Substantive Justice
Procedural Justice
Open Justice
Distributive Justice
Proportionate Justice
Enforceable Justice
Sustainable Justice
AI
+
-
Utopian Results
Dystopian Results
• Phase X
• Phase Y
• Phase Z
V1.3
Figure 3: AI & Law: Principles of Justice and AI Infusion
Source Author: Dr. Lance B. Eliot

Figure 14

Principles of Justice and Autonomous Levels of AI Legal Reasoning (AILR)

	Level 0	Level 1	Level 2	Level 3	Level 4	Level 5	Level 6
Descriptor	No Automation	Simple Assistance Automation	Advanced Assistance Automation	Semi-Autonomous Automation	AILR Domain Autonomous	AILR Fully Autonomous	AILR Superhuman Autonomous
Substantive Justice	*Traditional*	*Traditional*	*Traditional*	Emerging	Phase X Impacts	Phase Y Impacts	Phase Z Impacts
Procedural Justice	*Traditional*	*Traditional*	*Traditional*	Emerging	Phase X Impacts	Phase Y Impacts	Phase Z Impacts
Open Justice	*Traditional*	*Traditional*	*Traditional*	Emerging	Phase X Impacts	Phase Y Impacts	Phase Z Impacts
Distributive Justice	*Traditional*	*Traditional*	*Traditional*	Emerging	Phase X Impacts	Phase Y Impacts	Phase Z Impacts
Proportionate Justice	*Traditional*	*Traditional*	*Traditional*	Emerging	Phase X Impacts	Phase Y Impacts	Phase Z Impacts
Enforceable Justice	*Traditional*	*Traditional*	*Traditional*	Emerging	Phase X Impacts	Phase Y Impacts	Phase Z Impacts
Sustainable Justice	*Traditional*	*Traditional*	*Traditional*	Emerging	Phase X Impacts	Phase Y Impacts	Phase Z Impacts

Figure 1: AI & Law – Principles of Justice and LoA AILR by Columns

Source Author: Dr. Lance B. Eliot

V1.3

Figure 15

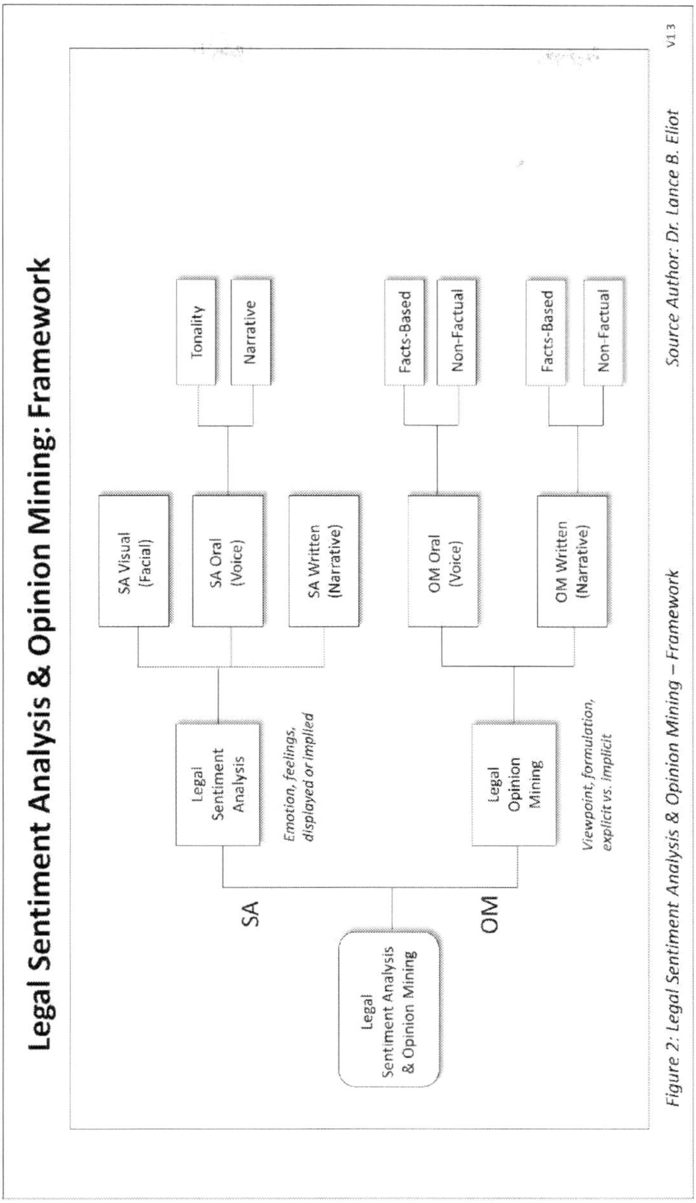
Legal Sentiment Analysis & Opinion Mining: Framework
Legal Sentiment Analysis & Opinion Mining
SA
OM
Legal Sentiment Analysis
Emotion, feelings, displayed or implied
Legal Opinion Mining
Viewpoint, formulation, explicit vs. implicit
SA Visual (Facial)
SA Oral (Voice)
SA Written (Narrative)
OM Oral (Voice)
OM Written (Narrative)
Tonality
Narrative
Facts-Based
Non-Factual
Facts-Based
Non-Factual
Figure 2: Legal Sentiment Analysis & Opinion Mining – Framework
Source Author: Dr. Lance B. Eliot
V13

Figure 16

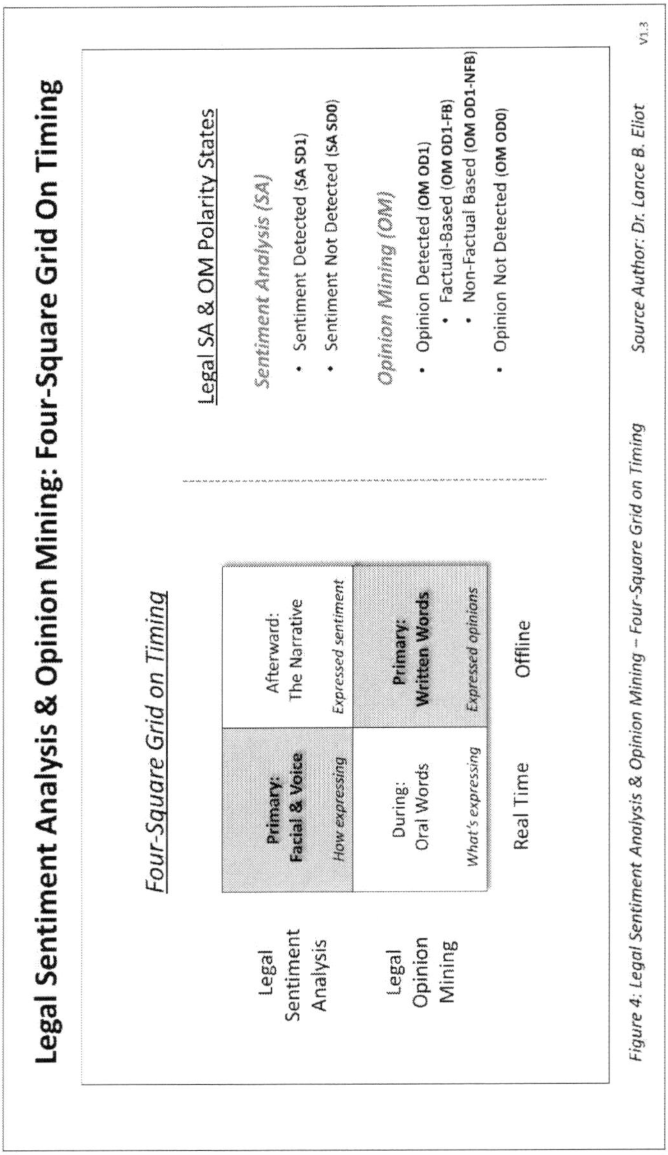
Legal Sentiment Analysis & Opinion Mining: Four-Square Grid On Timing
Four-Square Grid on Timing
Legal Sentiment Analysis
Legal Opinion Mining
Primary: Facial & Voice
How expressing
Afterward: The Narrative
Expressed sentiment
During: Oral Words
What's expressing
Primary: Written Words
Expressed opinions
Real Time
Offline
Legal SA & OM Polarity States
Sentiment Analysis (SA)
• Sentiment Detected (SA SD1)
• Sentiment Not Detected (SA SD0)
Opinion Mining (OM)
• Opinion Detected (OM OD1)
• Factual-Based (OM OD1-FB)
• Non-Factual Based (OM OD1-NFB)
• Opinion Not Detected (OM OD0)
Figure 4: Legal Sentiment Analysis & Opinion Mining – Four-Square Grid on Timing
Source Author: Dr. Lance B. Eliot
V1.3

Figure 17

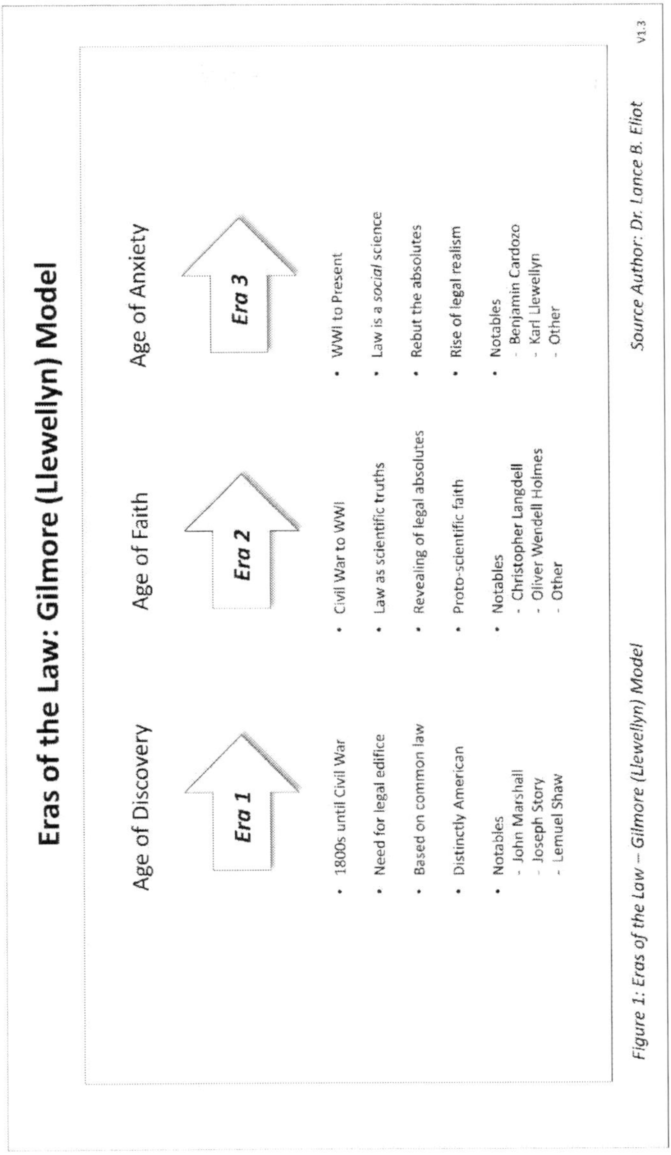
Eras of the Law: Gilmore (Llewellyn) Model
Age of Discovery
Era 1
1800s until Civil War
Need for legal edifice
Based on common law
Distinctly American
Notables
- John Marshall
- Joseph Story
- Lemuel Shaw
Age of Faith
Era 2
Civil War to WWI
Law as scientific truths
Revealing of legal absolutes
Proto-scientific faith
Notables
- Christopher Langdell
- Oliver Wendell Holmes
- Other
Age of Anxiety
Era 3
WWI to Present
Law is a social science
Rebut the absolutes
Rise of legal realism
Notables
- Benjamin Cardozo
- Karl Llewellyn
- Other
Figure 1: Eras of the Law -- Gilmore (Llewellyn) Model
Source Author: Dr. Lance B. Eliot
V1.3

Figure 18

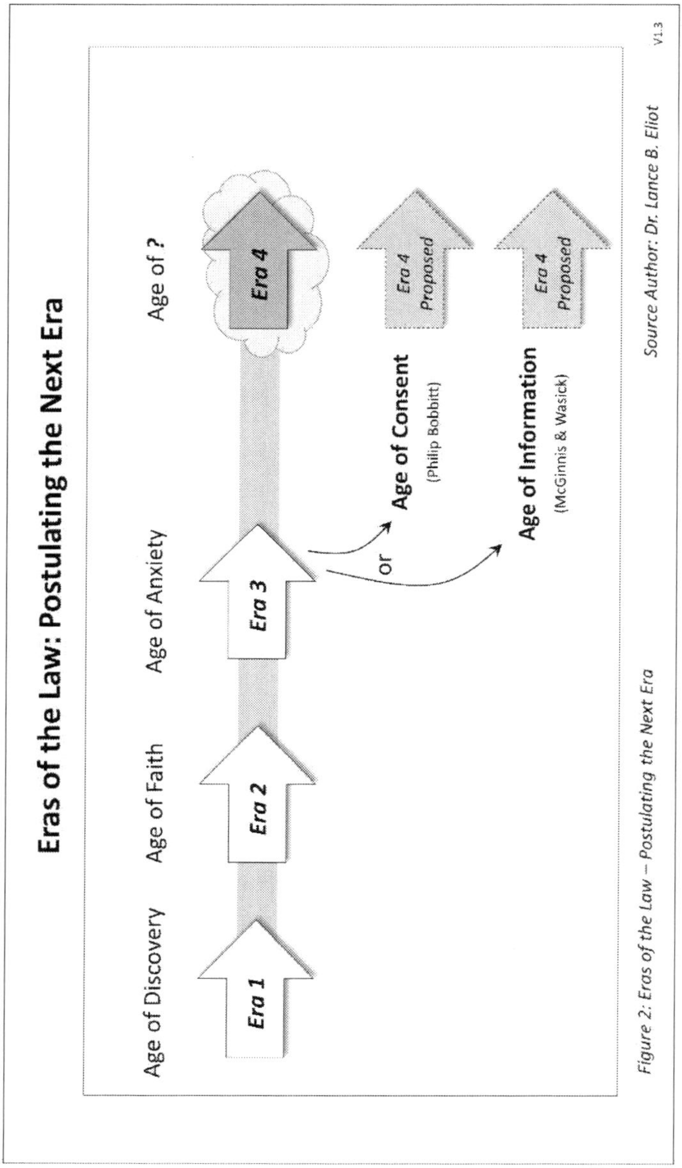
Eras of the Law: Postulating the Next Era
Age of Discovery
Age of Faith
Age of Anxiety
Age of ?
Era 1
Era 2
Era 3
Era 4
or
Age of Consent
(Philip Bobbitt)
Era 4
Proposed
Age of Information
(McGinnis & Wasick)
Era 4
Proposed
Figure 2: Eras of the Law – Postulating the Next Era
Source Author: Dr. Lance B. Eliot
V1.3

Figure 19

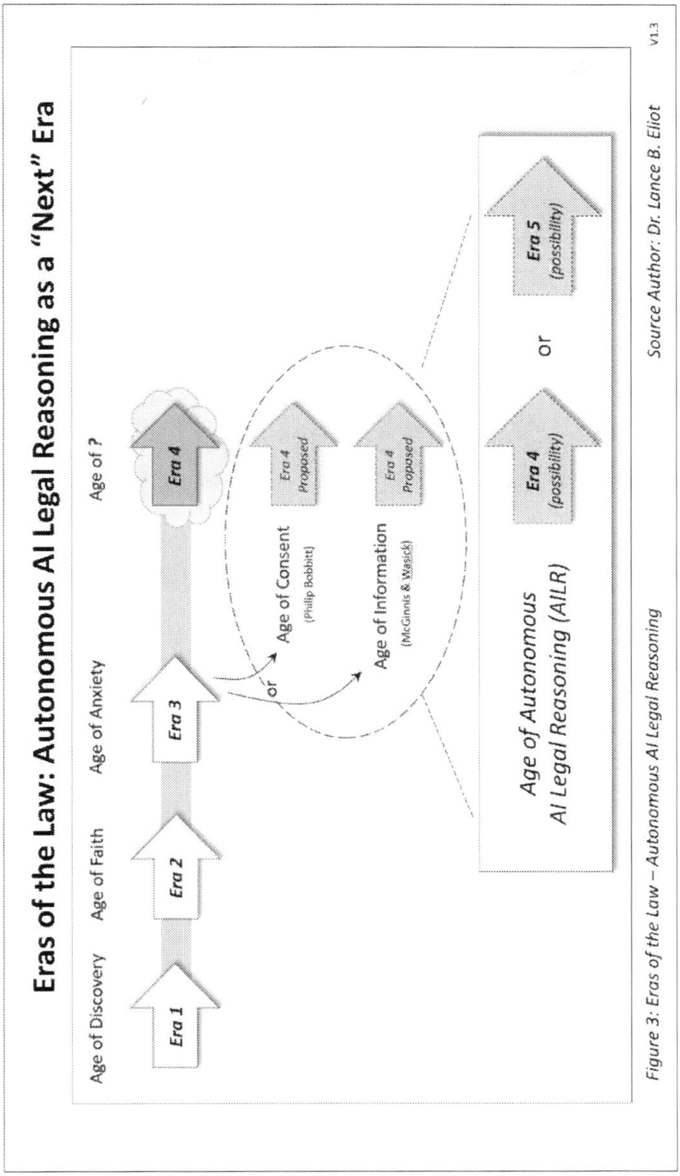

Figure 3: Eras of the Law – Autonomous AI Legal Reasoning

Figure 20

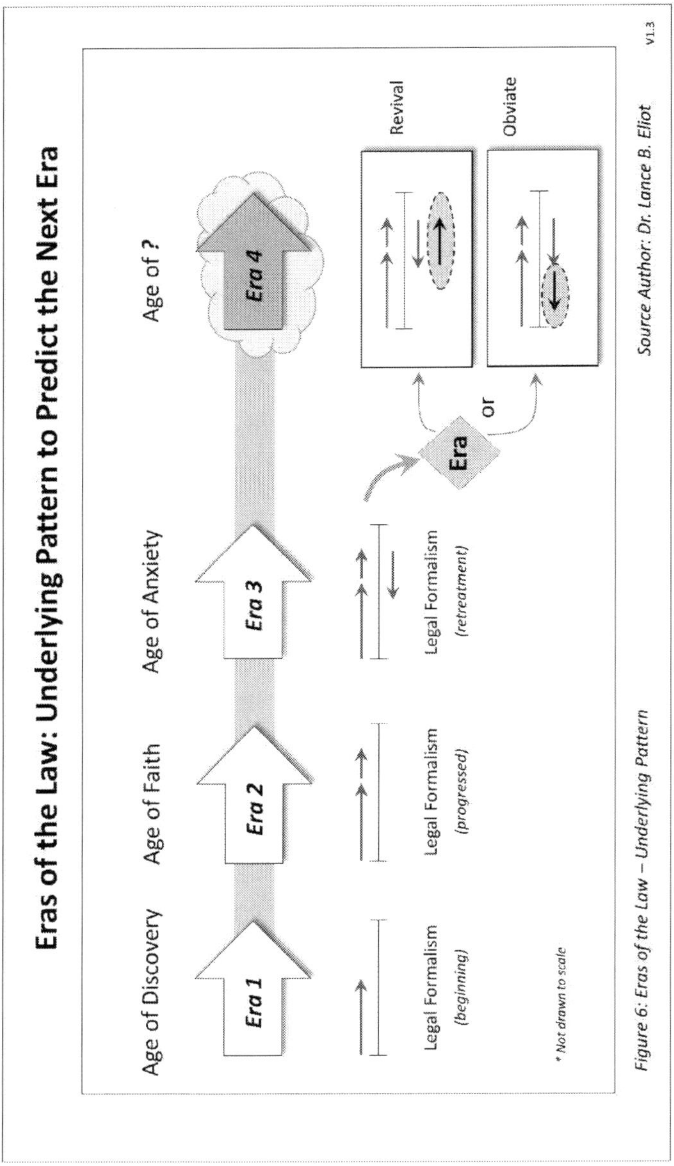
Eras of the Law: Underlying Pattern to Predict the Next Era
Age of Discovery
Age of Faith
Age of Anxiety
Age of ?
Era 1
Era 2
Era 3
Era 4
Legal Formalism
(beginning)
Legal Formalism
(progressed)
Legal Formalism
(retreatment)
Era
or
Revival
Obviate
* Not drawn to scale
Figure 6: Eras of the Law – Underlying Pattern
Source Author: Dr. Lance B. Eliot
V1.3

Figure 21

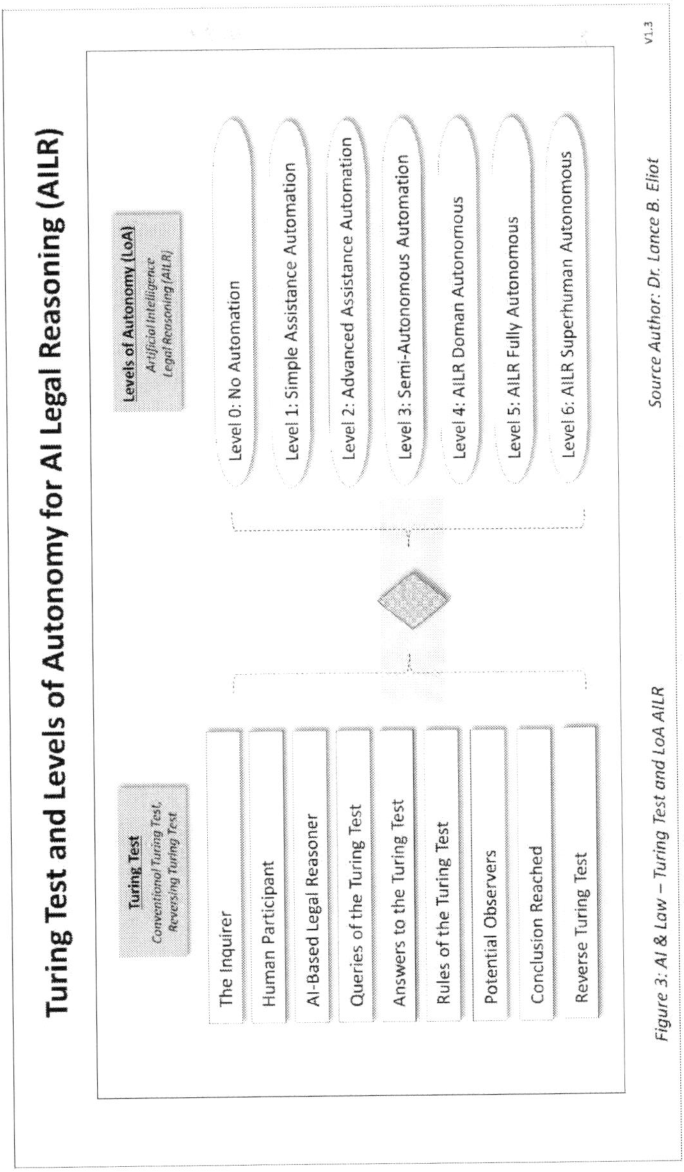
Turing Test and Levels of Autonomy for AI Legal Reasoning (AILR)
Turing Test
Conventional Turing Test, Reversing Turing Test
The Inquirer
Human Participant
AI-Based Legal Reasoner
Queries of the Turing Test
Answers to the Turing Test
Rules of the Turing Test
Potential Observers
Conclusion Reached
Reverse Turing Test
Levels of Autonomy (LoA)
Artificial Intelligence Legal Reasoning (AILR)
Level 0: No Automation
Level 1: Simple Assistance Automation
Level 2: Advanced Assistance Automation
Level 3: Semi-Autonomous Automation
Level 4: AILR Domain Autonomous
Level 5: AILR Fully Autonomous
Level 6: AILR Superhuman Autonomous
Figure 3: AI & Law – Turing Test and LoA AILR
Source Author: Dr. Lance B. Eliot
V1.3

Figure 22

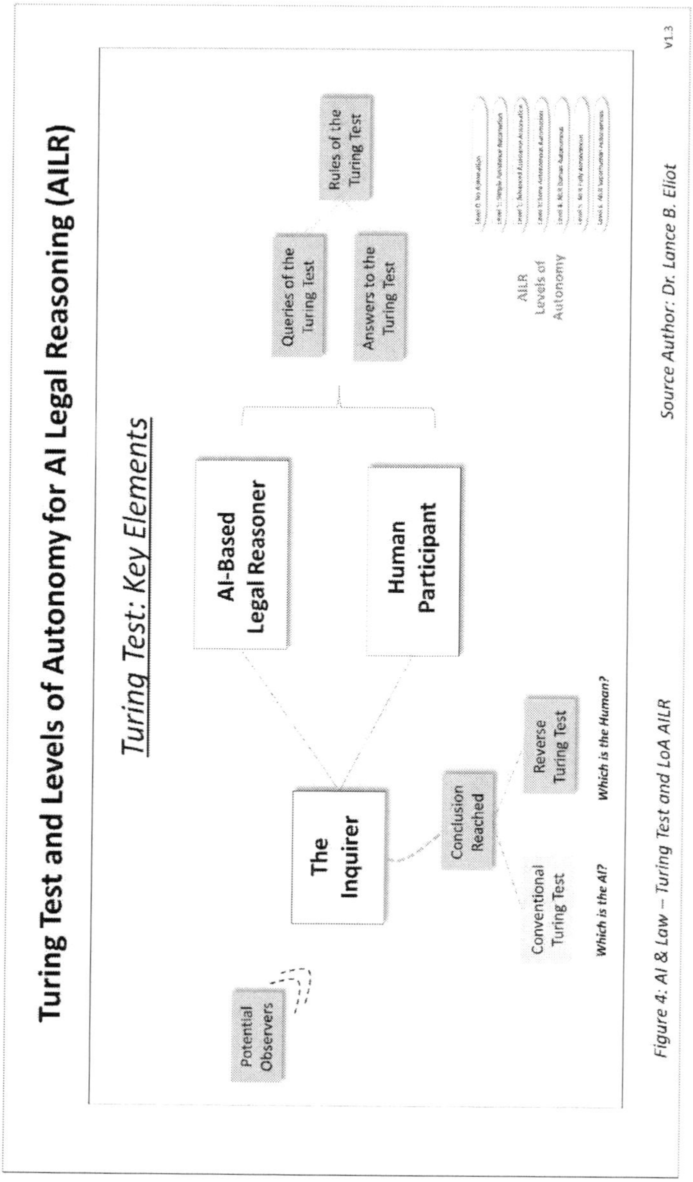
Turing Test and Levels of Autonomy for AI Legal Reasoning (AILR)
Turing Test: Key Elements
Potential Observers
The Inquirer
AI-Based Legal Reasoner
Human Participant
Queries of the Turing Test
Answers to the Turing Test
Rules of the Turing Test
Conclusion Reached
Conventional Turing Test
Reverse Turing Test
Which is the AI?
Which is the Human?
AILR Levels of Autonomy
V1.3
Figure 4: AI & Law -- Turing Test and LoA AILR
Source Author: Dr. Lance B. Eliot

Figure 23

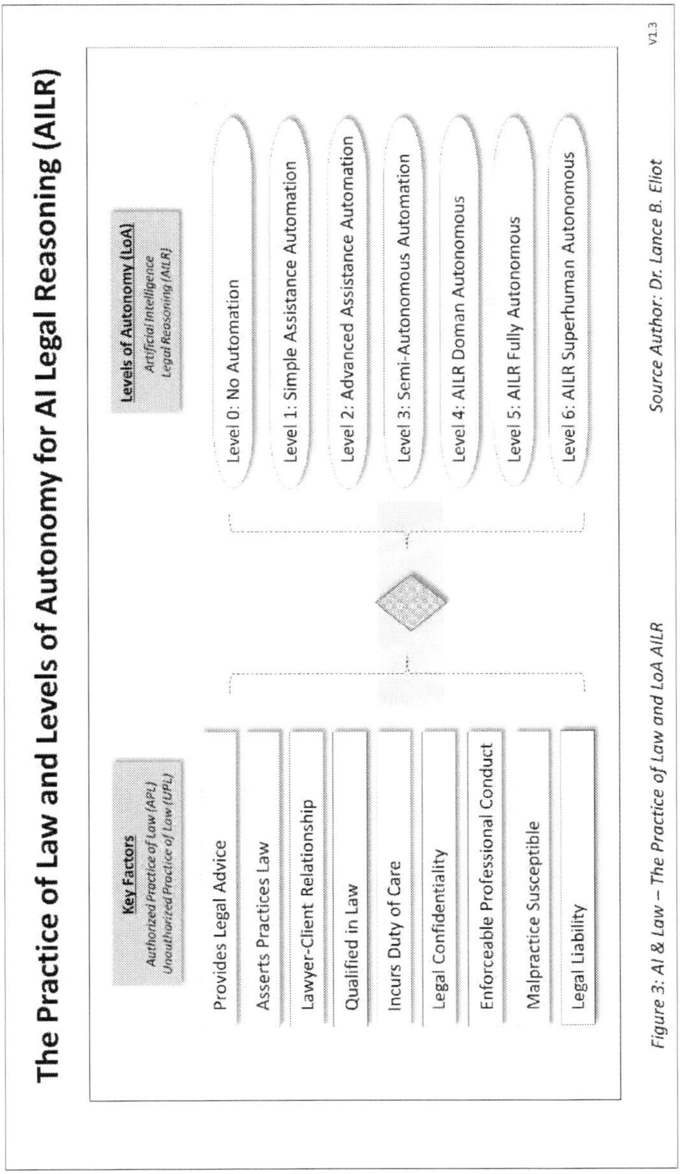
The Practice of Law and Levels of Autonomy for AI Legal Reasoning (AILR)
Key Factors
Authorized Practice of Law (APL)
Unauthorized Practice of Law (UPL)
Provides Legal Advice
Asserts Practices Law
Lawyer-Client Relationship
Qualified in Law
Incurs Duty of Care
Legal Confidentiality
Enforceable Professional Conduct
Malpractice Susceptible
Legal Liability
Levels of Autonomy (LoA)
Artificial Intelligence
Legal Reasoning (AILR)
Level 0: No Automation
Level 1: Simple Assistance Automation
Level 2: Advanced Assistance Automation
Level 3: Semi-Autonomous Automation
Level 4: AILR Doman Autonomous
Level 5: AILR Fully Autonomous
Level 6: AILR Superhuman Autonomous
Figure 3: AI & Law – The Practice of Law and LoA AILR
Source Author: Dr. Lance B. Eliot
V1.3

Figure 24

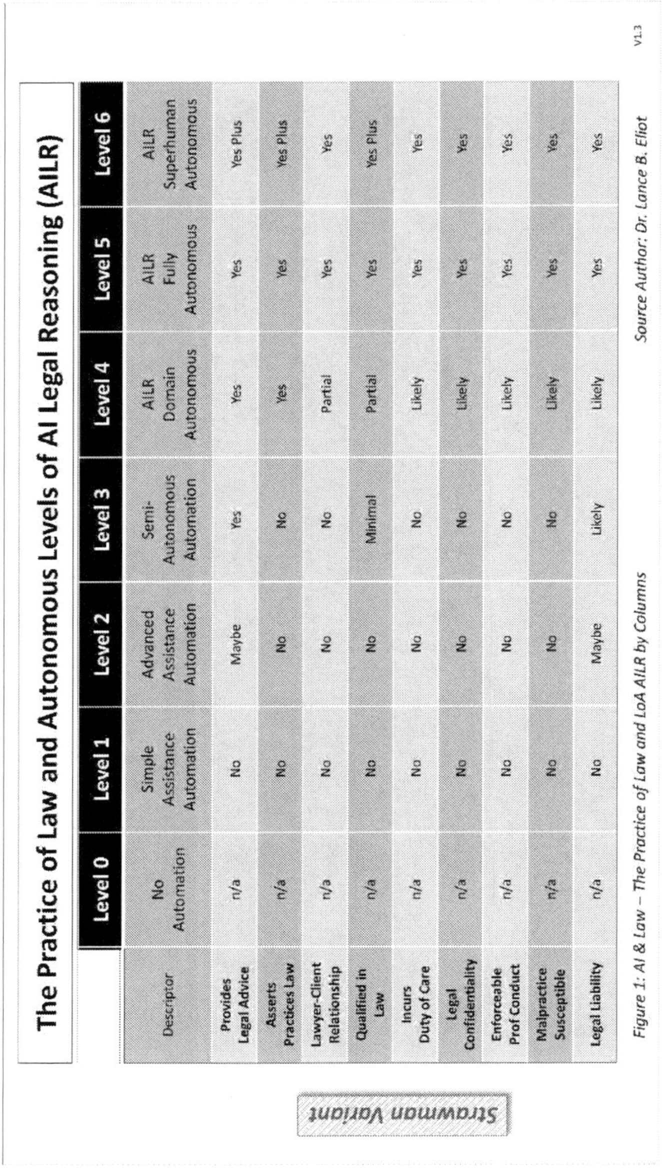

The Practice of Law and Autonomous Levels of AI Legal Reasoning (AILR)

Descriptor	Level 0	Level 1	Level 2	Level 3	Level 4	Level 5	Level 6
	No Automation	Simple Assistance Automation	Advanced Assistance Automation	Semi-Autonomous Automation	AILR Domain Autonomous	AILR Fully Autonomous	AILR Superhuman Autonomous
Provides Legal Advice	n/a	No	Maybe	Yes	Yes	Yes	Yes Plus
Asserts Practices Law	n/a	No	No	No	Yes	Yes	Yes Plus
Lawyer-Client Relationship	n/a	No	No	No	Partial	Yes	Yes
Qualified in Law	n/a	No	No	Minimal	Partial	Yes	Yes Plus
Incurs Duty of Care	n/a	No	No	No	Likely	Yes	Yes
Legal Confidentiality	n/a	No	No	No	Likely	Yes	Yes
Enforceable Prof Conduct	n/a	No	No	No	Likely	Yes	Yes
Malpractice Susceptible	n/a	No	No	No	Likely	Yes	Yes
Legal Liability	n/a	No	Maybe	Likely	Likely	Yes	Yes

Figure 1: AI & Law – The Practice of Law and LoA AILR by Columns

Source Author: Dr. Lance B. Eliot

Figure 25

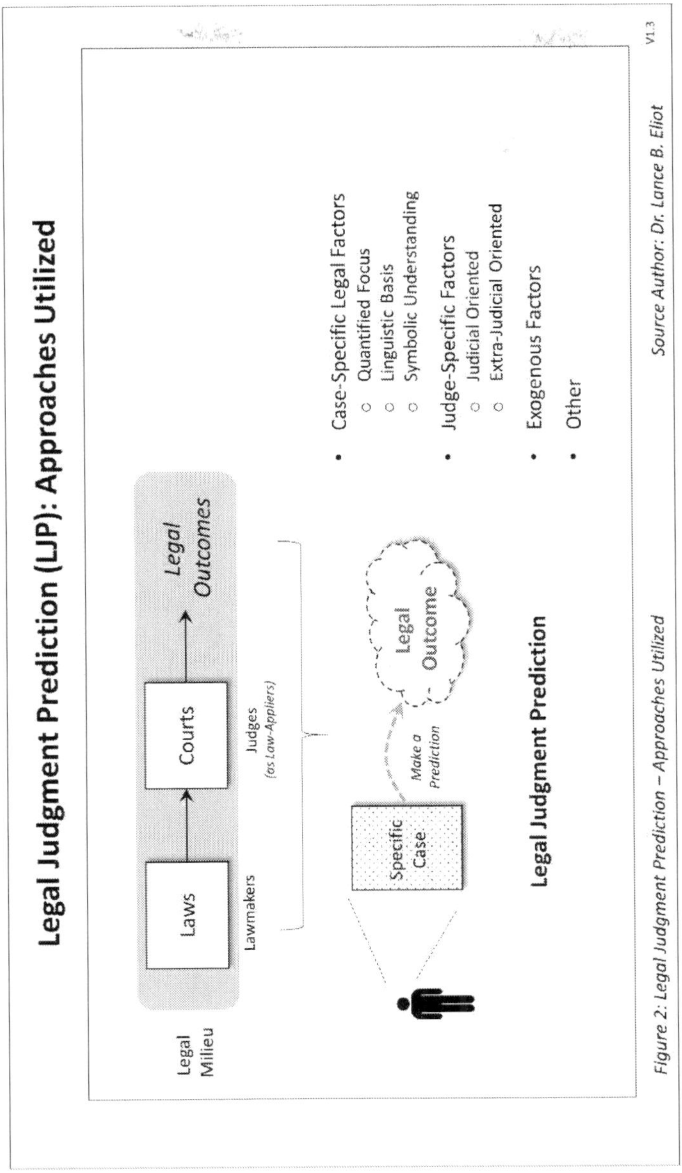
Legal Judgment Prediction (LJP): Approaches Utilized
Legal Milieu
Laws
Courts
Legal Outcomes
Lawmakers
Judges
(as Law-Appliers)
Specific Case
Make a Prediction
Legal Outcome
Legal Judgment Prediction
• Case-Specific Legal Factors
○ Quantified Focus
○ Linguistic Basis
○ Symbolic Understanding
• Judge-Specific Factors
○ Judicial Oriented
○ Extra-Judicial Oriented
• Exogenous Factors
• Other
Figure 2: Legal Judgment Prediction – Approaches Utilized
Source Author: Dr. Lance B. Eliot
V1.3

Figure 26

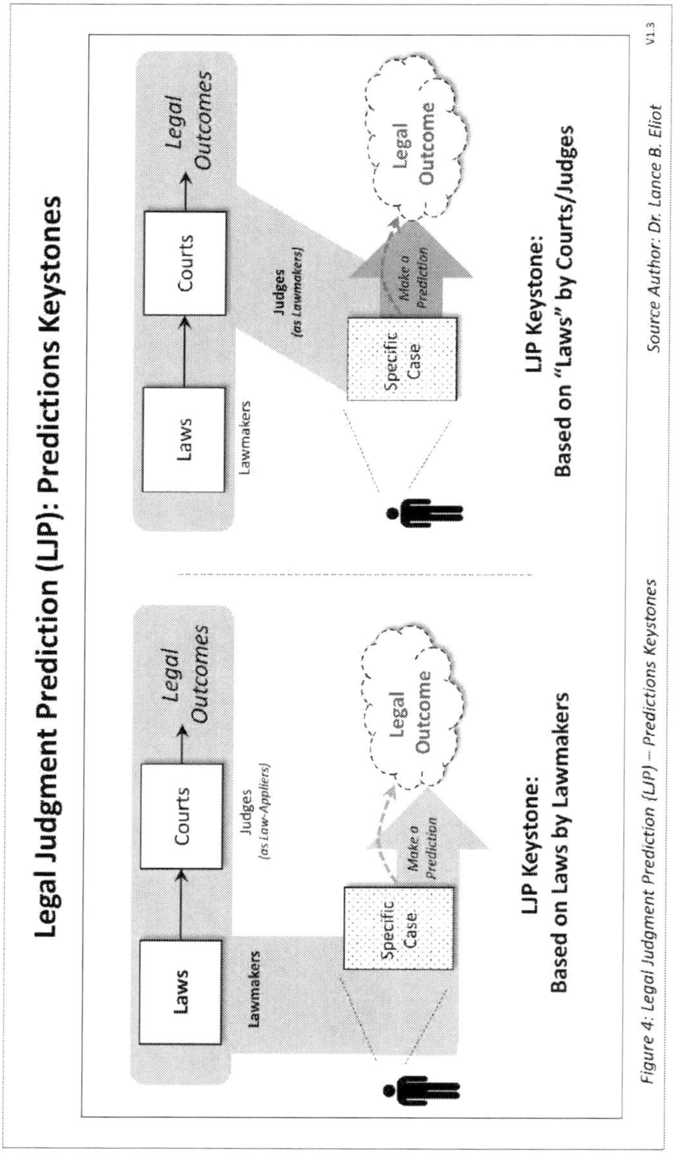
Legal Judgment Prediction (LJP): Predictions Keystones
Laws
Courts
Legal Outcomes
Lawmakers
Judges (as Law-Appliers)
Specific Case
Make a Prediction
Legal Outcome
LJP Keystone: Based on Laws by Lawmakers
Laws
Courts
Legal Outcomes
Lawmakers
Judges (as Lawmakers)
Specific Case
Make a Prediction
Legal Outcome
LJP Keystone: Based on "Laws" by Courts/Judges
Figure 4: Legal Judgment Prediction (LJP) – Predictions Keystones
Source Author: Dr. Lance B. Eliot
V1.3

Figure 27

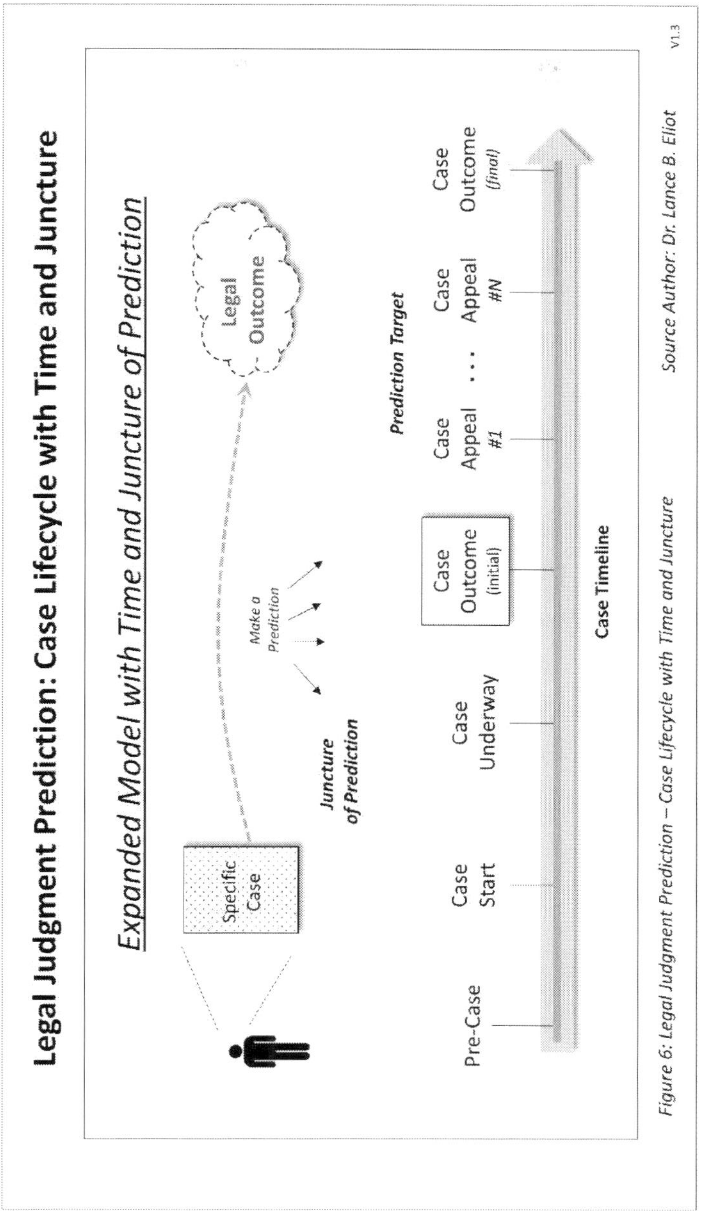
Legal Judgment Prediction: Case Lifecycle with Time and Juncture
Expanded Model with Time and Juncture of Prediction
Specific Case
Legal Outcome
Make a Prediction
Juncture of Prediction
Prediction Target
Pre-Case
Case Start
Case Underway
Case Outcome (initial)
Case Appeal #1
. . .
Case Appeal #N
Case Outcome (final)
Case Timeline
Figure 6: Legal Judgment Prediction – Case Lifecycle with Time and Juncture
Source Author: Dr. Lance B. Eliot
V1.3

Figure 28

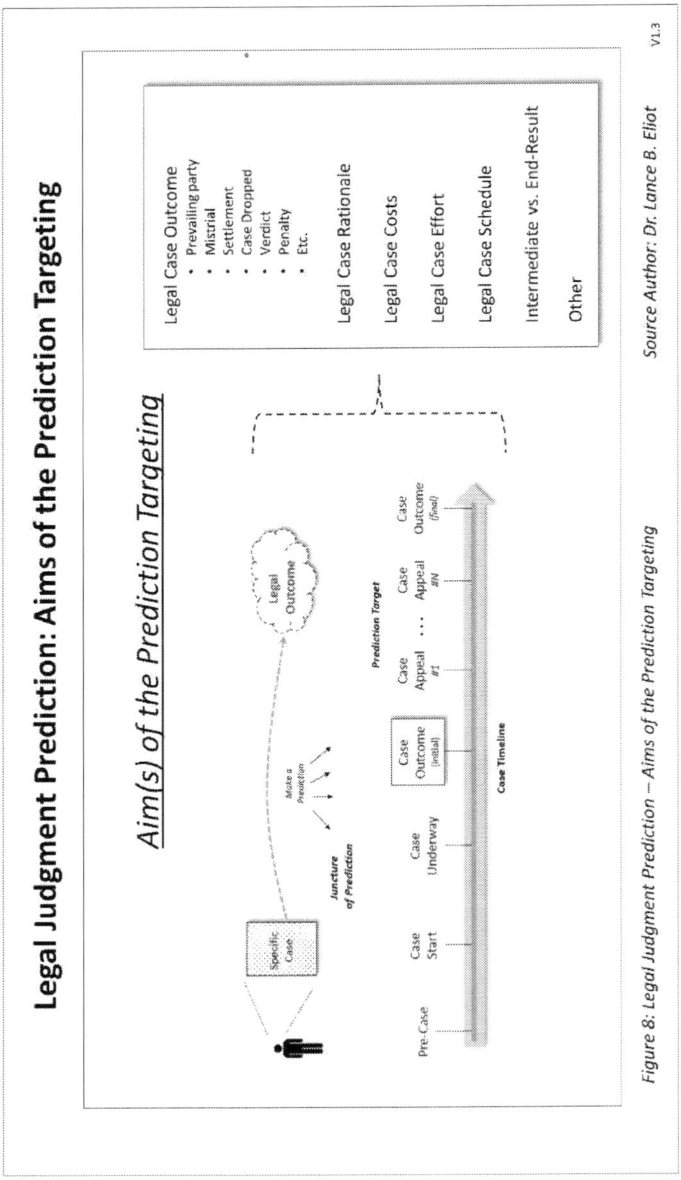
Legal Judgment Prediction: Aims of the Prediction Targeting
Aim(s) of the Prediction Targeting
Specific Case
Legal Outcome
Juncture of Prediction
Make a Prediction
Prediction Target
Pre-Case
Case Start
Case Underway
Case Outcome (initial)
Case Appeal #1
. . .
Case Appeal #N
Case Outcome (final)
Case Timeline
Legal Case Outcome
• Prevailing party
• Mistrial
• Settlement
• Case Dropped
• Verdict
• Penalty
• Etc.
Legal Case Rationale
Legal Case Costs
Legal Case Effort
Legal Case Schedule
Intermediate vs. End-Result
Other
Figure 8: Legal Judgment Prediction -- Aims of the Prediction Targeting
Source Author: Dr. Lance B. Eliot
V1.3

Figure 29

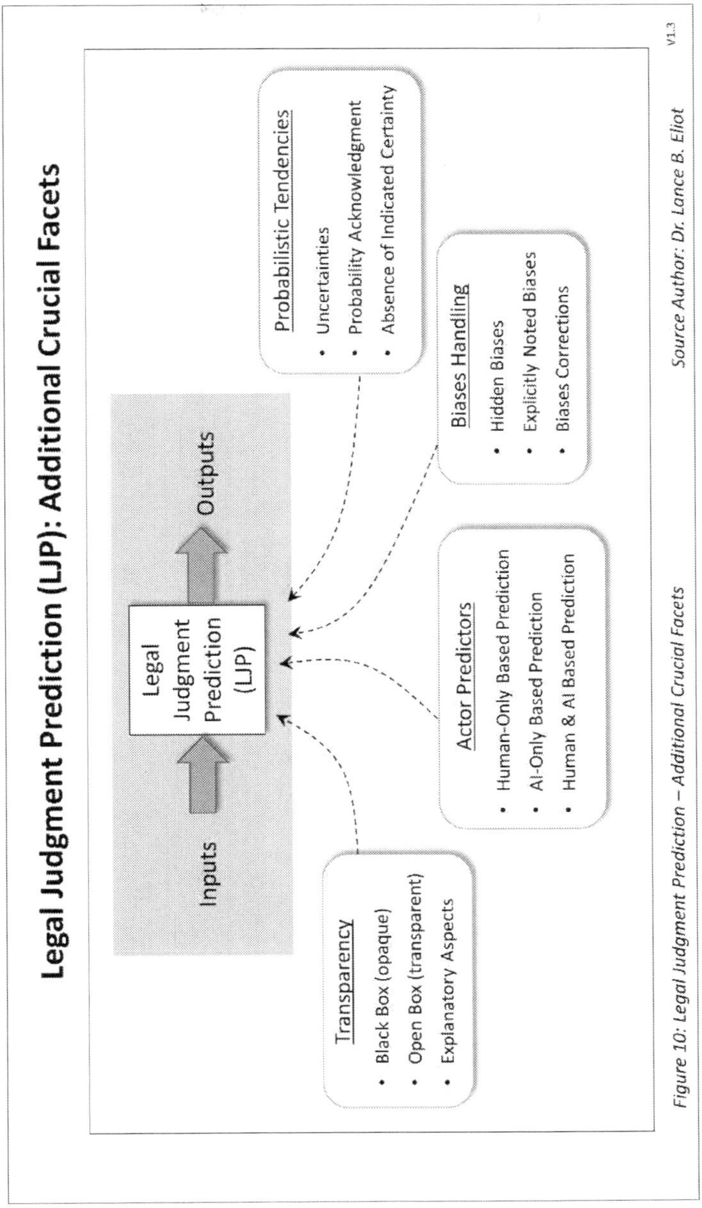
Legal Judgment Prediction (LJP): Additional Crucial Facets
Inputs
Legal Judgment Prediction (LJP)
Outputs
Probabilistic Tendencies
Uncertainties
Probability Acknowledgment
Absence of Indicated Certainty
Biases Handling
Hidden Biases
Explicitly Noted Biases
Biases Corrections
Actor Predictors
Human-Only Based Prediction
AI-Only Based Prediction
Human & AI Based Prediction
Transparency
Black Box (opaque)
Open Box (transparent)
Explanatory Aspects
V1.3
Figure 10: Legal Judgment Prediction – Additional Crucial Facets
Source Author: Dr. Lance B. Eliot

Figure 30

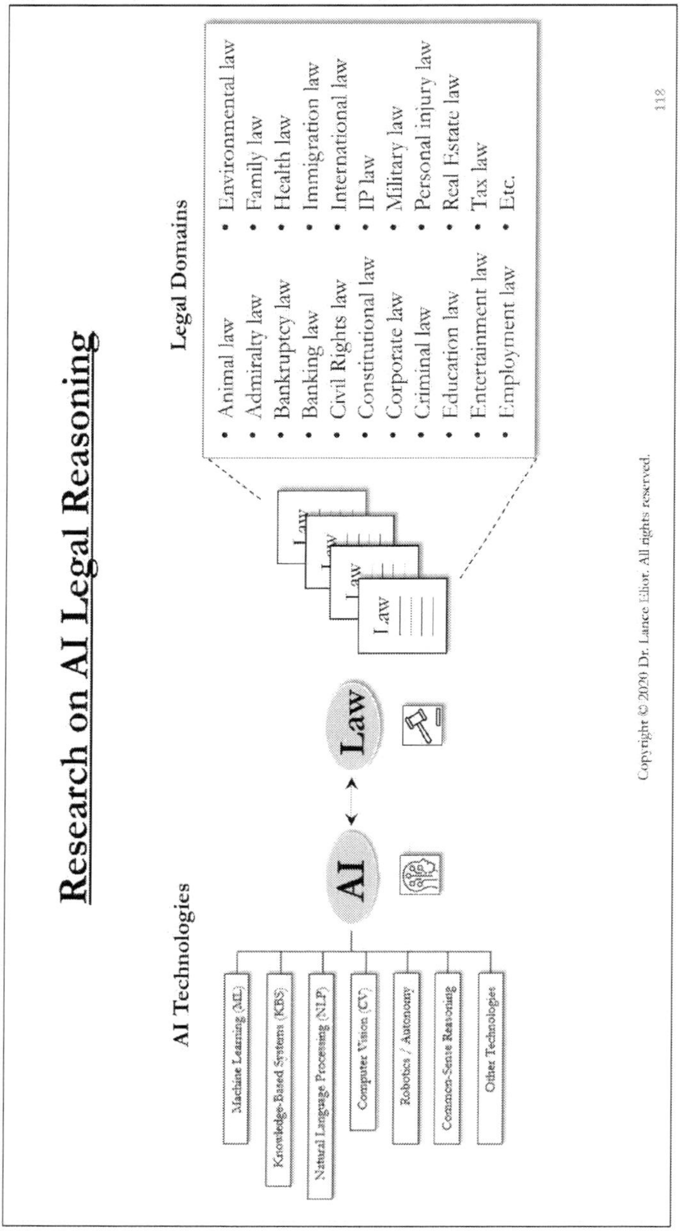
Research on AI Legal Reasoning
AI Technologies
Machine Learning (ML)
Knowledge-Based Systems (KBS)
Natural Language Processing (NLP)
Computer Vision (CV)
Robotics / Autonomy
Common-Sense Reasoning
Other Technologies
AI
Law
Legal Domains
Animal law
Admiralty law
Bankruptcy law
Banking law
Civil Rights law
Constitutional law
Corporate law
Criminal law
Education law
Entertainment law
Employment law
Environmental law
Family law
Health law
Immigration law
International law
IP law
Military law
Personal injury law
Real Estate law
Tax law
Etc.
Copyright © 2020 Dr. Lance Eliot. All rights reserved.
118

Figure 31

Companion Book By Dr. Lance Eliot

"AI And Legal Reasoning Essentials"

ISBN 978-1-73460165-7

Chapters

Available on Amazon and via other online book sellers

Companion Book By Dr. Lance Eliot

"Artificial Intelligence And LegalTech Essentials"

ISBN 978-1-7346016-3-3

Chapters

Companion Book By Dr. Lance Eliot

"Decisive Essays On AI And Law"

ISBN 978-1-73630310-8

Chapters

Available on Amazon and via other online book sellers

Companion Book By Dr. Lance Eliot

"Incisive Research On AI And Law"

ISBN 978-1-73630311-5

Chapters

Available on Amazon and via other online book sellers

Companion Book By Dr. Lance Eliot

"Ingenious Essays On AI And Law"

ISBN 978-1-73630312-2

Chapters

Available on Amazon and via other online book seller

Companion Book By Dr. Lance Eliot

"Compelling Essays On AI And Law"

ISBN 978-1-73630313-9

Chapters

01 Introduction to AI and Law
02 AI & Law: Echo Chambers In The Law
03 AI & Law: Role Reversible Judgment
04 AI & Law: When AI Is The Criminal
05 AI & Law: Apologetic AI Legal Troubles
06 AI & Law: Personal Digital Identity
07 AI & Law: Stockpiling Legal Postures
08 AI & Law: Law As Code
09 AI & Law: Lawyers As Coders
10 AI & Law: Agile AI And Law
11 AI & Law: Legal Advice By Nanosecond
12 AI & Law: AI-Based Co-Counsel
13 AI & Law: Deferential Behaviors In Law
14 AI & Law: Slowing AI Wheels Of Justice
15 AI & Law: Dehumanizing Lawyers
16 AI & Law: Gifting Of AI Legal Advice
17 AI & Law: When AI Is Evidentiary
18 AI & Law: Legal Maps
19 AI & Law: Posthumanization
20 AI & Law: AI Law Not Computable
21 AI & Law: Collective Intelligence
22 AI & Law: Limits Of Human Mind
23 AI & Law: Judicial Machine Readability
24 AI & Law: Legal Ecosystem
25 AI & Law: Oxford – Autonomous Levels

Appendix A: Teaching with this Material & Bibliography
Appendix B: Supplemental Figures and Charts
About the Author

Available on Amazon and via other online book sellers

Companion Book By Dr. Lance Eliot

"Topnotch Essays On AI And Law"

ISBN 978-1-73630314-6

Chapters

Available on Amazon and via other online book sellers

Companion Book By Dr. Lance Eliot

"Trendsetting Essays On AI And Law"

ISBN 978-1-95-738601-0

Chapters

Available on Amazon and via other online book sellers

<u>Companion Book By Dr. Lance Eliot</u>

"Pioneering Essays On AI And Law"

ISBN 978-1-95-738602-7

Chapters

Companion Book By Dr. Lance Eliot

"Trailblazing Essays On AI And Law"

ISBN 978-1-95-738602-7

Chapters

Available on Amazon and via other online book sellers

Companion Book By Dr. Lance Eliot

"Leading Edge Essays On AI And Law"

ISBN 978-1-95-738604-1

Chapters

Available on Amazon and via other online book sellers

Companion Book By Dr. Lance Eliot

"Jurisprudent Essays On AI And Law"

ISBN 978-1-95-738604-1

Chapters

Companion Book By Dr. Lance Eliot

"AI And Law Amid Ethical AI Trends"

ISBN 978-1-95-738607-2

Chapters

ABOUT THE AUTHOR

Dr. Lance B. Eliot, Ph.D., MBA is a globally recognized AI expert and thought leader, served as invited Stanford Fellow at Stanford University, an experienced top executive and corporate leader, a successful entrepreneur, and a noted scholar on AI, including that his Forbes and AI Trends columns have amassed over 9 million views, his books on AI are ranked in the Top 10 of all-time AI books, his journal articles are widely cited, and he has developed and implemented numerous AI systems.

He currently serves as Chief AI Scientist at Techbruim, Inc. and has over twenty years of industry experience, including serving as a corporate officer in billion-dollar-sized firms and being a partner in a major consulting firm. He is also a successful entrepreneur, having founded, run, and sold several high-tech firms.

Dr. Eliot previously hosted the popular radio show *Technotrends*, which was also available on American Airlines flights. He has made appearances on CBS's 60 Minutes, CNN, and C-SPAN, and has been a frequent speaker at industry conferences. His podcasts have over 500,000 downloads.

A former professor at the University of Southern California (USC), he founded and led an innovative research lab on Artificial Intelligence. He also previously served on the faculty of the University of California, Los Angeles (UCLA) and was a visiting professor at other major universities. He was elected to the International Board of the Society for Information Management (SIM), a prestigious association of over 3,000 high-tech executives worldwide.

He has performed extensive community service, including serving as Senior Science Adviser to the Congressional Vice-Chair of the Congressional Committee on Science & Technology. He has served on the Board of the OC Science & Engineering Fair (OCSEF), where he has also been a Grand Sweepstakes judge, and likewise served as a judge for the International SEF (ISEF). He served as the Vice-Chair of the Association for Computing Machinery (ACM) Chapter. Dr. Eliot has been a Shark Tank judge for the USC Mark Stevens Center for Innovation on start-up pitch competitions and served as a mentor for several incubators and accelerators in Silicon Valley and in Silicon Beach.

Dr. Eliot holds a Ph.D. from USC, an MBA, and a Bachelor's in Computer Science, and earned multiple high-tech certifications.

ADDENDUM

Latest Advances In AI And Law

Advanced Series on Artificial Intelligence (AI) and Law

By

Dr. Lance B. Eliot, MBA, PhD

For special orders of this book, contact:

LBE Press Publishing

Email: LBE.Press.Publishing@gmail.com

Made in United States
Orlando, FL
05 November 2026

90229834R10175